A War State All Over

A War State All Over

Alabama Politics and the Confederate Cause

BEN H. SEVERANCE

THE UNIVERSITY OF ALABAMA PRESS
Tuscaloosa

The University of Alabama Press
Tuscaloosa, Alabama 35487-0380
uapress.ua.edu

Typeface: Scala, Didot and Garamond

Cover image: Inauguration of Jefferson Davis on the steps of the capitol, Montgomery, Alabama, February 18, 1861; courtesy of the Alabama Department of Archives and History
Cover design: David Nees

Cataloging-in-Publication data is available from the Library of Congress.
ISBN: 978-0-8173-2059-1
E-ISBN: 978-0-8173-9295-6

To Tara, Beatrice, and Josephine

Contents

Illustrations

Figures

Tables

Acknowledgments

THIS BOOK IS A SPIN-OFF from my work on *Portraits of Conflict: A Photographic History of Alabama in the Civil War* (2012). The idea emerged from a conversation with Bob Bradley, a former curator at the Alabama Department of Archives and History (ADAH). While helping me with the research on *Portraits of Conflict*, Bob wondered whether the election of 1863 truly reflected the will of the people when so many potential voters—namely Alabama's soldiers—were not allowed to participate. In that book, I devoted just a few paragraphs to the election; this book devotes a great many more. So, let this serve as a word of encouragement or warning to all students of history. A diligent researcher can find a great deal to say about virtually any topic. Anyway, thank you, Bob, for posing the question.

Another colleague who deserves my gratitude is Chris McIlwain, who generously permitted me access to his vast collection of well-organized photocopies of virtually every Alabama newspaper from the Civil War era. Chris saved me many hours of scrolling through microfilm or scanning through digitized files. And like Bob, Chris is an enthusiastic conversationalist. Other friendly voices came from Mike Bonner, Ed Bridges, Michael Fitzgerald, and Ken Noe, all of whom offered valuable comments about various aspects of this project.

I owe a number of professional and civic organizations a round of applause for inviting me to share my preliminary findings through an assortment of presentations. They are here listed (with the sponsor) in no particular order: Auburn Civil War Society (Brett Derbes); Pensacola Civil War Roundtable (Larry Garrett); B. B. Comer Memorial Library in Sylacauga (Shirley Spears); Coosa County Historical Society (Lisa Bannister); ADAH Food for Thought Lecture Series (Amy Williamson and Alex Colvin); Prattville Historical Society (John Brown and Tyrone Crowley); South Carolina Historical Association (Lewie Reece); and Alabama Historical Association (Chris McIlwain).

As usual, library staff played an indispensable role in assisting me with my research. Specifically, I am indebted to Norwood Kerr, Nancy Dupree, and Scotty Kirkland from the Research Room at the Alabama Department of Archives and History; to Tommy Brown from Special Collections at Auburn University; to Samantha McNeilly from Special Collections at Auburn University at Montgomery; and to my colleague Terry Winemiller and the cartographers at the University of Alabama, for Terry's work in drafting the maps, and the cartographers' help in formatting them for the book.

I would be remiss not to mention the hardworking staff members of the University of Alabama Press, particularly Donna Baker and Dan Waterman (and the anonymous readers who gave my manuscript a hard and humbling critique). High praise also goes to Joanna Jacobs and Jessica Hinds-Bond for their thorough copyediting.

Finally, to my family—Tara, Beatrice, and Josie; Stan and Ginny Severance; John and Jeanette Harmon; "and the rest." I love you all.

A War State All Over

Figure 1. Alabama during the Civil War

Introduction

In October 1863, a little over two months after winning Alabama's gubernatorial contest, Thomas Hill Watts conducted a tour of the state that amounted to a grand wartime pep rally. The governor-elect urged Alabamians to fight on against the hated Yankee invader, to fight on for southern independence. A newspaper correspondent described Watts as "a war man all over." It was an apt description, not only for Watts, but for the entire polity of officeholders who orchestrated Alabama's war effort. Despite hardships on the home front—taxation, inflation, and starvation; despotic rule on the political front—conscription, impressment, and the suspension of habeas corpus; and setbacks on the battlefront—Gettysburg, Vicksburg, and the uncertain fate of Chattanooga; a majority of Alabama's politicians still wanted to win the war, were still willing to issue calls for sacrifice. This resolve came before the voters on August 3, and they elected enough men like Watts to keep Alabama on a total war footing. To be sure, many Alabamians believed that the cause was finished and that a negotiated peace was in order; but they were a minority. For better or for worse, Alabama's government was a war state all over, and it would remain so until the very end.[1]

In traditional political discourse, a state is an entity of sovereign power that encompasses both the administrative agencies of a government and the protective agencies of a military. Many Civil War historians agree that the eleven states of the Confederacy collectively waged an impressive total war through governmental authoritarianism. Sometimes referred to as *hard war*, the term *total war* encapsulates both the rapid centralization of state power and the mass mobilization of socioeconomic resources for the purpose of achieving a complete, nonnegotiable military victory. As early as the 1930s, Louise B. Hill argued that states' rights in the Confederacy gave way to state socialism, albeit "as a last resort and it was put into operation piece-meal, in true Anglo-Saxon fashion." This thesis, minus the Anglo-Saxon nonsense, entered the mainstream of Civil War scholarship in the 1960s. In a groundbreaking dissertation, John Brawner Robbins declared that southerners deliberately created a strong nation-state that could hold its own. "The Confederate Constitution established a government of considerable national power," he explains, one that was able "to fight a war of undreamed proportions—a modern war which would require all the energies of the nation." Frank E. Vandiver took the argument a step further with his observation that the war itself institutionalized central power in the South. In what he describes as "democratic militarism," Vandiver contends that the states voluntarily relinquished power to a national government, realizing that a unified war effort was imperative for success. In 1987, Richard Bensel extended the debate in an article appropriately titled "Southern Leviathan." According to this author, "the Confederate state attempted to direct a mobilization of men and material as complete and as centrally directed as any in American history." And by *state*, Bensel meant both the Davis administration that implemented total war policies and the Confederate Congress that willingly enacted them.[2]

An all-out war effort enjoyed ready support from local leaders, as well. "Having too much at stake to be hamstrung by the shibboleths of states' rights," William L. Barney notes in a provocative assessment of the Confederacy, "they demanded that other Southerners sacrifice for the war, and they ultimately compelled them to do so." This is not to say that long-standing ideas about federalism disappeared; rather, politicians at the national and state levels shared a commitment to victory, one affirmed through the democratic process. According to Curtis Arthur Amlund, "the central government secured authority from individuals *per se* through the election of officials to the executive and legislative branches" of the various states in rebellion. Most recently, the statist nature of the Confederacy has received some insightful commentary from Michael Brem Bonner: "Wartime circumstances pushed Confederate leaders to adopt a centralized, but flexible, system to support national survival." In saying this, Bonner presents yet another version of Confederate authoritarianism—"expedient corporatism"—whereby the government employed "ad hoc methods to temporarily satisfy wartime demands." Essentially, the public and private sectors of the South developed a remarkably effective partnership on behalf of the mutual goal of independence. Regardless of the terminology—socialism, militarism, leviathan, or corporatism—Alabama was part of an aggressive and expansive display of wartime political power.[3]

Did the average voter in Alabama understand, accept, and support this total war phenomenon? An answer can be found in the election of 1863. Elections, particularly during wartime, are an invaluable measure of a people's mood. Newly elected office holders presumably reflect the will of the people (a large though narrowly defined electorate of white men in nineteenth-century America), therefore any incumbent ousted at the polls ostensibly failed to meet the public's expectations. If so, then Alabama's returns reflected an inauspicious outcome for politicians that promoted all-out war. Watts defeated John Gill Shorter, the incumbent governor, who had rigorously enforced all of the Confederacy's controversial policies. Beyond the gubernatorial outcome, the congressional races saw two prowar hard-liners, Jabez Curry of Talladega County and John Ralls of Cherokee County, lose badly to antiwar rivals in their northeastern districts, while a third, James Pugh of Barbour County, barely held on to his seat. Finally, in the contests for the state legislature, the election brought to Montgomery many new delegates who were openly reluctant to continue the war. Later in the year, these "peace" lawmakers participated in the balloting that sent to the Confederate Senate two Alabamians who were known for their reservations about secession.

Not surprisingly, many historians regard the outcome of these state elections to be a repudiation of both secession and the war effort itself. They would probably hesitate to use the expression "a war state all over" to describe Alabama's polity in 1863. For instance, Malcolm C. McMillan, one of the leading authorities on Alabama during the Civil War, points out that "practically all of the important secession leaders of 1861 were voted out of office as Alabama changed horses in the middle of the stream." Bruce Levine agrees, observing that Alabamians elected "men who were even less enthusiastic about the war than the defeated incumbents." And then there is Armstead L. Robinson's bold assertion that "it was in Alabama that anti-Davis forces won their most sweeping victories," a development that he claims "testified to the power of the Peace Society" in the state. These statements, however, are troubling in three ways. First, a considerable number of secession leaders actually retained their seats, not to mention their majoritarian control. Second, the incoming politicians as a whole were not much different than the outgoing. Governor Watts proved no less vigorous than his unpopular predecessor in pressing the war effort, while the state's congressional delegation, as well as most of its legislators, sustained all of the decried war policies. Finally, in the wake of the election, several thousand more Alabamians donned the rebel uniform, either as Confederate regulars or as federalized militiamen, thereby raising the state's manpower contribution by the end of the war to over ninety thousand. This behavior is hardly that of a polity ready to throw in the towel. As Anne Sarah Rubin has said of white southerners as a whole, "they wanted the war to end, but they wanted it to end in victory . . . they longed for peace, but not at the expense of honor."[4]

Other historians see Alabama's election results as inconclusive, a product of wartime inertia rather than of outright defeatism. In his study of the state during the war, Christopher Lyle McIlwain concludes that nothing really changed after the election. An antiwar spirit certainly manifested itself, but it never translated into serious action against the Confederacy. Similarly, in an assessment pertaining to the entire South, George C. Rable states that "the voters rejected secessionist incumbents and peace candidates alike, generally preferring moderates." In short, Rable concludes, "the elections of 1863 became a crazy quilt of idiosyncratic, almost apolitical contests conducted before a largely apathetic though sometimes angry electorate." These more cautious observations appreciate the paucity of voter turnout. In 1860, when Alabamians confronted the prospect of a Lincoln presidency, 78 percent of the electorate cast ballots, a majority for the fire-eating candidacy of John C. Breckinridge. In 1863, by contrast, a mere third of eligible voters participated. Many factors account for this drop, including the difficulty of reaching polling places in precincts under military occupation, the thousands of war-related deaths by combat or disease, and the absence of soldiers for whom the state made no provision for balloting in the field. Consequently, it is difficult to draw definitive conclusions from the polls.[5]

All the same, a very real loss of will and its impact on the election cannot be easily dismissed. Besides the Confederacy's twin summertime military disasters at Gettysburg and Vicksburg, Alabama itself was beset by a legion of calamities. Beginning in spring 1862, Union forces had overrun much of the Tennessee River valley in the northern part of the state, confiscating or destroying thousands of bushels of grain, liberating slaves, and recruiting local unionists for the Federal army. Confederate efforts to drive out the Yankees produced a few tactical successes, but Union occupation by and large remained an unmitigated constant. "By the summer of 1863, civilians' confidence in their military had weakened," observes Joseph W. Danielson in his extensive study of north Alabama, "and their faith in the Confederacy had declined." To a lesser extent, the wiregrass region in the southeastern part of the state was similarly affected by the enemy presence in the Florida panhandle. And the whole state suffered economic privation due to the Union naval blockade of Mobile[6] (figure 1).

Unabated enemy activity exacerbated domestic policy. Beginning with the Conscription Act of April 1862, Confederate authorities implemented a series of war measures that were imperative for battlefield success but deleterious to the home front. Conscription violated individual liberty and fell especially hard on the state's yeomanry, or at least the portion that for whatever reason had not yet volunteered to serve. The law's subsequent twenty-slave exemption clause further complicated enforcement by prompting the cry, "rich man's war, poor man's fight." A gross exaggeration to be sure, this expression nonetheless created the enduring perception that slaveholders were forcing hardscrabble farmers to die for the peculiar institution. Planters, however, were hardly pleased by another controversial war policy—impressment. Enacted in March 1863, this law empowered the government to appropriate private property, including slaves, for military usage. Finally, the tax-in-kind law, passed in April 1863, required all citizens to furnish 10 percent of their agricultural produce to the government. Shortages in food and salt reached critical levels in early 1863. So-called corn women wandered rural Alabama in search of indigent relief, desperate residents of Mobile circulated petitions calling for "Bread or Peace," and folks living in occupied zones complained of despoliation by both friend and foe. Not surprisingly, desertion rates within the army noticeably increased. The conscription bureau reported in July 1863 that no fewer than eight thousand Alabamians had quit the ranks.[7]

Without a doubt, widespread privation and discontent influenced the August election. In her pioneering study of the Confederate home front, Georgia Lee Tatum insists that in Alabama "not only the disloyal but many of the loyal began to urge peace"; they saw the ballot box as the place to vent their frustration. This apparent loss of will manifested itself most prominently in the Peace Society. An antiwar movement, the Peace Society displayed varying degrees of strength and influence in many parts of the South, particularly in areas where the nonslaveholding white population predominated. In Alabama, members could be found in most of the hill counties north of the Black Belt, as well as in the wiregrass region along the Florida border. Believing that the rebellion was a failure, the Peace Society urged soldiers to desert; the Alabama wing organized itself into an unofficial and clandestine political party that in 1863 ran candidates in the more hard-pressed counties of the state. According to Bessie Martin, the Peace Society "was strong in voting and had considerable success in the election." Unhappiness with the war, however, was not necessarily disapproval of the cause, and the Peace Society hardly spoke for all Alabamians, let alone southerners more broadly. Again, Rubin offers poignant commentary: "The summer of 1863 reveals the myriad ways Confederates worked—and they worked very hard—at convincing themselves and each other that they were still winning the war, that independence was within their grasp." Rejecting narrow political explanations, as well as intimations of defeatism, Barney offers a guarded assessment of the South's midwar elections, going only so far as to say that "the 1863 returns did indicate a growing disenchantment with the war and an identification with those leaders who had been most reluctant to secede in the first place."[8]

Part of the difficulty in ascertaining the real public mood in 1863 is overcoming the variegated terminology that historians use in describing the political participants. The prowar camp is a jumble of hard-liners, Davis men, straight-out Democrats, and secessionists. The antiwar crowd is a muddle of defeatists, conservative Whigs, Jacksonian Democrats, and unionists. For example, Kenneth C. Martis, in his otherwise invaluable demographic breakdown of Confederate elections, makes the astounding claim that the "new legislature elected in the 1863 August elections was decidedly Unionist." It was not. Alabama unionists made up just 10 to 15 percent of the state's population and were confined mostly to the poorer counties (i.e., those with few slaves). Martis is understandably attempting to stress the election's significance, but his descriptor is careless. Unionists consistently hated everything about the Confederacy, a sentiment not shared by most who voted against Shorter or Curry. Most opponents of total war were not unionists but rather former cooperationists, who in 1861 had resisted the rush into secession. Cooperationists ranged widely in their enthusiasm for secession, but most were not averse to southern nationhood; rather, they were skeptical of the agrarian South's ability to win a war against the industrial North. Moreover, they worried that too few southern states would secede, thereby risking a stillborn Confederacy. Hesitation, however, gave way to enthusiasm after their new country grew to eleven states in summer 1861.[9]

A common scholarly approach to interpreting Alabama's 1863 elections is through the lens of prewar party politics. Most of Alabama's Democrats favored secession and its accompanying resort to armed rebellion, whereas many of the state's Whigs opposed disunion, or at least urged caution. Under the Confederacy, however, there was no formal party organization, a development that makes it difficult to categorize politicians on the war question. Nevertheless, the temptation to group wartime politicians according to their prewar political affiliation—Democrat or Whig—is natural, even irresistible. Foremost among historians doing just that is J. Mills Thornton III, whose brilliant work on antebellum Alabama delves briefly into the war years. Thornton sees the 1863 election as a triumph of level-headed Alabama Whiggery over the discredited policies of the state's reckless, fire-eating Democrats. In winning the gubernatorial race, for instance, Watts became the first Whig to ever win a statewide election in Alabama. Thornton attributes this outcome to the Democrats' mismanagement of the war effort, which he contends "produced a revulsion against the new rulers," one that enabled Watts and others like him to coast to victory on the mere hope that their Whig credentials would ameliorate the situation. This conclusion is reasonable, but it is based on a faulty premise, namely that the supposedly more rational Whigs never really embraced the Confederacy as their true country. In actuality, Alabama's Whigs could be just as fervent for the cause as their erstwhile Democratic counterparts. Whig victories in 1863 in no way undermined the state's commitment to total war.[10]

The Civil War unleashed an inchoate expression of nationalism in the South, one that transcended the old party ideologies. White southerners always exhibited reverence for the Revolutionary generation; hence they retained a vestige of love for the Union, but Yankeeism combined with abolitionism made coexistence impossible. Traditionally, Alabama's Democrats had followed the lead of Andrew Jackson and promoted *states'* rights. But with the sectional crisis over slavery, the party increasingly rallied around the so-called fire-eaters, who promulgated *southern* rights. For them, a nascent nationalism had already formed before the guns erupted over Fort Sumter. Traditionally, Alabama's Whigs supported national growth through government-sponsored economic programs. But with the rise of the antislavery Republican Party, their southern identity came to the fore. A defense of slavery unified the members of these two parties. Therefore, secession was a bipartisan act. When Jabez Curry, one of Alabama's fire-eating Democrats, railed against the Republican Party as "a standing menace" and Lincoln's election as "a declaration of war against our property and the supremacy of the white race," he was speaking for virtually all Alabamians, including the Whigs. The ensuing rebellion subsumed the remnants of the South's party system into a primal form of nationalism, one that compelled most Confederate politicians to accept drastic measures as vital to the defense of their homeland.[11]

After the 1863 elections, Alabama's congressional delegation and both houses of the state legislature comprised a generous mix of former Democrats and Whigs. Admittedly, some of the Democrats were old Jacksonians, sometimes dubbed Douglas men due to their support for pro-Union Stephen Douglas of Illinois in the presidential election of 1860, and some of the Whigs had rebranded themselves conservatives, in contradistinction to the hard-liners in their camp, but most of Alabama's office holders were sincere patriots of the Confederacy. "Party distinctions were marked before the war," Jabez Curry recalled years after the conflict, "but Whig, American, Democrat, were forgotten in the struggle, and all made common cause." Knowledge of prewar party lines is certainly useful information, but it provides limited insight into how people felt about the war in 1863. As Bensel notes, "public opinion, in the form of southern nationalism, abolished party competition in the South." In other words, voters cast their ballots more on whether they thought the conflict was still worth fighting and less on where a candidate stood on the issues of the 1850s. In an attempt to move past these old, misleading party labels, Rable proffers that Confederate politicians were either advocates of "national unity," with all its centralizing tendencies, or defenders of "individual liberty," where victory could never come at the price of freedom. These descriptions capture the essential differences within the Confederate polity, but they are a bit unwieldy in usage.[12]

For the sake of clarity, simplicity, and consistency, a new classification is in order: war Confederates and peace Confederates. (These labels are comparable to the actual divisions within the North's Democratic Party during the war.) Basically, war Confederates were those white Alabamians who were determined to push the military struggle to a successful conclusion—independence. They accepted the reality of a protracted war with its mounting casualties. They were disappointed by military setbacks but never dismayed by the need for more sacrifice, always believing that as long as the Confederacy maintained viable field armies then fortune could and would turn. They sympathized with the suffering families on the home front and understood the controversy surrounding the various war policies, but they fully endorsed all measures designed to produce victory. They were often critical of President Jefferson Davis's leadership, but they maintained unwavering loyalty to the government in Richmond. Some were once Democrats, others Whigs, but these appellations never detracted from the greater purpose of winning the war and creating a sovereign nation.

The peace Confederates comprise a more disparate body of Alabamians. Overall, their objective from 1863 onward was to somehow bring to an end their state's involvement in what they considered to be a futile war. The unionist minority obviously falls under this rubric; these men never wanted to secede, welcomed the Yankee invasion, and yearned for a decisive northern victory. Peace Confederates also included outright defeatists, citizens who may have initially supported the rebellion, but who could no longer endure further, seemingly senseless devastation. The largest set of peace Confederates consisted of men known as reconstructionists. This contingent sought a ceasefire for the purpose of negotiating a speedy reunification, one that would salvage as much as possible the South's agrarian economy. As the most influential group among the peace Confederates, reconstructionists were unrealistic about the terms the North would agree to after the war; they hoped to retain control of the freedmen as a labor force. The reconstructionist position developed an unwitting paradox in that it often entailed qualified cooperation with the war Confederates for the sake of military leverage at the bargaining table. In other words, peace Confederates had to pretend to win in order to surrender from a position of strength. All three outlooks—unionist, defeatist, and reconstructionist—could be found within the Peace Society.

No doubt there were differences within the ranks of both the war Confederates and the peace Confederates, but using these terms eliminates a great deal of confusion because the two groups so starkly despised each other, at least in terms of political ideology. To war Confederates, peace Confederates were at best "croakers"—dishonorable men who ranked self-interest above patriotism—or at worst traitors deserving a firing squad. To peace Confederates, war Confederates were basically lunatics bent on plunging the state ever deeper into an abyss of human carnage and economic ruin, all for an impossible dream of southern independence. Of the two, the war Confederates were more nationalistic and more cohesive. This did not guarantee unity of action, for ambitious and jealous men led this group. Still, their zeal inspired their followers and intimidated political opposition. Conversely, the peace Confederates were factionalized, particularly over their torn allegiance to Alabama itself. The unionist wing felt no love for the Confederacy, but most peace Confederates could and did periodically fall under the spell of patriotic sentiment and propaganda, despite their rational insistence that the idea of Dixie was fast becoming a meaningless concept.

The most important voice not heard at the polls in 1863 was the Alabama soldier. According to the state constitution, voters had to reside for three consecutive months in their home precinct. This technicality essentially disfranchised thousands of Alabamians who were away at the front fighting for their new nation. The vast majority of these men were volunteers who wanted to win no matter the cost. "Defeatism and open defiance of the Confederacy was much weaker in the armies than in the civilian population," Levine rightly notes, "partly because the men who were the most dedicated to the Confederacy had most readily put on uniforms and taken up arms." Had they been permitted to vote, Alabama's soldiers would have voted overwhelmingly for war Confederate candidates. "I think nothing can impede the progress of such men when prompted by patriotic motives," said Lieutenant William Owens of the Sixtieth Alabama Infantry shortly after the election of 1863, "our troops are now becoming eager to resent those wrongs so long heaped upon us by the Northern despotism." Instead, as Walter L. Fleming indelicately explains, "there were left at home as voters the old men, exempts, the lame, the halt, and the blind, teachers, preachers, officials, 'bombproofs,' 'featherbeds'—all, in short, who were most unlikely to favor a vigorous war policy." This characterization was harsh, to be sure, but most of the state's leaders were, indeed, in the army—a cruel twist of irony that denied them an opportunity to ensure that war Confederates ran the government.[13]

The electorate in Confederate Alabama, and everywhere else in America at the time, comprised only white men. Any invocation of the consent or will of the people must always take this reality into account. About 45 percent of Alabama's population was black, and half of the entire population was female. Whether they were chattel or dependents, black people and all women played no direct role in Alabama's polity. Stephanie McCurry rightly calls the Alabama of this time "an explicitly racial and patriarchal republic." Black people in Alabama were the most anti-Confederate segment in the state. As Steven

Hahn has noted, slaves engaged in a unique and informal communal politics that viewed the rise of the Republican Party "with anticipation rather than apprehension." The ensuing war offered slaves an opportunity to launch a quiet rebellion of their own against the peculiar institution, most commonly by simply running away to Union lines. This "second front" destabilized the plantations and contributed to the rationale behind the Confederacy's conscription exemption for overseers. So, while slaves had no voice in the polity, their defiance ironically intensified the rebel war effort by exposing the vulnerability of a system desperately in need of defending. Their opinion of the rebel war effort was most certainly negative, but as they were noncitizens, it was also irrelevant to Alabama's formal political structure.[14]

The political outlook of the state's white women, however, is another matter altogether. Women could not vote, hold office, or serve in the army, yet as mothers, wives, sisters, and daughters they exerted genuine, albeit hard to quantify, influence over their male counterparts. The fullest study of Alabama women during the war remains H. E. Sterkx's 1970 *Partners in Rebellion*. In this dated work, the author tends to highlight the patriotic contributions of the state's fairer sex while ignoring most instances of female defiance, such as the Mobile Bread Riots of 1863 and the numerous letters from yeoman wives beseeching their husbands to come home (i.e., desert). Nonetheless, more recent scholarship substantiates the long-standing supposition that most southern women, particularly among the planter class, were prowar. According to Laura F. Edwards, women bemoaned the mounting home-front hardships, but "they never doubted the principles that led them to support the Confederacy in the first place." In Victoria E. Ott's analysis, wartime suffering actually seemed to bind women more closely to the cause. "The only way to ensure the survival of their family and the future," she explains, "was to throw all their support behind the Confederacy." Rable points out that this support was often political in nature. "Women called for a strong and effective war policy," he says, adding that they wanted "bold and determined leaders." Alabama politicos such as Governor Shorter and Congressman Curry embodied these traits. Therefore, it stands to reason that had southern women enjoyed the franchise, a great many of them would have voted for war Confederates.[15]

This dismissal of black people and women from the political equation is not meant to minimize their agency, but rather to emphasize the difference between Alabama as a polity and as a society. In essence, a polity encapsulates the legitimate governing authority within a state, which for Alabama in 1863 was the purview of white men: officeholders, civil servants, military personnel, and even newspaper editors. As a polity, Confederate Alabama was very much a war state all over. Personal differences aside, its many members displayed a strong sense of duty that led them to put forth a rational and concerted effort to achieve the goal of independence. Societies are more diverse, comprising both the polity and just about everyone else. Unlike the polity, which formulated Alabama's role in the war and generated an incipient sense of nationalism, the people of Alabama mostly reacted to the vicissitudes of the conflict, oscillating between passion and despair. As a society of exploited slaves, patronized women, and hard-pressed white male civilians of all classes, Alabama was decidedly less consistent in its commitment to the contest. Nonetheless, Alabama's polity was the state in action, not its society. The polity instigated the rebellion and shaped its course; and it did so with the imprimatur of a democratic election, however limited its representation of the people. Antiwar sentiment pervaded many parts of Alabama's society, but it never took hold of the polity, the wavering of some elected officials notwithstanding.[16]

The ensuing chapters are oriented around Alabama's political leadership in the context of the 1863 elections. As such, they are a study of a white male polity in a state under wartime duress. Taking in turn the state's congressional delegation to the Confederate House, the gubernatorial contestants, the state legislators, and the Confederate senators, these chapters describe and analyze the political lives and wartime contributions of approximately 150 men who shaped Alabama's role in the Civil War. Most of these individuals have received scant attention by scholars, and so if nothing else this study is an overdue account of their part in the larger story of the Civil War. Chapter 1 starts at the national level with an examination of how and why Alabama's congressional leaders helped enact Confederate war policies. Chapter 2 then assesses how well the state's governors enforced these policies. Chapter 3 is especially important, for its analysis of the senatorial elections decisively establishes the breakdown between war Confederates and peace Confederates in the state legislature. Despite the existence of an antiwar contingent, these first three chapters reveal that the majority of Alabama's politicians were "war men all over." As participants in an all-out rebellion, they knowingly expanded the power of the government. As southerners beset by Yankee aggression, they readily embraced Confederate nationalism. As members of a democracy, they willingly placed their records before the judgment of the people. They may have seceded in order to protect slavery (a purely self-interested motive), but they waged a total war in order to create a new country (from the Confederate perspective, a much more noble goal). They were alternately idealistic and pragmatic, patriotic and skeptical, courageous and anxious. Ultimately, they were gamblers who tried to increase the odds through legislative action before eventually going all in. The fourth and final chapter addresses the political actor who was absent in plain sight—the soldier. Though disfranchised, Alabama's fighting men exerted enormous influence over the political process. As the soldiers were citizens willing to put their lives on the line for a genuine cause, their opinion arguably counted for more than even those who actually cast ballots.

The election of 1863 in Alabama is an instructive lesson in wartime morale. Undeniably, the election reflects consternation about the whole idea of rebellion, with its attendant cost in treasure and blood, but too many scholarly conclusions belie the historical record. Scrutiny beyond the face of the returns reveals not a repudiation of the war, but rather a stoic affirmation of the cause. While not exactly producing a mandate, the election shows that a majority of those who voted wanted to press on with their state's revolution. In a statement intended to apply to the entire Confederacy, Rable once again ably, if somewhat morosely, captures the truer political attitude in the election's aftermath: "Defeatism occasionally cropped up in floor debates and private discussions, but there remained a grim determination to see the war through to its ineluctable end." This determination can be seen in the post-election behavior of the politicians themselves, for Alabama continued its participation in a war that raged for nearly two more years. Whether in Richmond or Montgomery, the politicians upheld all of the military policies heretofore enacted, placing an ever-greater strain on the home front. Evidence of disillusion aside, a pro-Confederate mentality prevailed at the polls in 1863, thereby ensuring that Alabama's government remained a war state all over.[17]

1
The Congressional Races

It was the shocker of the 1863 elections in Alabama. Congressman Jabez Curry, the state's most prominent war Confederate, suffered defeat at the polls, losing to the political tyro Marcus Cruikshank, whose campaign message called for a negotiated cease-fire and an "honorable peace" with the North. Less startling, but no less disheartening to the prowar crowd, was Congressman John Ralls's loss to the avowed upstate unionist Williamson Cobb. Even war Confederate victories seemed to bring more relief than joy. In the state's wiregrass region, for instance, hard-liner James Pugh retained his seat with a narrow plurality. Measured against these developments, the congressional elections in Alabama were a disaster for politicians promoting a total war effort. The voters—the people—had apparently lost the will to fight on for independence and would no longer tolerate leadership that demanded ever more sacrifice. Or so a cursory examination of the returns would suggest. Viewed more broadly, to include scrutiny of the other contests, the elections also reveal that the citizenry in many parts of the state was still strongly committed to winning the war.

Curry, Ralls, and Pugh were but three of Alabama's nine congressmen in 1863. Their congressional districts ran roughly north to south in numerical order: 1) Thomas Foster; 2) William Smith; 3) John Ralls; 4) Jabez Curry; 5) Francis Lyon; 6) William Chilton; 7) David Clopton; 8) James Pugh; and 9) Edmund Dargan (figure 2). This was Alabama's delegation to the House of the First Confederate States Congress, a chamber with 106 members. The delegation's role in shaping wartime policy faced the verdict of the people at the ballot box, and so the congressional elections of 1863 serve as a unique midwar plebiscite on the performance of the Confederate government. Much in general has been said about these elections throughout the South, yet much investigation remains to be done. In his contribution to the collection of essays *Why the North Won the Civil War*, David M. Potter agrees: "Though history has neglected the elections most scandalously, we do know that they constituted a sharp rebuke to the [Davis] administration and its followers." It seems a bit presumptuous, however, for Potter to claim to know what something means when the research has been "most scandalously" absent. Actually, there are several good studies of the congressional races in the South.

Among them are *The Confederate Republic* by George C. Rable, which offers a detailed overview, and the article "The Essential Nationalism of the People" by Rod Andrew, which scrutinizes the elections in Georgia. Nevertheless, basic questions remain to be explored, especially for Alabama: Who were the candidates, both those seeking reelection and those running against them? What were their views on the war and the Confederacy as a whole? Why did they win or lose in 1863? And what do the elections tell us about home-front morale? Unfortunately, recent scholarship notwithstanding, the general approach to the elections has not changed substantially since Potter's observation; too many historians continue to promulgate the thesis that they demonstrate a popular denunciation of the war effort.[1]

Like the elections, the Confederate Congress itself receives little coverage in most studies of the Civil War. When it does, the scholarly assessment is usually unkind. Richard Bensel observes that southern congressmen "are often seen as faceless, petty figures with relatively undeveloped political philosophies." The historiography bears this out. "As a body the Confederate Congress was a disappointment," asserts E. Merton Coulter, housed as it supposedly was by a large number of small-minded members "who wasted their time on trivialities." Wilfred Buck Yearns further contends that the Congress "was unable to make a good reputation for itself" because it was overshadowed by a domineering executive branch. Frank E. Vandiver faults it for becoming "isolated in Richmond," and thereby disconnected from the very people that its members were expected to represent. More recently, James M. McPherson claims that the Confederate Congress "made few positive contributions to the war effort," preferring instead to engage in "grandiloquent or billingsgate oratory." Allan Nevins declares that it "was far inferior in both brains and character to its counterpart in Washington." Reid Mitchell simply states that the Confederate Congress "never inspired much confidence."[2]

The undeniable talents of these many historians notwithstanding, their unflattering portrait of the Confederate Congress is overly harsh, needlessly dismissive, and even flat out wrong. Congressional legislation profoundly affected both the soldier and the civilian of the South. Indeed, the First Confederate Congress, the one that faced reelection in 1863, shaped the course of the rebellion more than any other political institution in the South. In four sessions from February 1862 to February 1864—the crucial years of the war—its members, including the nine from Alabama, debated and passed the most significant laws in the Confederacy's short history: conscription (April 1862), impressment (March 1863), and tax-in-kind (April 1863), among many others. Furthermore, on two occasions in 1862 (February and October), they also granted President Jefferson Davis the temporary power to suspend the writ of

Figure 2. Alabama's congressional districts in 1863

habeas corpus. Each of these laws enjoyed full legitimacy under the Confederate Constitution. Enacting wartime policies of this kind was not the work of mediocre men blindly following the direction of their commander-in-chief, but the product of intelligent, deliberative politicians who strived to balance the necessities of war with the principles of liberty. Nearly two-thirds of the 106 delegates possessed parliamentary experience at the state or national level going into the war. Among the Alabamians, only Thomas Foster and John Ralls had never held political office prior to their service in Congress. Six of the Alabamians—Clopton, Curry, Dargan, Lyon, Pugh, and Smith—could boast at least one term in the House of the old Union.[3]

Conceding that the First Confederate Congress actually did a creditable job under the duress of war, many of the same historians who roundly criticize the legislative branch find themselves also coming to its defense. Most congressmen were "desirous of winning the war," admits Coulter, and they displayed "a boldness of imagination as [they] faced unprecedented problems." Yearns observes that "Congress gave the impression of a devoted body hard at work," where all concerns "were secondary to winning the war." Similarly, Vandiver concludes that the controversial laws demonstrate that southern congressmen were "willing to do what seemed necessary to win the war." Even Nevins makes an about-face when he describes the South's resort to conscription as "a bolder law than the North dare make . . . a more Spartan measure than any other English-speaking land had ever enacted." Some historians, such as Scott Nelson and Carol Sheriff, are now beginning to think that the Confederate Congress was arguably more united and focused in its efforts to wage war than even the US Congress.[4]

Most of Alabama's delegates to the Confederate Congress voted with the majority on war legislation. And it was their stance on these extraordinary measures that came before the electorate in August 1863. Unfortunately, scholarly commentary on these elections produces a great deal of confusion. Without providing any detail, Walter L. Fleming states that the results of 1863 produced a congressional delegation that "was of a decidedly different temper" than the gung ho secessionists who prevailed in 1861. Frank L. Owsley is less coy, claiming that in Alabama alone the voters elected six "avowed unionists" to Congress, an outcome that he interprets as an unmistakable sign of defeatism. Bessie Martin concurs, arguing that the growing strength of the Peace Society in Alabama turned the people against the cause, hence against their state's war Confederates. More recent scholars share this pessimistic interpretation. Paul D. Escott, a historian who has long viewed Confederate nationalism as more myth than reality, reduces the number of Alabama's peace Confederates from six to four, and he classifies them not as unionists, but as proponents of reconstruction. Nevertheless, he insists that the elections in Alabama and elsewhere in the South "revealed broad-based discontent," and that the presence of so many antiwar politicians promised "more difficult days" ahead for President Jefferson Davis. In his dissertation on Confederate politics, John Brawner Robbins pegs Alabama's incoming peace delegation at just three, yet he still maintains that the elections reflected a profound rejection of hard-war policies. In a newer work, David Williams tries to differentiate between voter opposition to Confederate policy and the Confederacy itself, but he ultimately asserts that the elections mark a decisive shift against both, an opposition that only grew stronger during the latter half of the war.[5]

The election-as-defeatism theme, however, hardly enjoys consensus among historians. In *Why the South Lost the Civil War*, Richard E. Beringer et al. note that although most of the freshman congressional winners in 1863 had opposed secession in 1861, these ostensible unionists rarely offered any meaningful dissent about the Confederate war effort. Therefore, the elections did not reflect "a true peace movement," because Congress continued to "warmly support the war." With his usual appreciation for political complexity, Rable acknowledges that the elections of 1863 produced significant turnover, but he sees the outcome more as a halfhearted protest without any real substance; the incoming peace Confederates had no clear manifesto for change, and war Confederates continued to dominate in Richmond. Similarly, Bruce Levine notes that the influence of the Peace Society is overstated and instead argues that the congressional elections constituted "a widespread if largely unfocused mood of disappointment and dissatisfaction." In other words, the voters were angry not so much with the Confederacy per se, but with certain political leaders.[6]

Overall, the tendency among historians is to present the congressional elections as a vague yet profound expression of popular discontent that ultimately proved politically irrelevant and yet is worth stressing all the same, when it came to affecting how Congress waged the war. This scholarly ambiguity affirms Potter's original charge that the topic remains scandalously neglected. A central flaw with all these studies is that they focus almost entirely on the races that were lost by war Confederates. The districts that sent war men back to Congress are largely ignored. This is especially true for Alabama, where the Curry-Cruikshank contest often becomes the sole example in virtually every discussion on the matter. Taken in isolation, Curry's defeat does indeed suggest a pronounced loss of will in Alabama's fight for independence. But it cannot be taken in isolation, any more than that the face of the returns can be taken without qualification. An examination of all nine congressional districts in Alabama is necessary to reach a final verdict on this particular state's attitude toward the Confederate war effort. Reorienting the focus produces a markedly different conclusion. There were not six peace men who won at the polls as Owsley says, nor four as Escott says, nor even three as Robbins says, but only two—Marcus Cruikshank and Williamson Cobb. Admittedly, William Smith often inclined toward peace, as did Thomas Foster toward the very end of the war, but both men always evinced loyalty to their new country. The other five, including four incumbents, proved staunch war Confederates. Rather than marking the emergence of defeatism in the worst-case analysis or merely discontent in the best case, the congressional elections support the argument that Alabama's polity generally remained a war state all over.

ALABAMA'S CONGRESSIONAL INCUMBENTS IN 1863

Five former Democrats represented Alabama in the First Confederate Congress: Jabez Curry, John Ralls, David Clopton, James Pugh, and Edmund Dargan. All five espoused the doctrine of states' rights, but while many historians consider this ideology to be a political liability for the Confederacy, it is not incompatible with a push for total war. To these Alabamians, the concept of states' rights within the context of federalism was not a belief in limited or weak government, but was rather concerned with the locus of power within government. Such power was best wielded at the state level, especially during times of peace, but there was nothing inherently wrong with yielding to a national authority in a time of crisis, particularly during the revolutionary struggle that they were currently undergoing. Paradoxically, total war was the most logical means of safeguarding states' rights against a numerically and materially superior northern foe. In this sense, it is more appropriate to speak of these five Alabama congressmen as advocates of southern rights (not states' rights), where the Confederacy epitomized a newer, bolder, and more righteous version of the American republic, one that evidently could only be forged through an all-out military effort. This spirit of Confederate nationalism recognized that states' rights would mean nothing if the Yankees won the war.[7]

Given his starring role in virtually every study of the wartime congressional races in Alabama, Jabez Lamar Monroe Curry offers a good place to start (figure 3). In 1863, he was perhaps the most prominent Alabamian in the Confederate capital. The historians Ezra J. Warner and Wilfred Buck Yearns describe him as "a strong Confederate nationalist." True enough, but Curry also epitomized the idealized notions of southern manhood—genteel and eloquent on the one hand, defiant and chauvinistic on the other. Like the Revolutionary generation before him, Curry believed in an "aristocracy of merit," where society's best men—like him—ruled, and did so in accordance with the political philosophy of John C. Calhoun, one that elevated southern rights and south-

Figure 3. Jabez Lamar Monroe Curry, studio portrait by Julian Vannerson, 1859. (Courtesy of Library of Congress)

ern honor into articles of faith. To the manor born (specifically a Georgia plantation in 1825), Curry moved with his family to Talladega County in 1838. There, he came of age as his father's favorite son, eventually becoming the master of nearly fifty slaves. In the process, Jabez received one of the finest educations that a nineteenth-century man could obtain, first graduating from the University of Georgia and then earning a law degree from Harvard.[8]

Although a lawyer by training, Curry was a politician by choice. While still in his twenties, he won election to the state legislature as a progressive-minded Democrat. He quickly established himself as an advocate of public education, a passion that became his mission later in life. He also promoted internal improvements, believing that Alabama's transportation system was woefully inadequate for the needs of a growing cotton economy. In 1857, the voters from the central-eastern counties of the state sent young Curry to Washington, DC, as their representative. On the national stage, Curry garnered instant attention throughout the country with his uncompromising defense of slavery. In his first floor speech, the thirty-two-year-old congressman averred that the controversial, proslavery Lecompton Constitution was perfectly legitimate, and so he demanded the admission of Kansas into the Union as a slave state. He feigned surprise both at the North's unfavorable reaction to the Kansas-Nebraska Act of 1854 and at its subsequent outrage over the "Bleeding Kansas" travesty that followed. To him, the westward extension of slavery comported with Calhoun's "common property" theory, which held that all federal territory was owned collectively by the American people and was hence free and open to settlement by any citizen, slaveholder or otherwise. In the wake of this speech, Curry became one of Alabama's most popular fire-eaters.[9]

The centrality of racial slavery to Curry's idea of southern rights became more pronounced in the months and years that followed. In December 1859, he pilloried the rising Republican Party in a lengthy floor speech. "The real cause of the agitation in the public mind, the radix of the excitement," Curry explained in reference to John Brown's recent raid on Harpers Ferry, "is the anti-slavery sentiment of the North," which the Alabamian blamed squarely on the Republicans. He rejected that party's pledge to abide the institution of slavery where it already existed, arguing instead that everything about the Republican platform was "of imminent danger to the Constitution, and the South, and the country at large." "All who cannot pronounce the *shibboleth* of Republicanism," he further warned, "are to be proscribed and banished from all influence in our Government." Accordingly, in the presidential election of 1860, he backed the overtly proslavery ticket of John C. Breckinridge and traveled the state on his behalf. Expounding a politics of fear, Curry warned one audience that the Republicans would "lay waste your fields, emancipate your negroes, and amalgamate the poor man's daughter and the rich man's buck-nigger before your very eyes!" After Lincoln won, a dismayed Curry worried that the US government had indeed fallen into the hands of "an abolition dynasty." He called for the immediate secession of the southern states. While Alabamians back home convened a convention to debate that very issue, the fire-eating congressman eagerly served as a secession commissioner to Maryland. In an apocalyptic letter to the political leaders of that state, Curry predicted that "under an abolition government the slave-holding states will be placed under a common ban of proscription . . . to be assaulted, humbled, dwarfed, degraded, and finally crushed out." Maryland ultimately remained loyal, but Curry did not; in mid-January he resigned his seat in Congress and returned to Alabama, newly free and independent.[10]

Curry's restructured congressional district comprised the counties of Calhoun, Randolph, and Shelby, as well as his home of Talladega. Beyond a general disdain for the Republican Party of the North, the citizenry there was not of one mind on secession. Calhoun County was straight-out, befitting the character for whom it was named, but the other three counties contained sizeable pockets of cooperationism. Nonetheless, when Alabama formally seceded, the people of the Coosa River valley exhibited strong patriotism. Curry had little difficulty transferring his congressional seat from the US Congress to that of the Confederacy. He served first in the Provisional Congress, where he played a vocal role in drafting his new country's constitution. As a framer, Curry insisted that the document explicitly vouchsafe the sovereignty of the states so as to prevent "selfish majorities" (essentially what the North's Republican Party amounted to) from undermining political liberty. In fall 1861, he ran unopposed for the permanent Congress and garnered 3,112 votes.[11]

Jabez Curry relished his role in the Confederate revolution and rarely wavered in his commitment to victory. As an advocate of states' rights, he had once warned that in a federalist system, "the centripetal tendencies have been found to be greater than the centrifugal." But without the slightest hint of irony, Curry endorsed most of the Confederacy's total war policies. Evidently, his constitutional ideals were for peacetime only; a revolutionary war demanded pragmatism. On March 5, 1862, he took the floor in support of a bill authorizing the government to destroy property lest it fall into enemy hands and delivered one of the chamber's most truculent speeches. According to one newspaper correspondent, "Mr. Curry said that if there was any man in Alabama who was so avaricious that he would not, with his own hands, put the torch to every lock of cotton rather than that the Lincoln Government should get it, he hoped the Yankees would burn him." Given such bellicosity, it is not surprising that the firebrand later voted without hesitation for conscription and demanded that it be enforced in a spirit of shared sacrifice. To that end, he opposed many of the subsequent amendments that created exemptions and authorized substitutions. Curry considered the twenty-slave clause to be especially obnoxious, rightly predicting that it would inflame class discord on the home front. On impressments, he was again in the majority. Curry owned forty-seven slaves, yet he willingly acceded to their conditional use as military laborers. The congressman also supported the tax-in-kind. As a member of the House Commerce Committee, he saw this measure as preferable to the folly of printing more paper currency, which he mockingly referred to as "pictured rags." Knowing, however, that the tax-in-kind would fall hardest on the families of soldiers, he donated thousands of bushels of corn from his own plantation for indigent relief and called on his fellow planters to do likewise. Only on the suspension of habeas corpus did he balk at increasing federal authority. But rather than speak out or vote against it, Curry absented himself from the chamber when the matter came up for a vote—a tacit acceptance perhaps of the law's military necessity.[12]

By 1863, Curry's enthusiasm betrayed a few signs of waning. He came to regard many of his congressional colleagues as lesser men who were possessed of inadequate "civic ability," and he increasingly complained of the "futility in debates" and the "dullness in proceedings." Interestingly, several Confederate politicians blamed Curry himself for this congressional malaise. Both Vice President Alexander Stephens and Senator Louis Wigfall viewed Curry as a political lightweight who disguised his mediocrity behind a veil of pedantry. Congressman Franklin Sexton, however, considered Curry "a good & able man," while Senator Williamson Oldham admired the Alabamian's "eloquence and statesmanship." In any event, Curry began eating more, taking on a physical "plumpness" that made him sometimes feel unfit to represent a nation in arms. In his youth, Curry had served briefly in the Mexican War, and he now yearned to volunteer again, confessing to President Davis that he felt "a strong desire to share in the excitement and perils" of fighting for freedom. Several of his brothers were in the ranks, and Curry took every opportunity to visit them at the front. During an inspection of the Army of Tennessee in summer 1862, he noted that the soldiers were "hopeful and confident," ever ready to take on the enemy, even though they expressed little faith in their commander, General Braxton Bragg. Despite his fascination with all things military, Curry resigned himself to a life of politics. "Congressmen had probably better stick to their vocations," he stoically explained.[13]

When not pushing legislation or visiting army camps, Curry took to delivering public lectures that were partly propaganda against the Yankees but were mostly indictments of the southern people's supposedly insufficient wartime mettle. In one such presentation, "The Two Wants of the Confederacy," composed in 1862, he blamed the South's military woes not on its soldiers, but on its citizens and politicians. Far too many civilians, according to Curry, were ill informed about what was at stake in the war, and so they whined about every hardship. Similarly, too many political leaders lacked what Curry called "liberal Christian statesmanship," and so they failed to appreciate the revolutionary nature of the conflict, one that required vision and faith. Curry's solution entailed a public acceptance of aristocracy, where men of "courage and virtue" (presumably men like himself) would govern through the "triumph of reason, deliberation and accountability." In January 1863, Curry went a step further, denouncing the moral weakness of a democracy at war in a lecture titled "Social and Political Quicksands," which was derived in part from conversations with the esteemed writer Augusta Jane Evans of Mobile. With so many of the South's finest men in the ranks, he explained, the home front had fallen prey to profiteers, defeatists, and mountebanks and was a place where politicians pursued "what is popular instead of what is right . . . the criterion of the demagogue." He urged the public to be wary of false rumors and false promises, and instead to rededicate itself to core values such as education, slavery, constitutionalism, and Christianity. Until then, Curry warned that holding too many elections in a time of crisis was unwise lest men unworthy of the people's trust gain political office. The lecture never suggested that the August elections be canceled, but Curry apparently worried that he might not retain his seat.[14]

In contradistinction to Curry, Congressman John Perkins Ralls was a latecomer to the world of politics, just as he was a latecomer to the idea of secession. A well-educated physician and slaveholder (he owned twenty-eight slaves) from Gadsden in Cherokee County, Ralls exemplified the stereotype of the kindly, middle-aged country doctor. When not tending the sick, he pushed temperance as an active member of the Methodist faith. Politically, he leaned Democrat, but he never engaged in politics until his election to the Alabama Secession Convention in 1861. Charged to support the cooperationists, he gravitated toward the straight-out camp, especially after Florida and Mississippi seceded. To Ralls, these developments rendered irrelevant any further attempts to stall Alabama's own secession. And so he voted for and subsequently signed the official ordinance.[15]

Having established himself as pro-Confederate, Ralls went on to defeat for Congress Williamson Cobb, the Second District's longtime incumbent and a prominent unionist. The tally was 3,754 to 1,917 and included a healthy soldier vote for the winner. According to Private James Stephens of the Seventh Alabama Infantry, "Dr. John P. Ralls received evry vote cast in the two companies allowed to vote in his district . . . over 90 votes in all." In Richmond, Ralls displayed an early zeal for the cause when on March 3, 1862, he introduced a "Declaratory Resolution" that stated that it was Congress's "unalterable determination" to see the war through to a successful conclusion and that the delegates would "NEVER politically affiliate on any terms with a people who are guilty of an invasion of their soil and the butchery of their citizens." The resolution passed, 69–0. In keeping with his truculent rhetoric, Ralls compiled a generally prowar record as a representative. He voted for conscription (but opposed the later twenty-slave clause), the various suspensions of habeas corpus, and the tax-in-kind law. He either abstained or was absent when impressment came before the floor, though he subsequently expressed approval of the government's use of slaves as military laborers. Ralls was a thoughtful legislator who voted his conscience, but he was always loyal to the Confederacy. Unlike a great many in the House, he never voiced any criticism of the Davis administration or objected to the final passage of any laws. Instead, he tended to go quietly about his duties, enjoying the occasional invitation to open a session with prayer. As a member of the Committee on Hospitals, he periodically visited Richmond's growing network of medical facilities, finding them generally well managed though frequently in need of medicine and other supplies. One of the few times when he took the floor was to propose a modest one-cent tax on unginned cotton. For all his devotion, Ralls displayed no dynamism, a personality shortcoming that would adversely affect his prospects for reelection.[16]

Voters in Alabama's Seventh District (Chambers, Macon, Russell, and Tallapoosa Counties) could hardly have found a more principled representative than David Clopton. During his first term in Congress, the Honorable Clopton adeptly balanced the conflicting obligations, faced by all Confederate politicians, to protect the people's liberty and to promote effective war legislation. Born in 1820 into a family of wealthy Georgia planters and physicians, Clopton received a first-rate education at Virginia's Randolph-Macon College before settling in Tuskegee (Macon County), where he established a successful law practice in the 1840s and over time acquired a dozen slaves. A true believer in the ideology of southern rights, Clopton proudly identified with the South's fire-eaters and began clamoring for Alabama's secession as early as 1852. Soon thereafter, he ran for public office as a Democrat, helping his party thwart Whig inroads into the district. Despite his frail physique, the black-haired Clopton displayed talent as a stump speaker and apparently enjoyed "great personal popularity." In 1859, he won election to the US House.[17]

Clopton hated the Republican Party of the North, believing that it stood for abolition and racial equality. When Lincoln won the presidency in 1860, the Alabama congressman could barely contain his disgust. During the ensuing secession crisis, he readily accepted a special gubernatorial commission to bring the case for disunion to the slaveholders of Delaware. While doubting that this particular state would join the South, he warned its residents all the same about the Republicans' supposed plans "to disseminate insurrectionary sentiments among a hitherto contented servile population." When Alabama seceded, Clopton gladly resigned his seat in Congress. Just before doing so, however, he visited the War Department and brazenly asked for the plans to the federal arsenal in Mount Vernon, Alabama, in order to expedite his state's seizure of that important facility. Needless to say, his request was denied. Once back in Alabama, he enlisted as a private in the Twelfth Alabama Infantry, serving until his unanimous election (he ran unopposed) to the Confederate Congress in fall 1861. Clopton may have accepted a position in government over service in the military, but two of his brothers remained with the army, ultimately giving their lives for the cause. Thus, the war was never far from Clopton's thoughts.[18]

As a patriotic politician, Clopton sought to empower the Davis administration with everything that it needed to win the war, yet to do so without placing undue burdens on the citizenry. His long-standing belief in limited government would inform, but not handicap, his legislative record. Case in point: the Conscription Act of February 1862. As a matter of principle, he rejected it; as a matter of military necessity, he voted for it. In explaining his apparent apostasy to the states' rights purists in the House (and to the voters back home), Clopton pointed out the obvious. Federal forces were rapidly advancing through Tennessee at the very moment that the one-year volunteer enlistments were beginning to expire. To allow the rebel army to essentially disband in the face of an enemy invasion would be the height of stupidity, if not treason. Therefore, under such trying circumstances, Clopton proclaimed that "conscription was necessary to the salvation of the country." Thereafter, the congressman returned to his convictions, voting against later amendments to the conscription law, lest the policy "drain the country of its strength." Still, Clopton worried about the deficient size of the Confederate military; he believed that the South needed a field army of at least six hundred thousand men. His solution was for Congress to place every white man into certain categories and then "authorize the President to call upon the classes for troops as they might be needed." Clopton never explained how exactly this proposal differed from conscription.[19]

Clopton further demonstrated his blend of pragmatism and principle on subsequent war measures. He reluctantly voted for impressment, seeing no other reasonable way for the government to obtain much-needed war material, but he insisted that officials compensate civilians at market value. The congressman rightly worried that any such compensation would come in the form of increasingly worthless Confederate banknotes, but he was unsure how to prevent this issue. He accepted a state's prerogative to print money but rejected the central government's power to do so, voting against all paper currency bills and moving in vain to get them repealed once enacted. Similarly, Clopton balked at the Confederate taxation policy, which he considered to be impressment in a different guise. He voted against the tax-in-kind law of 1863. On the issue of habeas corpus, Clopton generally opposed this measure, and he acceded to its suspension only on the condition that the House create an oversight committee to investigate alleged abuses. He personally served on this committee and happily reported that the government was never guilty of any egregious violations of the law. Clopton's concern for civil liberty, however, did not extend to the Yankees. In January 1863, he suggested that Union soldiers captured in the act of plundering private property or harming civilians should be remanded to state authorities for trial as common criminals. Later in May, he voted for the bill Retaliation on Prisoners, a draconian measure that authorized military commanders to execute any Union officer that was captured while leading black soldiers. Other than his nay vote on taxation, Clopton would pursue reelection as an undeniable war Confederate.[20]

From Alabama's Eighth District (the southeastern counties) came James Lawrence Pugh, one of the state's most outspoken war Confederates (figure 4). At the time of the election, he was a proud member of the planter class, owning a multistory mansion—Liberty Hall—on the south side of Eufaula in Barbour County. But Pugh came from common Georgia stock. Born in 1819, he traveled with his family to Pike County, Alabama, in 1824. Orphaned at age eleven, the future congressman never received a formal education, but he compensated with tireless ambition. In 1841, Pugh moved to Barbour County, where he worked as a postman until becoming a lawyer. He soon started acquiring slaves and then dabbled in Whig politics. By the end of the decade, however, he switched to the Democratic Party and soon developed a passion for the political philosophy of John C. Calhoun, with its strident emphasis on states' rights and the defense of slavery. It was the polemics around the antislavery Wilmot Proviso that ignited his political transformation, as well as his realization that the surest route to sociopolitical status in Alabama seemed to go through the Democratic Party. In any event, by 1848, Pugh was a welcome member of the Eufaula Regency, a gathering of prominent Alabama planters who propounded states' rights and dreamed of a southern nation free from meddlesome northern abolitionists.[21]

Throughout the 1850s, James Pugh was obsessed with slavery and could fairly be described as one of the South's most vocal fire-eaters. On the eve of the Civil War, he owned sixty slaves, but he was apparently a benevolent master. According to one of his domestic servants, a woman named Matilda, Pugh showed great affection for his chattel, allowing his children to play with those from the slave quarters. In keeping with the South's concept of paternalism, Pugh genuinely believed that slavery was a positive good for both white and black people. Not surprisingly, he viewed the rise of the Republican Party in the North as his state's greatest concern. In 1859, he successfully ran for the US House with a slogan that encapsulated the fire-eater mentality:

Figure 4. James Lawrence Pugh, studio portrait by Matthew B. Brady, 1859. (Courtesy of Alabama Department of Archives and History)

"Union among Ourselves for the South." On the stump, Pugh was a formidable campaigner. Because he stood six feet in height with tremendous girth, a fellow planter dubbed him "a great bronze battering ram." Drawing on Calhounite arguments, Pugh proclaimed to his constituents that the North and the South were two "concurrent sovereignties," and that secession was a permissible political option. When Lincoln won the 1860 presidential election, Pugh knew that the time for radical action had come. In a letter coauthored with Jabez Curry to the Secession Convention, he stressed the urgency of the situation: compromise with the "Black Republican party" was impossible due to its "hostility to slavery." Once the deed was done, he resigned his seat and departed Washington, DC.[22]

Back in Alabama, Pugh enlisted in the Eufaula Rifles, a company that later melded into the First Alabama Infantry. Eagerly serving as a private, he joined the throng of Alabamians stationed at Fort Barrancas, Florida, before easily winning election in 1861 to the Confederate House (he won 4,215 votes running unopposed). The Davis administration could not have asked for a more supportive congressman. According to the historians Warner and Yearns, Pugh "was a staunch advocate of legislation to strengthen the central government." As a member of both the Committee on Military Affairs and the Committee on Currency, Pugh had a direct hand in shaping most of the government's military policies. Virtually any bill that increased the war powers of the government received his yea vote: conscription, impressment, tax-in-kind, suspension of habeas corpus, the destruction of property. Displeased by the proliferation of draft exemptions, Pugh sponsored a failed bill that sought to tax anyone not in the uniform and then redistribute the proceeds to the families of soldiers. Of all these war measures, however, the Alabama congressman was especially proud of the tax-in-kind. In a series of speeches both on the House floor and to his constituents back home, Pugh defended the tax as not only necessary but equitable, in that it affected the South's producers (not its poor) and targeted provisions rather than landed property. Resorting to total war hyperbole, Pugh also claimed that whereas the Confederacy was asking for a mere 10 percent, a triumphant North would extract 90 percent through plunder and devastation. In short, compliance with the tax was a patriotic imperative. To offset the deleterious impact that the tax would have on the South's yeomanry, he tried unsuccessfully to exempt the households of those with Confederate military service. Pugh went into the election season confident that his record was both solidly pro-Confederate and sympathetic to the suffering of the voters back home.[23]

The last former Democrat among Alabama's Confederate delegation was Edmund Spann Dargan. Born in 1805, Dargan was the son of a poor Baptist minister whose flock consisted of yeoman farmers in rural North Carolina. Orphaned as a young teenager, Dargan worked various menial jobs about the state before heading west to Alabama in 1829. An autodidact, Dargan earned a living as an itinerant schoolteacher until the 1840s, when he moved to Mobile, opened a law practice, and entered politics as a Democrat.[24]

If first impressions are truly important, then Dargan should never have achieved any political success (figure 5). He was habitually disheveled in appearance; his apparel was shabby, wrinkled, ill fitting, even unlaundered; his shoes were worn out and frequently unlaced. Dargan's hygiene was little better, particularly his receding shocks of hair, which were usually uncombed and just as often unwashed. A political foe once remarked that on the stump

Figure 5. Edmund Spann Dargan, studio portrait by Reed and Wallace of Mobile, Alabama, 1860s. (Courtesy of Alabama Department of Archives and History)

Dargan could be found consorting with "one-gallows' fellows, *picking the ticks off of his legs.*" Behind this slovenly exterior, however, lay a sharp mind and an eloquent tongue. Dargan was a formidable politician who, in the age of Jackson, skillfully parlayed his lack of sophistication into a common-man appeal that helped him win numerous elections. His most noteworthy victory came in 1845 when he ran for Congress and soundly defeated William Dunn, a rich and well-connected Whig. Dargan served just one term, but he gained immediate notoriety as one of the War Hawks of 1846, a vocal group of legislators who strongly supported the expansionist agenda of President James Polk. After finishing his term, he won election to the Alabama Supreme Court, presiding as chief justice from 1849 to 1852.[25]

Around this time, Dargan gravitated into the southern rights wing of the Democratic Party. It may be going too far to call him an outright fire-eater, but he was certainly worried about the future of slavery, an institution that Dargan considered to be vital to the southern way of life. He never personally aspired to become a big planter, preferring instead the mercantile atmosphere of Mobile, but he did own thirteen household slaves and defended the right of white society to hold black people as chattel. In a property case in 1848, Dargan ruled against a petition of manumission where a deceased master had stipulated in his will that his slaves be given the option of freedom. Dargan disagreed, declaring that slaves "did not have the legal capacity or power to choose." Nor would they ever, as far as the judge was concerned. To Dargan, slavery was crucial to race order; tampering with it, whether through a private will or more alarmingly through federal decree, augured race war. "Dissolve the relation of master and slave, and what would become of that race?," Dargan asked on a later occasion. "They would either be destroyed by our own hands . . . or we ourselves would become demoralized and degraded."[26]

By the early 1850s, Dargan grew disillusioned with national politics. He returned to his legal practice and watched with fatalistic detachment the increasingly rancorous bifurcation of the North and the South over the extension of slavery in the territories. To Dargan, compromise over the issue was a fool's errand; a resort to secession was just a matter of time. That moment came in 1860, when Abraham Lincoln won the presidency. In December, Dargan spoke before a gathering of the Young Men's Secession Association of Mobile. Stenciled on the club's flag were the words "ALABAMA * The time has come." Dargan gestured toward the banner and dramatically repeated its message three times, slowly and deliberately. He then departed for Montgomery as one of Mobile's delegates to the Secession Convention. For Dargan, the rationale for disunion was obvious: sovereignty for the sake of "African Slavery." After the ordinance passed with his support, Dargan then urged the delegates to brace for a revolutionary struggle. "I have thought that war would be inevitable," he explained, "that our redemption would have to be worked out by war." With the die cast, Dargan beseeched all Alabamians to set aside old grievances and commit totally to the state's bid for independence. The voters in and around Mobile agreed with their delegate and elected him to the First Confederate Congress. In winning Alabama's Ninth District seat with 2,891 votes, Dargan bested the combined tally of two impressive rivals: John W. Portis, a planter from Clarke County (1,594 votes), and Percy Walker, a prominent Mobile politico and erstwhile leader of the city's Know-Nothing Party (1,228 votes).[27]

As a congressman, Edmund Dargan produced a decidedly war Confederate voting record. And he did so in his typically eccentric style. Colleagues recalled him sitting quietly for lengthy periods, wearing "a peculiar gravity of expression," before suddenly rising with a loud "Mr. Cheer-man, Mr. Cheerman" whenever he felt moved to present his views or respond to those with whom he disagreed. Conscription enjoyed his unswerving support. To him, a wartime draft was not merely imperative as an emergency measure; it was wholly permissible, even noble, under the Constitution. When Confederate prospects for victory improved in the latter half of 1862, Dargan favored "putting forth the whole strength of the country now" in the hopes that "one more blow" would produce "sweet beams of peace." He scorned those who objected to conscription. His greatest nemesis on this matter was Henry S. Foote of Tennessee, a defeatist politician who went out of his way to make himself obnoxious to anyone who promoted a total war approach. Foote frequently consumed floor time denouncing conscription, and conscripts themselves, as hypocritical and disgraceful to a democratic polity. Dargan would have none of it. In August 1862, he interrupted one of Foote's stem-winders and blurted out, "If the country was saved by conscripts that mark would be the greatest mark their country could place upon them." The gallery erupted in applause, and a fellow congressman referred to Dargan's retort as "a very sound & eloquent speech." Two months later Dargan again engaged Foote, this time in what one observer called "a disgraceful scene." Evidently, Foote decided to interrupt one of Dargan's speeches, referring to his political adversary as a "damned rascal." Dargan abruptly charged Foote, grabbed him by the collar, and threatened him with a penknife before others intervened to separate the two. Richmond newspapers sensationalized the incident as an assassination attempt that had Dargan wielding a bowie knife.[28]

Along with conscription, Dargan backed every other major piece of war legislation. Impressment and tax-in-kind received his yea vote. Of the two, impressment momentarily troubled the congressman. Dargan considered the appropriation of private property to be "the highest prerogative of government," but as long as such power was "in the hands of the wisest and the best men," by which he presumably meant Jefferson Davis, then its execution could be trusted. Dargan also exhibited caution about suspending habeas corpus, an act that more than any other risked military despotism. He conceded that the army would perforce assert tremendous power over civil authority in any war zone, but he maintained that martial law did not permit arbitrary arrest. Accordingly, Dargan joined the chorus of other politicians who insisted that the Confederacy's suspension laws be limited by time and place, and only target those citizens engaged in crimes against the war effort, such as evasion of the draft. Finally, in financial matters, Dargan supported a variety of plans to pay for the war. He chaired the committee that secured the Erlanger Loan from France and even voted to make Confederate notes legal tender, although—in what one colleague described as "a very strange speech"—he muttered that doing so was unconstitutional. As his record indicates, Dargan was a staunch war Confederate, but he was no lackey to the Davis administration. All of his votes reflected a genuine respect for the seriousness of the policies being enacted.[29]

By summer 1863, Dargan's typically morose demeanor betrayed signs of despair. The loss of Vicksburg in July crushed his spirit. "Mississippi is very nearly subdued and Alabama is nearly exhausted," he opined to secretary of war James Seddon, "by winter both States will be overrun." He alternately blamed the Davis administration and General John Pemberton for the Confederacy's failure to hold the river citadel. Dargan also worried about his young son, Moro, who was a staff officer in the Army of Tennessee. He had once told President Jefferson Davis that he "would Black boots to save my country," but he now believed that only European intervention could save the South. To that end, Dargan recommended that the Confederacy embark on selective emancipation to recruit black people for the rebel army. He specifically had in mind the "Creole Negroes" of Mobile and New Orleans, whom he claimed were "as true to the South as the pure white races." Dargan was not alone in these views, but the Davis administration dismissed his suggestions as the desperate lamentations of a man who had lost his faith. "Ill health and liquor made him crazy," explained one official in the War Department, while another simply remarked that "Mr. D. had an unhappy disposition." To be sure, Alabama was not quite exhausted, but Dargan apparently was: "We are without doubt gone up." His fatalism having returned, the incumbent abruptly declined to seek a second term mere weeks before the election. War Confederates in the Ninth District would have to find a new representative, and do so on short notice.[30]

Three former Whigs represented Alabama in the First Confederate Congress: Thomas Foster, William Chilton, and Francis Lyon. The role of southern Whiggery as a persistent force of antisecessionism has enjoyed scholarly sanction over the years, but this thesis is no longer valid, at least not for Alabama, and certainly not when discussing the Confederate war effort. A great many of Alabama's erstwhile Whigs, including the three in Congress, became strong southern nationalists who seamlessly transferred their allegiance from the Stars and Stripes to the Stars and Bars. Accordingly, they were perfectly comfortable with clothing their nation's executive branch with extraordinary authority. To the extent that Alabama's Whigs embraced federalism, the threat to liberty came not from Richmond, but from Washington, DC. The Confederate States of America was their "Union" now.[31]

Representing Alabama's First District, Thomas Jefferson Foster was a relatively obscure political figure. Born in 1809 to a prominent family of Tennesseans, Foster became an Alabamian in 1836 through his marriage to Virginia Watkins, the daughter of a big slaveholder from Lawrence County. The marriage elevated Thomas to instant planter status, and for the next quarter century he enjoyed a comfortable lifestyle among the rich and famous of the Tennessee River valley. In 1861, no fewer than 128 slaves worked his lands between Courtland and Moulton in Lawrence County. Foster also showed an interest in industrial development, regularly voting the Whig ticket in the hopes that his region might receive the benefits of internal improvements. Personally, he eschewed politics, holding no office despite his vast wealth and influence. During the secession crisis, however, Foster could no longer sit on the sidelines. He urged caution, worrying with good reason (at least until Tennessee also seceded) that his backyard would become the frontline should war ensue. He shared the valley's desire for a popular referendum on secession, but he dropped his reservations after the convention rejected that proposal; and after the Battle of Fort Sumter, he displayed genuine enthusiasm for the cause. Over the summer, Foster helped raise a company for the Twenty-Seventh Alabama Infantry Regiment, and he briefly served as a staff officer overseeing the construction of Fort Henry in Tennessee. In November 1861, he stood for election to the Confederate Congress. It was his first political contest, and it proved a close race with four men vying for the seat. Foster's most formidable opponent was Henry C. Jones, a cooperationist delegate to the Secession Convention who voted against the ordinance and then refused to sign it. But Foster prevailed with a plurality of 2,077 votes against 1,836 for Jones. Another 1,200 votes were divided between the other two candidates. The valley region was certainly cooler toward secession than were other parts of the state, but Foster's victory demonstrates that a sizeable number of Alabamians in the First District wanted a representative who was committed to giving the Confederacy a chance.[32]

Like many Confederate congressmen, Foster was a man torn between his belief in both states' rights and southern nationalism, as his legislative record reveals. On the matter of conscription, in April 1862, he opposed it as an infringement on individual liberty and voted with the minority against the original act. Later that autumn, however, when the war had indeed come to his backyard in the form of Union gunboats and cavalry incursions, Foster dramatically changed his position. Grandstanding on the House floor, the congressman exhibited appalling hyperbole when he ridiculed all legal objections to expanding the draft. “If the Constitution stood between him and his country's freedom,” a gallery observer reported, “he would burn the Constitution.” It was an unusual exhibition of verbal ardor from the normally reserved Foster, but true to its rhetoric he voted for the second conscription act. Interestingly, he argued against the so-called twenty-slave clause, perhaps to avoid possible censure from his yeoman constituency, but probably to gain as many white men as possible in the ranks.[33]

As Federal forces overran more and more of his home district, Foster shifted into the camp of the war Confederates. On numerous occasions from autumn 1862 through summer 1863, he bombarded the governor's office and the Davis administration with updates on the latest depredations by “our fiendish enemy” in the valley region; and he demanded that more be done to protect his constituents. In this sense, Foster conformed to the political pattern whereby congressmen from war-torn or occupied parts of the South proved to be the most strident in their calls for total war policies. Nevertheless, his record sometimes belied his rhetoric. Whereas the congressman voted without hesitation for the Impressment Act, he vacillated over the suspension of habeas corpus. He acceded to the first suspension in February 1862, and he seemed amenable to doing so again in October 1862 but ultimately voted nay. Similarly, when legislation on the tax-in-kind came to the floor in spring 1863, he openly agreed with the bill's proponents, yet he abstained on the final vote. The congressman wanted to win the war, but he apparently fretted over the means to that end.[34]

Unlike Foster, William Parish Chilton of Alabama's Sixth District was a well-known and well-respected state politician (figure 6). Chilton was born in 1810 in Kentucky, where his father was a Baptist minister who taught young William the importance of duty, courtesy, and amity, three traits that proved of enormous value to his subsequent rise in politics. Friends described him oxymoronically as “grave but cheerful.” Chilton furthered his education whenever he could and, after the untimely death of his parents, left home as soon as he could. Immigrating to Alabama in 1831, he earned a living first as a teacher and then as a lawyer, opening a firm in Talladega County. Soon thereafter, Chilton entered politics as a Whig, holding several local offices before winning election to the state supreme court, a position that he held from 1848 to 1856. In reaching this lofty position, the tall and lanky Chilton became one of many examples of the all-American self-made man. Like most southern professionals of his day, Chilton acquired slaves, though his eight bondsmen left him well below the status of the planter class. His precise political views as a Whig prior to the Civil War are unclear, though they were likely in accord

Figure 6. William Parish Chilton, copy print, photographer unknown, 1850s. (Courtesy of Alabama Department of Archives and History)

with the national party's platform. He was, however, an avowed defender of the peculiar institution. In the wake of John Brown's raid in 1859, then state senator Chilton authored a bill in the legislature that helped create a military corps, a body whose purpose was to defend the state against rumored abolitionist conspiracies. And in 1860, he moved to Montgomery, where he joined the firm of the radical states'-rights proponent William Yancey. Nevertheless, during the secession crisis, he espoused the cooperationist position. He shared Yancey's dream of a southern nation, but he considered "unwise" the fire-eating tactics of men like his law partner. Once the deed was done, however, the Confederacy could hardly have found a more dedicated citizen.[35]

Chilton won appointment to the Provisional Confederate Congress and thereafter won election outright as the unopposed representative of Alabama's Sixth District. As a congressman, Chilton reveled in the political life of his new country. His failed effort to keep the national capital in Montgomery barely dampened his zeal. In Richmond, he was a constant presence, rarely absent from House sessions and always involved in the legislative discourse. Fellow Alabamian Jabez Curry applauded not only Chilton's remarkable work ethic, but his unfailing optimism. Behind the amiable demeanor lay a serious war Confederate. On most of the major military bills, Chilton voted aye. He not only voted for conscription but pressed the War Department to implement the law with speed and vigor. "I would have every man assist in the defense of the country if necessary," Chilton declared, insisting that exemptions were neither privileged nor permanent; even congressmen might be called on to shoulder arms. He was similarly committed to the policies of impressment and taxation, calling on planters to forego cash crops for personal profit in favor of foodstuffs for the army and the people. In keeping with his prewar Whiggery, Chilton was also one of the first Confederate politicians to champion homegrown industrial development under government supervision. Only on the suspension of habeas corpus did Chilton reveal any dissent, voting against the measure out of concern that such a law made the president "absolutely and essentially a dictator." With the growing encroachment of enemy forces into southern territory, however, he hardened his prowar stance. In October 1862, he presented a resolution that declared, "all Federal officers captured within our limits shall be treated as felons" subject to capital punishment. One astonished colleague exclaimed that Chilton had raised the "black flag" of retaliation. Going into the election of 1863, no one could mistake Chilton as anything other than a war Confederate.[36]

Rounding out the Whig faction of Alabama's delegation was Francis Strother Lyon (figure 7). A gray-haired, blue-eyed lawyer and Whig politico from Demopolis in Marengo County, Lyon was one of the state's largest planters. He, his wife, and their two daughters resided in comfort at Bluff Hall, a white, two-story mansion on the Tombigbee River, while 189 slaves tilled two thousand acres of surrounding cotton fields. His personal wealth notwithstanding, Lyon was a frugal and meticulous man who disdained financial fraud and waste. Born in North Carolina in 1800, Lyon moved to Alabama in 1817, initially earning a living as a clerk before passing the bar in 1821. The next year, young Francis attained the job of secretary of the Senate, where he won praise for his neatly written and lucidly summarized minutes of all of the proceedings. Politics beckoned in the 1830s, and Lyon twice won election to the US House, serving from 1835 to 1839. In the late 1840s, the state appointed Lyon as a special commissioner whose task was to rectify years

Figure 7. Francis Strother Lyon, copy print, photographer unknown, 1850s. (Courtesy of Alabama Department of Archives and History)

of mismanagement in the offices of the Bank of Alabama. By all accounts, Lyon speedily and efficiently cleaned the ledgers, reducing the amount of indebtedness by almost $9 million, thereby restoring public confidence in the state's financial structure. From then on, he was regarded as something of a genius in money matters.[37]

Throughout the 1850s, Lyon closely monitored the rancorous debates over the fate of slavery in the nation, though he usually kept his views private. A nationalist on economic policy, he was a southerner when it came to defending the peculiar institution. Following the demise of the Whig party as a national institution, Lyon joined the ranks of the South's fire-eaters, befriending William Yancey and serving in 1860 as chairman of the Democratic state convention. This convention promulgated a platform that required the state's delegates to walk out if the party did not pledge to protect slavery in the territories. During the proceedings, the normally equipoised Lyon lambasted the Republican Party and lauded the Dred Scott decision. "Let no man call this a disunion movement," he exclaimed at one point; "It is a movement to uphold the constitution." Semantics aside, Lyon strongly favored Alabama's secession in 1861. And the voters evidently liked the newly radicalized Lyon, electing him to Congress by a comfortable majority over the combined tally of two other candidates—Jack F. Cocke, a unionist Whig planter and Thomas H. Herndon, a fire-eating Democrat.[38]

Congressman Lyon was among the earliest advocates of total war policies. According to the historians Warner and Yearns, "Few members showed as much awareness of the Confederacy's needs." This assertion is not an exaggeration. On the major war measures that passed through the House, Lyon could always be found with the majority. He voted for all of the various bills on conscription despite his opposition to the twenty-slave exemption clause. He voted for impressment, including the government's use of slaves for military purposes, and for the tax-in-kind. Lyon voiced support for the suspension of habeas corpus, though he urged the president to invoke this power only in areas directly threatened by Union invasion; he appears to have been absent, however, when the matter came to a vote in October 1862. In a letter to President Davis, Lyon even intimated that military control of the South's railroads might prove to be a wiser course than permitting such a vital transportation system to remain in private hands. Lyon's consistent support may have influenced the War Department's decision to make Demopolis an important military center for the western theater.[39]

It was on the issue of fiscal policy that Francis Lyon displayed his greatest zeal for the cause. As a leading member of both the Ways and Means Committee and the Currency Committee, Lyon sought to pay for the war through policies that were designed to generate revenue without jeopardizing the solvency of the Confederacy. To this end, he favored direct taxation, supplemented by an occasional and conservative resort to loans, along with a national currency that he hoped might supplant the diverse banknotes of the states. Lyon was instrumental in enacting the war tax of August 1861. Levied against the states and based on property values, this tax eventually generated over $17 million for the Confederacy. Lyon's advocacy of taxation, however, encountered resistance from treasury secretary Christopher Memminger. The secretary agreed that taxation was probably the most responsible approach but believed that collection was too time consuming and that such monies would prove inadequate to wartime needs. Rather than tax the states, Memminger preferred to borrow money from them, doing so through hefty loans that struggled to reconcile the complicated exchange rates between state currencies and the newly printed Confederate treasury notes. These notes functioned as "bills of credit," promising cash interest only after the war had been won. An alarmed Lyon rightly considered Memminger's plan to be a recipe for fiscal chaos and runaway inflation. By July 1863, $400–500 million treasury notes were in circulation, and their value in gold had diminished by 90 percent since the early months of 1861. Reluctantly concluding that a single currency was probably unconstitutional, Lyon nevertheless strove to establish the Confederate dollar as legal tender in all transactions between the national and state governments. In pursuing this policy, he calculated that treasury notes would gradually replace state notes (over $20 million of which were circulating) through required usage. This indirect attempt to centralize the South's financial structure ran afoul of politicians who believed that Lyon's currency ideas would undermine the sovereignty of the states.[40]

While waiting and wondering whether Congress would embrace his currency ideas, Lyon renewed his efforts to fund the war through taxation. On this topic, friend and fellow congressman Warren Akin of Georgia noted that Lyon's speaking style was often "very dry" but that his command of the issue was always respected. In April 1863, the Alabamian helped draft the bill that became the much-criticized tax-in-kind. The law authorized the government to collect up to a tenth of all farm produce and iron production and 8 percent of all cash crop harvests. In defending this policy before Congress, Lyon stressed the usual refrain of military necessity, but he also explained that appropriating real commodities in lieu of money payments made perfect sense if for no other reason than that the South's multifarious paper currency was fast becoming worthless. Opponents countered that a tax-in-kind would place yet another burden on an already oppressed citizenry. Texas congressmen Franklin Sexton, for instance, admired Lyon's passion on the topic but believed that the Alabamian's speech "was really a good argument against the bill." Lyon grumbled that no one seemed happy with the bill's language, but he was satisfied when his version of it finally passed. When the session ended at the end of April, Lyon was proud of his role in shaping Confederate war policy. For the voters back home, their incumbent was an undeniable war Confederate.[41]

The odd man out in the Alabama delegation was William Russell Smith (figure 8). A political independent, Smith is difficult to classify as either a war Confederate or a peace Confederate; his words and deeds suggest that he fluctuated between the two. Born in Kentucky in 1815, Smith was orphaned at eight years of age and removed to a foster family in Tuscaloosa, the city that he called home for most of the rest of his life. A studious yet outgoing youth, he showed an aptitude for law, which he subsequently practiced even though he yearned to become a famous writer. In 1833, Smith published a collec-

Figure 8. William Russell Smith, studio portrait, photographer unknown, 1850s. (Courtesy of Alabama Department of Archives and History)

tion of poems about his college days at the University of Alabama, the first of nearly twenty literary works. The arts, however, were only one of Smith's ambitions. The savant also wanted to be a warrior, his short, wiry frame notwithstanding. In 1836, he helped raise a militia company, hoping to see action in the Creek War. With the abrupt end of that conflict, he sought passage to Texas, where one of his brothers had been killed at the Goliad massacre. But the revolution there ended before young Billy could arrange transportation. Having failed to satiate his martial fantasies, Smith moved into publishing, first as the owner of the literary magazine *Bachelor's Button*, which went bankrupt, and then as editor of the *Tuscaloosa Monitor*. His work as a newsman ignited a passion for politics, one that he soon realized he would never satisfy, but that would forever beckon.[42]

In a pattern that was indicative of his restlessness, Smith experimented with all of the leading parties of the antebellum period. In 1839, he joined the Whigs, winning several local elections before growing disenchanted with that party's call for protective tariffs. It had taken a few years for Smith to clarify his political principles, but by 1843 he espoused a strict constructionist view of the Constitution. Therefore, he logically found the Democrats appealing, joining that party and winning a few more elections. The rise of the fire-eaters, however, with their obsessive fixation on slavery and their incessant talk of secession, disturbed him. Smith was a Union man. So, in 1854, he became a member of the Know-Nothings, embracing that party's efforts to steer Americans away from the internal discord over slavery and direct their attention against the supposed dangers of Catholicism and unregulated immigration. Winning a seat in the US House in 1855, Smith further distanced himself from his erstwhile party by denouncing the spread of slavery into Kansas. Significantly, he was one of few southerners who voted to censure South Carolina's Preston Brooks for a brutal assault on Massachusetts's Charles Sumner in May 1856. Independent in his actions, Smith was unfailingly gracious and good-humored with his words. In response to those who criticized his seeming lack of constancy, he glibly replied, "they can't make political parties any faster than I can join them." It was a fair enough statement until the Republican Party formed; this entity was one that even Smith found repulsive. In the 1860 election, he cast his ballot for the Constitutional Union ticket of John Bell.[43]

The Alabama Secession Convention in January 1861 proved the defining moment in William Smith's political career. Elected to the convention as a cooperationist, he quickly emerged as a leader of that faction. Moreover, Smith's detailed minutes of the proceedings established him as an invaluable chronicler of this pivotal event. From the outset, Smith made it clear to everyone that he held in contempt both president-elect Abraham Lincoln and the Republican Party, but he also rejected the straight-out call for immediate secession. To the straight-out majority, he posed what he termed the "naked question," namely whether the incoming Republicans had committed an overt act of tyranny simply by winning an election. If so, then Smith would acquiesce; if not, then he found no cause for severing the Union. Annoyed by the fire-eating rhetoric of such delegates as William Yancey, Smith retorted with cool sarcasm. He referred to the straight-outs as a "meagre majority," contending that the cooperationists reflected the true mind of Alabama's citizenry. Throughout, Smith conceded that Alabama enjoyed the right of revolution, but he believed that the current rush to secession was unwarranted. In the end, he voted against the ordinance and later refused to sign the document. Nevertheless, Smith pledged allegiance to the outcome and at the close of the convention gave way to a bout of patriotic sentimentalism. The ladies of Montgomery had sewn a new state flag, one that depicted a sword-wielding heroine holding aloft a banner containing the state's name and one star. Arcing over Lady Liberty were the words "Independent Now and Forever." When the flag was unfurled in the convention hall, a noticeably moved Smith exclaimed, "though it glows with but a single star, may that star increase in magnitude and brilliancy, until it out-rivals the historic glories of the Star-Spangled Banner!"[44]

Shortly after secession, Smith raised the Twenty-Sixth Alabama Infantry and became its colonel. For a man often described as a staunch opponent of secession, Smith's evident willingness to kill those who sought to suppress the rebellion suggests that his primal loyalty was always to the South. Just as his martial aspirations came to naught in 1836, so too would his dream of leading men into battle against the northern invader. In autumn 1861, he won election to the Confederate Congress. It was a narrow plurality over three other candidates, including runner-up Newbern H. Browne, Tuscaloosa's leading fire-eater. Smith was already in Richmond at the time on other business. To his family and his regiment, he delivered a rather ambivalent farewell: "I can serve our unhappy country more effectually here than in the field."[45]

As a congressman, Smith maintained his political independence, a task made a bit easier given the absence of a party system. While most of the Alabama delegation supported some form of war socialism, Smith could never reconcile military necessity with his political principles. On the matter of conscription, for instance, he acknowledged the South's desperate need for manpower but believed that compulsory service was an unacceptable step toward despotism. He abstained on the measure when it first came up and voted against subsequent bills. On September 9, 1862, Smith questioned the constitutionality of the second conscription act, warning that its passage "would produce eternal antagonism between the Confederate and State governments." He abstained on the policy of impressment, but when it came to the suspension of habeas corpus and the tax-in-kind, Smith could not stay neutral; he voted against both measures. Curiously, he did support the destruction of property bill and approved of Castle Thunder, a makeshift jail in Richmond that in May 1863 came under congressional scrutiny for alleged mistreatment of residents accused of disloyalty. On fiscal policy, Smith's old Whiggery resurfaced when he voted to create a single national currency. His roll call votes aside, Smith does not appear to have engaged in much floor debate, a stark contrast to his outspoken conduct at the Secession Convention. By the end of 1862, he appears to have grown disillusioned by the rebellion, though he usually kept his opinions to himself. In an October letter to his wife, he opined that "the men who inaugurated this war are unwilling to admit the possibility of failure." Smith soon concluded that only British and French intervention could save the South from destruction.[46]

Smith was clearly dubious of the cause, but he was no peace Confederate. Instead, he was a southerner troubled by a sense of impending doom. He could sound defeatist, as he did in a letter to his wife in February 1863: "There is nothing original in this movement, not the building up of a new government, but a mere transfer of principles and a change of rulers and boundaries." But he could also exhibit visceral nationalism, such as when he expressed outrage over the Emancipation Proclamation. Smirking at that document's supposed emphasis on liberation, Smith ranted that Lincoln's real intent was slave insurrection and race war. (Smith owned five slaves.) He found solace in the military heroism of his son Sidney Binion Smith. The boy served as a lieutenant in the regiment that his father helped organize, the Twenty-Sixth Alabama Infantry. He also earned a reputation for reckless bravery, suffering a grievous wound at Gaines's Mill in June 1862, a battle that was fought mere miles from the Confederate capital, where a nervous father waited. Congressman Smith privately worried that the courage displayed by his son, and that of thousands of other young southern men, was not matched by an economy capable of keeping them properly armed and supplied.[47]

Indignation and familial pride are poor substitutes for genuine nationalism. Try as he may, Smith could never conjure any durable enthusiasm for the Confederacy. He even seems to have grown bored with the whole business of war. "Congress is literally doing nothing," he complained to his wife in March 1863, "I groan under the thought of a long session." He avoided the halls of Congress as much as possible and increasingly sought refuge in his writing. In 1863, he published *The Royal Ape*, a "gossipy" comedy about the Lincoln administration. The title character is, of course, the enemy president himself, depicted on stage as a hapless commander-in-chief who by day shamelessly flirts with the White House domestics and who by night suffers nightmare deliriums that suggest that his wartime policies are misguided. Certainly no literary masterpiece, *The Royal Ape* does have humorous and insightful moments. It also reveals the playwright's deep love for the South, an attitude that was not always apparent in his political discourse.[48]

As one of the few examples of Confederate literature, *The Royal Ape* deserves fuller explication. First performed in spring 1863, the play is set in 1861. While intended to bring some levity to war-weary citizens, it also serves as blunt propaganda with its undisguised affirmations of the Confederate cause. Lincoln, when not parodied as an ape, is exposed as a royal—the autocrat that the South always knew him to be. "A state of war is one of despotism," Lincoln lectures a group of Republican senators in an early scene, "there should be, to control it, but one will, and that must be untrammel'd. Tyranny, brutal, remorseless tyranny is needful to bring success." (Smith was no doubt aware that his own president, Jefferson Davis, had been charged in the southern press for having exhibited similar sentiments.) But not to fear, the playwright reassures his audience that the enemy is no match for southern manhood. Lincoln himself acknowledges this fact, telling the portly Winfield Scott that whereas that old general's 1848 campaign in Mexico had been against "Lilliputians," the current war pitted northern boys against southern "Brobdignags." There follows a farcical reenactment of the First Battle of Manassas, with Yankee recruits bumbling around the stage while Confederate soldiers march with parade-ground precision. In one particularly outrageous scene, ten Union soldiers are led by a colonel in the struggle to capture a single rebel private. "Do me a little fresh arithmetic," the southerner asks rhetorically; "How many will it take to conquer us?" The prisoner then miraculously overpowers his guards, killing one, chasing away the others, and capturing the colonel.[49]

The play also makes a mockery of the North's supposed crusade against slavery. The abolitionist senator Henry Wilson of Massachusetts becomes the straw man for Yankee righteousness. Prior to the Manassas battle scene, the senator betrays the true face of abolitionism: "It is not that I love the slaves so well, but, that I hate their masters." Brandishing a child's pop-gun musket, Wilson proceeds to accompany the Union army into combat, but he becomes lost in the ensuing chaos. There follows one of the play's most bizarre scenes. Wilson runs into the characters Sambo and Hercules, "negroes in grotesque Confederate uniform." Wilson is taken aback by their demands that he surrender. "I sent this army to fight for you; don't you want to be free?" the shocked senator asks, adding, "I bring you liberty and equality." Sambo responds curtly, "Oh! darn your *quality*. No, hoss I am already free. You know de law in dis new federashun, dat ebery nigger dat captivates a Yankee is to be free. So you see, boss, you are *my* prisoner—my *contraband*." Never was the positive good argument more ludicrously presented.[50]

The last two acts of *The Royal Ape* return to the antics of the Lincoln White House. The rebels are marching on Washington, DC, and the president is preparing to flee the capital. Displaying a total lack of priorities, he orders Mary Todd to "bring up my manuscripts," lest these supposedly precious documents fall into enemy hands. The First Lady hurries on stage with a large bundle of books whose titles reveal the true intellectual passions of the Great Emancipator: *Bathsheba's Bath, Fatal Flirtations, Coquetry on Stilts, The Magic Touch of Whiskers,* and *Kentucky's Bright Eyed Heloconides,* among many other ridiculous works that are proudly described by the president as "master pieces in the opinion of Smithsonian critics." After safeguarding his essential library, Mr. Lincoln affixes a phony mustache and makes for the exit. In the meantime, Mrs. Lincoln beckons her son Robert to round up the family servants. "Go, knock up all the women—everyone," she exclaims in one the play's funniest moments. "Did ever a mother so advise a son?" Robert quips in an aside. The comedy comes to an end with the first family hastily boarding a carriage, Mary Todd toting a carpetbag of her husband's books, Robert sporting a dress and a wig of blond curls, and the president himself further decked out in Scotch cap and striped pants. "If this ain't despotism, then pray what is," a stupefied driver asks, as Robert Lincoln faces the audience and exclaims, "I played the *girl,* and dad, he played the *ape.*"[51]

It is unclear how the play was received or how long it ran. Smith privately hoped that it might bring him some fame, though he complained to his wife that the acting troupe was inferior. At the very least, however, it enabled the congressman to escape the ennui of political life in Richmond. It also permitted him to share indirectly his cynical yet melancholy view of war. For instance, at one point he presents General P. G. T. Beauregard, delivering a martial exhortation to a regiment of Alabamians. "An absent arm will be the badge of glory," the general shouts, assuring the men that the folks back home "will honor the deformities that sword and bullets make on brave and daring men." This homage is overly dramatic to be sure, written perhaps with the wounded Sidney in mind, but it reveals tacit doubt as to whether glory was indeed worth the potential loss of a beloved son. At another point, Smith has a DC resident reflecting dourly on the North's political leadership. "These politicians bring on the wars, but when it comes to fighting they greatly prefer the smell of a steam pipe and the snort of an engine to the sulphurous breath and obstreperous lungs of a cannon." It would come as no surprise to Smith's audience that Yankees were waging the war as a mere means toward their ultimate goal of corporate industrial capitalism. One final example shows two White House domestics fighting for the affection of Robert Lincoln. At last, one relents, "Well, let him choose between us; Love scorns force." This last line is the rebellion in microcosm. How could the real Lincoln think that the South would ever consider reunion at the point of a gun barrel? Although a simple comedy, *The Royal Ape* exposes the author's romantic view of the Confederacy. As a rational politician, Smith strove to restrain the inexorable forces of secession and total war. But as an artist, he reveled in the

South's bold and quixotic gamble for independence. In his heart, Smith was a war Confederate.[52]

LEGISLATIVE ANALYSIS

Going into the election of 1863, most of Alabama's congressmen ran on a nationalist platform that conformed to their voting records back in Richmond. Whatever states' rights ideologies they may have professed at the beginning of their terms had clearly been cast aside in favor of total war. In one of the few targeted studies of Alabama's congressional delegates, however, Helen Jeanette Jackson argues that none of them ever really supported a centralized war effort. Alabamians remained "firm in their conviction of the supremacy of state sovereignty," she explains, and so they never developed "the fervent patriotism so needed by the South during these trying times." Yet Jackson's own evidence, as well as the House journals of the Confederate Congress, strongly suggests precisely the opposite. On every critical war policy, most of the Alabamians unmistakably leaned toward centralized authority. This is especially true for conscription. The first act passed 54–26 in the House in April 1862 with seven Alabamians in the majority (Foster voted against it, and Smith abstained). The second act passed 49–39 in September 1862 with five Alabamians in the majority. This time around, Foster voted for it, while Clopton, Curry, and Ralls dissented over discrepancies regarding exemptions and substitutions, not the need for conscription itself. So, disagreeable elements within the law notwithstanding, eight of Alabama's nine congressmen supported conscription. Impressment reveals a similar prowar slant. When it passed 52–7 in March 1863, seven Alabamians were among the overwhelming majority. Ralls and Smith were either absent or abstained; no Alabamian opposed this measure. On the tax-in-kind, which passed the House 47–37 in April 1863, five Alabamians voted yea. A sixth, Ralls, had voted for an earlier House version but was absent for the final vote. Therefore, six Alabamians supported this law in some form. Clopton, Foster, and Smith (a Democrat, a Whig, and an independent) voted against it. Even on lesser war policies, Alabamians backed the hard line. Eight of them voted for destruction of property, which passed the House in March 1862 by a 72–13 margin. The usual outlier, Smith, did not cast a vote for this bill. Finally, on the matter of suspending habeas corpus, the Alabamians evinced genuine misgivings, but in the end they still either helped grant the president this power or kept their opinions to themselves. Helen Jackson herself goes so far as to say that "probably the state least openly critical at this time was Alabama." There is no extant record of the first vote on suspension. The second act passed the House 38–29 in October 1862, with only Dargan, Pugh, and Ralls in the majority.

Chilton, Clopton, and Foster had approved an earlier House version, leaving only Curry, Lyon, and Smith (a Democrat, a Whig, and an independent) as possible opponents of the bill. Smith abstained, however, while Curry and Lyon were absent prior to the vote (though both later voted for a postelection act of suspension in February 1864). If these records are any indication, and they assuredly are, then Alabama's delegation to the First Confederate Congress was decidedly prowar. Of the five policies discussed above, Dargan and Pugh voted for all of them; Curry, Lyon, and Foster for four; Chilton, Clopton, and Ralls for three. Smith is the only one who never voted yea, but then he seldom voted at all.[53]

This prowar voting pattern belies many of the older guides for why Confederate politicians acted as they did. Prewar party affiliations offer practically no insight as Alabama's five Democrats and its three Whigs displayed bipartisan support for total war. Jeffery A. Jenkins corroborates this bipartisanship for the South at large, asserting that "former party labels had no impact on voting in the no-party Confederate House." To be fair, however, old party allegiances did manifest themselves on fiscal and judicial topics. The Whigs (including Smith in a reiteration of his erstwhile connection) advocated the creation of a single, legal tender for the South. Lyon understood that the constitution forbade eliminating the state currencies, but he helped push through a bill that required all citizens to accept Confederate notes as payment. Foster went so far as to advocate conscripting anyone who refused to accept such notes. Conversely, the Democrats generally opposed federal monetary policies, an issue that historian Don E. Fehrenbacher notes was one of few during the war for which the states' rights doctrine successfully reared its head. Only Curry and Dargan expressed any interest in a centralized currency, but neither actually voted their support. Ralls dismissed legal tender as "exceedingly unjust," while Clopton thought that a more aggressive prosecution of counterfeiters was a smarter financial strategy. Similarly, in debates over whether to create a supreme court for the Confederacy, the Whigs (especially Chilton) urged doing so, whereas the Democrats all objected. Neither legal tender nor a supreme court was ever established.[54]

The Alabama case study also turns on its head the enduring "interior" versus "exterior" thesis of Thomas B. Alexander and Richard E. Beringer. These scholars contend that Confederate congressmen from exterior (i.e., battleground) states, such as Kentucky and Virginia, voted disproportionately for harsh policies because they were already being ravaged and so had nothing to lose from imposing greater demands on the citizenry. Conversely, interior (i.e., resource) states generally opposed total war because they were yet untouched and so had very much to lose from policies that required extraordinary sacrifice. Not so the interior state of Alabama, whose delegates proved as hawkish as their brethren in the front-line states. Admittedly, Foster fits into the exterior category; his Tennessee River valley district suffered frequent Yankee depredations. Lyon and Chilton, however, represented virtually untouched interior districts, and yet both are classified by historians as two of the staunchest war Confederates in the entire South. It was precisely because Alabama had so much to lose that these men supported a total war. Alabama's political leaders intuitively understood that conscription, impressment, and all the other controversial laws for which they voted were imperative means of avoiding the physical destruction unfolding in neighboring regions.[55]

Further profiles of Alabama's nine congressmen reveal a commitment to the Confederacy that crosses other sociopolitical models. They were all mature, family men. Lyon was the elder at sixty-three, and Curry the babe at thirty-eight. The other seven were in their forties or fifties. If there is a prewar trend to be found it is that the three Whigs were all over fifty, whereas no Democrat besides Dargan was older than forty-three. Like virtually every other southerner in Congress, they were all slaveholders, collectively owning at least 437 chattels. Five boasted planter status: Lyon and Foster, former Whigs, were at the top of the tier, followed by Pugh, Curry, and Ralls. Therefore, the fate of the peculiar institution arguably weighed heaviest on the old Whigs, but it was of great importance to all nine, regardless of previous party or political outlook. Jeffery Jenkins is absolutely correct when he says that these lawmakers "had a financial incentive to see the Confederacy succeed." The Alabamians were mostly Christian gentlemen, though of varied denominations. Chilton, Curry, and Dargan were Baptists; Clopton and Ralls (both Democrats) were Methodists; Lyon and Pugh were Episcopalian; Foster's specific faith is unknown; and the contrarian Smith was unchurched, though in later life this one-time Know-Nothing ironically embraced Catholicism. So again, there is no real pattern pitting Whig against Democrat. And it is certainly mere coincidence that the two most devout in practicing their faith—Curry, a future Baptist minister, and Ralls, an active minister—were the only incumbents to lose their bids for reelection. Finally, most of these Alabamians had a direct familial stake in the war's outcome. Dargan, Lyon, and Smith each had sons in the rebel army, while Clopton and Curry had brothers in the ranks. These men were not asking others to die for a cause that they were not similarly willing to sacrifice for.[56]

Another significant indication of Alabama's congressional support for the war is found in the delegates' generally cooperative respect toward President Jefferson Davis. Much has been alleged about the lack of rapport between the Confederacy's president and its congress, and there were certainly politicians who disliked Davis. Most historians, however, agree that the legislative branch rarely denied its commander in chief the laws that he needed to wage war to the fullest. To the extent that there was an anti-Davis cabal in Congress, Alabamians were not part of it. Other than Senator Yancey, who developed a tempestuous relationship with Davis, congressional Alabamians almost never spoke ill of the president. In fact, the state's other senator, Clement Clay, was a close friend of Davis's. To be sure, the Alabamians could be critical at times, but their opinions were never insidious and never conducted in open forums. For instance, in private conversations Curry complained of the president's haughty style: "We were apparently expected to put into statutes what he deemed best for the interests of the Confederacy." But in public, Curry called Davis "a noble fellow" who was better qualified for the office than virtually anyone else in the South. In short, Curry "believed in team play" and steered clear of the president's enemies. Similarly, Pugh was known to gossip about the administration with fellow congressmen with whom he shared a boardinghouse in Richmond, but his disdain was aimed more at specific cabinet members, particularly Judah Benjamin, than at the president himself. Foster complained that he and other congressional delegates had been "treated cavalierly" on occasion by departmental bureaucrats, but he never implicated the president in this shabby behavior. Smith quietly dismissed Davis as "old, ailing, and lacking in self-confidence," but he still respected the office of the presidency.[57]

On one occasion an Alabama congressman did get into hot water with the president. Chilton faulted the executive branch for various inefficiencies, especially its maladroit enforcement of conscription, but he avoided as much as possible getting into quarrels with his commander in chief. As a member of the Post Office Committee, however, he was drawn into a ludicrous dispute between the president and Senator Yancey over a postmaster appointment for Montgomery. Because Chilton favored Yancey's man over the president's, the congressman briefly endured the latter's wrath, but the matter soon blew over. More often than not, Alabama's delegates developed a cordial relationship with the president. Lyon, for instance, went out of his way to entertain the president at his plush home in Demopolis whenever Davis visited the state. The lack of any significant friction between Davis and his colleagues from Alabama should come as no surprise, for they were really of one mind; they wanted to win the war. In fact, the majority of Alabamians were part of what Richard Bensel calls a "statist coalition" within Congress, one that did not always like the person of Jefferson Davis but that consistently set aside its states' rights ideology in favor of increased executive war powers.[58]

Based on this study of Alabama's congressional delegation, the sole question worth asking any Confederate politician in 1863 was how badly did he want to win the war? As the research demonstrates, the main divide in Congress was not between former Whigs and Democrats, or between states' rights purists and centralizing pragmatists, or between those who liked Davis and those who did not, or between "the politics of individual liberty" and "the politics of national unity," as George Rable would have it. Rather, congressmen split into two basic camps: war Confederates and peace Confederates. The former thought victory both desirable and possible and so were willing to promote authoritarian laws to achieve it; the latter cherished the idea of victory but were dubious of the military prospects and so approached legislation with an eye toward damage control. This division into two camps also reflected the frame of mind of the voters back home, most of whom cared little about prewar politics or political philosophies, at least not while their communities and loved ones were in the throes of an all-out war. The people were going to vote either for men who wanted to press on in the forlorn hope of independence or for men who wanted to cut the South's losses before an inevitable Yankee triumph. As Wilfred Buck Yearns aptly notes in his study of the 1863 elections, "the administration program, particularly the peace issue, dominated every race." All of Alabama's congressmen, with the exception of Smith, were willingly, even proudly, complicit in the Confederacy's war policies. None of them, even Smith, were tainted by the defeatism of the state's nascent Peace Society. Whatever their prewar views on states' rights and secession, total war was their de facto platform in 1863, and the election was a plebiscite on whether these politicians still reflected the popular will (table 1).[59]

THE CONGRESSIONAL RACES

The race most scrutinized by observers at the time, and by historians since, pitted Jabez Curry against Marcus Cruikshank in the Fourth District. Curry had good reason to be concerned about his prospects for reelection. The people acknowledged the incumbent's intellectual talents, but a great many no longer shared his total war convictions. Moreover, the Peace Society had made inroads into the district, while deserter bands roamed the rural county precincts, particularly in Randolph, where some four hundred men allegedly engaged in banditry. Curry's condescending public lectures about moral turpitude on the home front and the "quicksand" of popular democracy, though honest and candid, likely only infuriated these dissident groups all the more. Emerging to challenge Curry for his seat was Marcus H. Cruikshank, a lawyer and newspaperman from Talladega, who in 1863 was also the mayor of that city. In the prewar years, Cruikshank promoted the Whig agenda in the pages of his *Alabama Reporter*, and during the secession crisis he strongly opposed

Table 1. Alabama's Congressional Returns—1863 (by District)

County	Candidate	Candidate	Candidate	Candidate
District 1	**Foster (I)**	**Unknown**		
Franklin	nvr	nvr		
Lauderdale	337	141		
Lawrence	389	236		
Limestone	333	nvr		
Madison	396	nvr		
Morgan	402	nvr		
Total	**1,857**	**377**		
District 2	**Smith (I)**	**Fowler**		
Blount	87	134		
Fayette	342	177		
Jefferson	331	229		
Marion	134	131		
Tuscaloosa	672	301		
Walker	190	124		
Winston	0	12		
Total	**1,756**	**1,108**		
District 3	**Cobb**	**Ralls (I)**	**Sheffield**	
Cherokee	596	413	69	
DeKalb	587	136	88	
Jackson	126	134	94	
Marshall	229	79	219	
St. Clair	573	204	12	
Total	**2,111**	**966**	**482**	
District 4	**Cruikshank**	**Curry (I)**		
Calhoun	605	761		
Randolph	850	567		
Shelby	582	439		
Talladega	1,199	532		
Total	**3,236**	**2,299**		
District 5	**Lyon (I)**	**Cocke**	**Misc.[a]**	
Bibb	493	nvr	8	
Choctaw	180	169	1	
Greene	467	nvr	12	

Continued on the next page

Table 1. *Continued*

County	Candidate	Candidate	Candidate	Candidate
Marengo	379	29	nvr	
Perry	408	nvr	nvr	
Pickens	285	nvr	16	
Sumter	296	nvr	nvr	
Total	**2,508**	**198**	**37**	
District 6	**Chilton (I)**	**Lane**		
Autauga	263	327		
Butler	190	643		
Coosa	422	849		
Dallas	731	52		
Lowndes	529	70		
Monty	806	553		
Total	**2,941**	**2,494**		
District 7	**Clopton (I)**	**Cadenhead**	**Misc.**[b]	
Chambers	611	385	8	
Macon	832	237	5	
Russell	571	273	4	
Tallapoosa	484	922	nvr	
Total	**2,498**	**1,817**	**17**	
District 8	**Pugh (I)**	**Jones**	**Wiley**	**Starke**
Barbour	538	305	245	82
Coffee	95	202	166	119
Covington	99	162	131	26
Dale	154	375	160	29
Henry	258	49	275	17
Pike	422	280	385	113
Total	**1,566**	**1,373**	**1,362**	**386**
District 9	**Dickinson**	**Langdon**	**Hall**	**Smith**
Baldwin	49	101	55	nvr
Clarke	414	54	17	nvr
Conecuh	113	193	36	2
Mobile	546	952	146	nvr
Monroe	384	146	10	nvr
Washington	86	48	3	1
Wilcox	274	166	7	60
Total	**1,866**	**1,660**	**274**	**63**

Table 1. *Continued*

[a] Miscellaneous votes in District 5: James Webb, 8 from Bibb; James Dowdell, 1 from Choctaw; Turner Reavis, 8 from Greene; Thomas Herndon, 2 from Greene; Augustus Benners, 1 from Greene; James Taylor, 1 from Greene; William Smith, 16 from Pickens; 37 total.
[b] Miscellaneous votes in District 7: Samuel Dailey, 8 from Chambers and 5 from Macon; Alpheus Baker, 3 from Russell; John Gill Shorter, 1 from Russell; 17 total.
Note: Incumbents indicated with (I); "nvr" signifies that no vote was recorded.
Source: Election Files of the Alabama Secretary of State, folders 12 and 13, SG002475, Alabama Department of Archives and History.

disunion. He frankly believed that the South had no chance of prevailing in a military contest with the North. To him, the war would only jeopardize the institution of slavery (he owned eleven slaves himself). As the wartime mayor, Cruikshank frequently reminded the people of Talladega to watch their chattel closely and decreed that "Negro gatherings be strictly prohibited." Sharing this outlook was one of his close friends, Lewis Parsons, a fellow Whig from Talladega and an aspirant for the state legislature. Together, they represented the Peace Society of the Coosa River valley. And together, they strove to unseat Curry as the first step in a program for reconstruction—a ceasefire with the North followed by a negotiated reunification, ideally with slavery still intact. Supporters expressed private hopes that peace Confederates would "make a clean sweep." Cruikshank, however, was careful not to overplay his antiwar message lest he appear craven. In public statements, he always praised the valor of the Confederate soldier and often referred to Abraham Lincoln as "the miserable creature." But he stressed that the war had gone on for too long at too high a cost in lives and treasure. "No possible effort," he therefore declared, "should be spared to secure an *honorable peace*."[60]

Curry agreed that Cruikshank was popular with the voters and "a very worthy man" in general, but he was appalled by his opponent's antiwar platform. The incumbent brashly countered by describing himself as "a secessionist in favor of a vigorous prosecution of the war." Notions of "reconstruction" and "honorable peace" were nothing more than euphemisms for "humbly begging the Yankees to abandon their wicked purposes." Anything less than complete independence, he averred, "was a proposition too monstrous to be tolerated by any Southerner." Curry tried in vain to draw his rival into a series of public debates, so he canvassed the district alone. On the hustings in Talladega, he railed against the Peace Society and insinuated that men like Cruikshank and Parsons were cowards. Such comments appear to have ignited a family feud, one involving Parsons's son George and Curry's brother Mark, both of whom were serving in Company A of the Eighth Confederate Cavalry. During a card game one evening in camp, Lieutenant Mark Curry cast aspersions against Private George Parsons's father. The latter became enraged and shot Curry. Fortunately, the lieutenant suffered only a minor wound. An ensuing court-martial ultimately acquitted the private of any wrongdoing; George was upholding family honor. Whether or not he was influenced by this incident, Congressman Curry did tone down the personal attacks and instead relied on his newspaper surrogates to campaign for him. The *Jacksonville Republican* (Calhoun County) and the *Democratic Watchtower* (Talladega County) aggressively defended Curry's legislative record, stressing his vote to increase the pay of soldiers, eliminate the twenty-slave exemption, and reduce the salaries of congressmen. Conversely, these newspapers dismissed the political views of Cruikshank, claiming that they undermined social order and unity. The *Watchtower* admonished its readers that a Cruikshank victory at the polls would constitute a "great public calamity."[61]

When the polls closed in the Fourth District and the ballots were counted, Cruikshank soundly defeated Curry, 3,236–2,299. The incumbent won the fire-eating county of Calhoun but lost badly everywhere else, particularly in Talladega County, where Curry trailed his opponent by more than six hundred votes. This outcome was not wholly unexpected, but it reverberated through the entire country; a stalwart war Confederate had gone down. The *Montgomery Advertiser* lamented that Cruikshank was "without that experience in the affairs of legislation which would fit him at this time to be the successor of such a man as Mr. Curry." One of Curry's dearest friends, the Mobile novelist Augusta Jane Evans, expressed profound regret. "How *grieved* and *astounded* I was, to hear of your defeat," she wrote to Curry later that autumn, "that the fatuity of your quondam constituency could reach the extreme of sending Cruikshank to Congress, I was utterly skeptical." She was essentially accusing the voters of stupidity. Most other observers, however, agreed that it was Curry's unabashed support for hard-war policies that wrecked his candidacy. Major W. T. Walthall, a conscription officer stationed in Talladega, reported that followers of the "Peace Party"—and apparently a "host of deserters"—flocked to the polls in large numbers. Curry himself could barely contain his disappointment. "A statesman preaching patriotism, courage, endurance, taxation, plighted faith, national honor," he opined, "falls a victim to any such Demagogue of the hour who flatters and cheats and betrays." The *Montgomery Mail* blamed the "reconstructionists of the Talladega district" for deceiving the people and betraying the state "by voting for submission to the Lincoln government." This newspaper went on to speculate that had soldiers been allowed to vote, then they would have swept the incumbent to victory.

Curry wholeheartedly agreed, and forever after he believed that he had been robbed by an antiwar minority.[62]

The race in the Third District saw the return of one of Alabama's most unusual politicians: Williamson R. W. Cobb. A longtime Democrat from Jackson County, Cobb polled a majority over the combined tally of the incumbent, John Ralls, and a third contestant, war hero James Sheffield. In winning the district, Cobb deprived the rebellion of one of its more reliable war Confederates. Prior to the Civil War, Cobb served fourteen years in the US House. His background typified the American image of a self-made man—from working as a local traveling salesman (a clock peddler) to walking the halls of Congress. Cobb's folksy demeanor appealed to the yeoman farmers and rural poor of Alabama's hill country. So too did his Jacksonian commitment to defending the common man from the state's wealthy elites. His campaigns featured a good-natured mix of class-based jokes and banjo music. A crowd favorite was his "Homestead Song," especially the stanza, "Uncle Sam is rich enough to give us all a farm." Friends described him as a "whole-souled fellow," whose tall and muscular frame conveyed honest strength and empathy for voters who worked with their hands. His critics, however, regarded him as an irascible populist. The district's leading planters were appalled by his uncouth manners (he reportedly ate raw onions before delivering stump speeches), and they ridiculed him as an unlettered rube and a low-born huckster. But they mostly hated how Cobb beat one high society candidate after another for seven consecutive elections. Clement C. Clay, the most prominent and peeved among the losers, explained that Cobb's success derived from his ability to "command the vote of those who can't or don't read."[63]

In actuality, Cobb was a capable, if unrefined, political figure who made good on his pledge to make federal land available to lower-class Americans. In 1854, he surprised his opponents by skillfully maneuvering a land reform bill through Congress. After becoming law, the Graduation Act lowered the price of seventy-seven thousand acres of public land. For this reason, Cobb's seat was considered a political lock—until the secession crisis. The hill counties were noticeably less ardent in their allegiance to the new Confederacy, but the yeomen there were still generally supportive of secession. Cobb, however, would have none of it. When the Alabama delegation resigned its seats in Congress, Cobb refused to participate. Rather than remain a pariah or a man without a country, however, he eventually left as well, but not before delivering an impassioned speech on behalf of his "country, greater than any other the sun ever shone upon . . . perhaps severed forever." Such overt unionism cost him his seat. In 1861, the "hitherto invincible" Cobb lost badly to John

Ralls, 1,917–3,754. For the next two years, he worked his farm and awaited his opportunity for revenge.[64]

In summer 1863, Cobb surmised that Ralls's identification as a war Confederate made him politically vulnerable. Voters in the Third District had grown cool toward the cause. Moreover, the nascent Peace Society operated throughout much of the region, encouraging desertion, protecting draft dodgers, and urging folks to vote out all war Confederates come election day. Cobb rightly suspected that his unionist credentials were no longer anathema but instead the perfect platform for reclaiming his old seat. He was also confident that his inimitable hillbilly charm would contrast favorably to the stolid personality of Congressman Ralls. It is unclear whether Cobb actually canvassed the district, but he made no effort to hide his controversial visits across enemy lines, ostensibly to discuss matters of reconstruction with federal authorities. For his part, Ralls did little to reassure voters. A fortnight before the election, he issued a hurried, written defense of his legislative record. In it, he apologized for having neglected to visit the district during his time in office but pointed out that he had tried to balance the rights of the people with the needs of the military. Furthermore, Ralls was proud to state that he had voted to give soldiers a pay raise.[65]

Many war Confederates from the district, including active-duty soldiers away at the front, had good reason to fear defeat. Convinced that Ralls did not have a chance against Cobb, they persuaded Colonel James L. Sheffield to stand for election. And so a third man entered the race. Sheffield was a merchant, a lawman, and a small planter (he owned twenty-two slaves) from Marshall County, who in the mid-1850s served in the state legislature as a Democrat. His last-minute candidacy held real promise; he had qualities that could appeal to both sides in the election. As a delegate to the 1861 Secession Convention, he voted against the ordinance, a plus with the peace Confederates, but he later signed the official document, a plus for the war Confederates. "With the South," he said in explaining his change of heart, "driven to the wall, the present struggle, is obviously one of life and death." The thirty-four-year-old Sheffield was also a bona fide war hero. In 1862, he spent $50,000 of his own money to raise the Forty-Eighth Alabama Infantry Regiment, and he then won election as its colonel. At a celebration welcoming the unit into the Confederate army, Sheffield vowed that he and his men would defend the South "while the life blood coursed their veins." The colonel made good his promise, leading the regiment through some of the war's most grueling battles as part of the vaunted Army of Northern Virginia. On the eve of the election, Sheffield was returning from the blood-soaked fields of Gettysburg, where his regiment had engaged in furious fighting at Little Round Top.[66]

Had a true party system ever formed, then the war Confederates might have nudged Ralls aside in favor of Sheffield. Instead, two prowar men ran against Cobb, splitting their votes and guaranteeing a peace Confederate victory. The official tally saw the unionist win 2,111 votes, the incumbent 966, and the warrior 482. Cobb won solid majorities in Cherokee, DeKalb, and St. Clair counties, though Ralls put up a fight in his home of Cherokee; he scratched out a narrow plurality over Sheffield in Marshall; and he finished second in a tight race in Jackson. There is a dearth of local commentary on the election, and even this is frustrating in its lack of specificity. For instance, Sarah Espy of Cherokee County noted in her diary that her daughters attended a rally where "Dr. Ralls spoke" on July 9, and that two of her sons later "went to the election." Unfortunately, she never explains the family's political outlook beyond vague lamentations: "The death struggle is now to be made. Would an all powerful God stand up for our help they [Union forces] would yet be put to confusion; but it seems he has given us over into the hand of our cruel foe." Regardless, in defeating Ralls, Cobb could hardly boast of having dethroned a Confederate titan like Jabez Curry, but his achievement was an important victory for the antiwar movement all the same. And it was a personally satisfying moment of vindication for Cobb himself.[67]

Alabama's remaining incumbents fared much better at the polls. In the Seventh District, David Clopton does not appear to have conducted much of a campaign, preferring instead to deliver his message through the local newspapers. The *South Western Baptist*, a pro-Clopton organ from Tuskegee, circulated a letter from the candidate that laid out his Confederate credentials. Besides reiterating his legislative record, to include a reminder that he had voted to increase soldier pay, Clopton viciously denounced the Yankee foe. "Their avowed determination is extermination," he insisted; "the alternative presented is subjugation or independence." For Clopton, the choice was obvious: "Eternal separation is the only ark of safety." This time around, however, the incumbent did not run unopposed. His primary challenger was John H. Cadenhead, who like Clopton was a lawyer and small slaveholder from Macon County. Cadenhead's platform is unclear. Given his majoritarian support among voters in Tallapoosa County, where antiwar sentiment was quite pronounced, he was likely a peace Confederate. He did serve in a local militia unit, where he was apparently fond of brandishing a double-barreled shotgun, but at thirty-one years of age, Cadenhead should probably have been in the army instead of running for office. Furthermore, he was an utter political neophyte. It came as no surprise that Clopton won reelection by a clean majority: 2,498–1,817. (Three other candidates picked up a scattering of seventeen votes.) Still, the actual returns reveal genuine disillusion by a substantial segment of the electorate. Clopton won handily in the counties of Chambers, Macon, and Russell, but he lost badly in Tallapoosa. Nonetheless, his victory affirmed the Seventh District's overall commitment to the war.[68]

In his bid for reelection in Alabama's Eighth District, James Pugh never expected a fiercely contested race. War Confederates loved him, but not everyone in the district was a war Confederate. The lone candidate in 1861, Pugh faced three challengers in 1863, all of whom enjoyed varying degrees of popular support. The incumbent would have to fight hard to persuade an increasingly disillusioned electorate that he was still the right man for the job. Foremost among Pugh's challengers were two physicians: Joseph Jones of Barbour County and J. McCaleb Wiley of Pike County. There is little information about Jones. Wiley, however, was known as "an old fashioned" Whig. He opposed secession, but he had not actively engaged in politics for nearly two decades. Wiley also enjoyed a modicum of local fame for his small but exciting part in the Texas Revolution of 1836. Evidently, while visiting the Republic of Texas, Wiley was press-ganged as a surgeon into Santa Anna's Mexican army. Refusing to partake in the generalissimo's expedition against the Texans, he was imprisoned and then sentenced to be shot, a punishment that was averted only by the American victory at San Jacinto. Released from captivity, Wiley was again ordered to serve the Mexican army, but he deserted at the first chance. As a politician in 1863, Wiley was unclear in his message to the voters, besides issuing a general call for peace. The fourth man in this congressional race was Alexander W. Starke. A state legislator and newspaperman from Troy in Pike County, the thirty-three-year-old Starke was the youngest of the four. A secessionist Democrat before the war, Starke edited the *Southern Advertiser* until its owners backed Stephen Douglas in 1860. He then formed the short-lived *States Rights Advocate,* which trumpeted Breckinridge for president. After secession, he briefly served as a lieutenant in the Fifteenth Alabama Infantry, but he was mustered out due to "lung disease." Starke was an out-and-out war Confederate who thought that he could promote the rebellion more effectively than even Pugh.[69]

On the day of the election, all four men received votes from across the district's six counties, but Pugh eked out a plurality with 1,566 votes, thereby winning the race and retaining his seat. The key to his victory was the polling in Barbour and Pike Counties, Black Belt counties that displayed martial ardor throughout the war and whose leading constituents undoubtedly shared Pugh's proslavery views. In the wiregrass counties, however, Jones and Wiley did well. With the exception of Henry County, the people of the wiregrass professed much discontent with the war effort. In fact, Covington County elected an open unionist—Alfred Holley—for the state legislature. Dr.

Jones's strong showing in that county suggests that he too was a peace Confederate. Starke ran a distant fourth, and his race mostly siphoned votes away from Pugh. If Jones and Wiley truly were opposed to the war, and if one had stepped aside in favor of the other, then a peace Confederate might have won the Eighth District with over 2,700 votes. Even if the ballots for Starke are added to Pugh's tally, the incumbent would still have not cracked two thousand votes. Here then is an example of how the lack of a party system may have hurt the antiwar movement in Alabama. It should be noted, however, that hundreds of soldiers from the district did not participate; they were at the front defending their homeland. As will be explained in chapter 4, most of them shared Pugh's hard-line attitude, and so, had they voted, Pugh likely would have polled an outright majority. Speculation aside, Pugh still won and maintained his political zeal for the cause all the way to the end.[70]

With Edmund Dargan's retirement from politics, the race in the Ninth District was wide open. In April 1863, the *Mobile Register* called for "the services of a full grown and masculine statesman" to fill Dargan's seat. Four men came forth in response. War Confederates rallied around the candidacy of one of them, James Shelton Dickinson. A wealthy lawyer and slaveholder (thirteen chattels) from Clarke County, the forty-five-year-old Dickinson had lived in Alabama since 1821, when his family arrived from Virginia. In contradistinction to Dargan's unkempt mien, Dickinson was a man of elegant tastes and immaculate apparel. He was polite and respectful to a fault; as a devout Baptist and member of the local temperance society, he reportedly never cursed or drank. Nonetheless, Dickinson enjoyed a reputation as a social bonhomie who hosted lavish parties at his "Italianate" mansion in Grove Hill, where he and his wife also raised nine children (along with a purportedly "fierce dog" as the family pet). Though refined in his manners, he was a radical in his politics. Convinced that the South had been swindled by the Compromise of 1850, he officially joined the Democratic Party in 1853 and became an advocate of immediate secession. Slavery was the crux of the matter, and Dickinson publicly proclaimed it to be "a *moral*, *social* and *political good*, and not an *evil*." In 1860, he endorsed the Breckinridge ticket, and after Alabama seceded, he spent his own money to raise a company for the Confederate army—the Dickinson Guards, later Company E in the Twenty-Fourth Alabama Infantry, whose motto was Victory or Death. For the first two years of the war, he served as a food commissioner for the southwestern counties of Alabama, distributing more than three thousand bushels of corn to needy families. When Dargan stepped aside in 1863, Dickinson felt it his duty to uphold the district's commitment to the rebellion. The *Clarke County Journal* immediately endorsed its native son as a man "thoroughly imbued with the earnest spirit of resistance to Yankee domination." Dickinson denounced any effort at reconstruction with the North, making his campaign message music to the ears of any war Confederate. "All my hopes and all my prayers," he informed the voters in July, "are for the success of our brave soldiers, the triumph of our arms, and for the final independence of these States—and all my efforts shall be devoted to that object."[71]

Of Dickinson's three rivals, two were among Mobile's finest: Robert Hardy Smith and Charles Carter Langdon, both former Whigs and both members of the city's newly formed Confederate Society (an incipient counter to the Peace Society). Smith was the initial favorite among the city's residents. A prominent politician before the war, Smith expressed some misgivings about secession, but he believed that it was still an appropriate course after Lincoln's election. To this end, he served as one of the state's secession commissioners to North Carolina. Thereafter, he contributed to the cause by serving first as the district's representative in the Provisional Confederate Congress, where he displayed a noteworthy spirit of nationalism, and then as colonel of the Thirty-Sixth Alabama Infantry. Physical maladies, however, compelled him to return home before seeing any action, and he does not seem to have fully recovered by 1863. His participation in the race was driven more by his friends than by any burning desire to reenter politics. Apparently, Mobilians recognized this disinterest, and by July most of them had shifted their support to Langdon. Charles Langdon was a bona fide Connecticut Yankee, arriving in Alabama as a young man to work at his older brother's dry goods store in Macon County. Commercial interests later took Langdon to Mobile, where he embraced the political dynamism of the city and joined the Whig party. He ran the *Mobile Daily Advertiser* for a number of years and then served as Mobile's mayor in the early 1850s, before moving on to the state legislature. Other than a brief association with the Know-Nothings—out of concern over the influx of Catholic immigrants to the city—Langdon remained a conventional Whig in outlook. Always vocal in his opposition to secession, he stumped the state in 1860 for the Constitutional Union candidate John Bell. Nevertheless, he supported the Confederacy once the war began. The fourth candidate in the race was Garrett Hall, a slaveholder from Baldwin County. Little is known about his background or his rationale for running.[72]

The outcome in the Ninth District was a tight plurality for Dickinson, who edged out Langdon by two hundred votes (1,866–1,660). The *Clarke County Journal* unleashed constant reminders that Dickinson was the truest southerner in the contest, whereas Langdon's patriotism was ostensibly tainted by his New England blood. In an effort both to rebuff this aspersion to his loyalty and to differentiate himself more forcefully from Dickinson, Langdon belatedly called for the "Black Flag," a war without quarter, to include the summary execution of enemy prisoners. It was an atypical display of hypernationalism, but it apparently played well with the residents of a city under direct blockade. For his part, Dickinson eschewed the topic, preferring to vouchsafe support for the war policies already enacted by the Confederate Congress. As the returns make clear, Langdon prevailed in the bay area, taking Mobile itself by a comfortable margin, but Dickinson dominated in the rural counties, including obtaining a landslide in his home county of Clarke. The obscure Garrett Hall polled nearly three hundred votes, while the ailing Robert Smith garnered a mere sixty-three. It was perhaps fortuitous for the winner that Smith was in poor health, for had the colonel been more interested and campaigned with vigor, he might have drawn enough votes from Dickinson's column to give Langdon the victory. To be sure, Langdon was hardly a peace Confederate, so this hypothetical cannot be read as a success for the antiwar movement. Dickinson, however, was definitely a war Confederate, and his district would remain one as well.[73]

The election in Alabama's First District was pretty straightforward. The incumbent Thomas Jefferson Foster ran largely unopposed and won. Foster had evinced a generally prowar stance in Congress, and the voters back home apparently liked what they saw in their representative. There was a scattering of votes for a few unidentified candidates, but the final tally was decisive: 1,857–377. Foster's victory, however, does require some qualification. Voter turnout in the district was almost three thousand fewer than in 1861, in no small part because much of the electorate was displaced by the presence of the Union army. There were no returns from Franklin County, and the number of precincts that actually opened in the other counties is unclear. What is clear is that Foster won handily among those who did cast ballots.[74]

The safest Congressional seat in Alabama was Francis Strother Lyon's in the Fifth District. Lyon's legislative record, especially his views on fiscal policy, may have encountered some opposition in Richmond, but his performance greatly pleased the voters back home. The *Alabama Beacon* noted that the incumbent was "too generally and favorably known to the voters of the District to require any newspaper endorsement." Lyon did not bother to stump the counties; there was no need. His only serious rival in 1863 was Jack F. Cocke, whose candidacy the newspapers barely acknowledged. A planter from Perry County, Cocke had served in the state Senate as a Whig throughout the 1850s. In 1861, he ran a distant second against Lyon for Congress. His political platform is unclear, but he appears to have been an indifferent supporter of both secession and the war. In the end, Lyon crushed Cocke at the polls, winning every county in the district by so great a margin—2,508–198—that the word *landslide* is an understatement. Only in Choctaw was the race close, with Lyon winning 180 votes to Cocke's 169. (Six other candidates picked up a scattering of thirty-seven votes across the district.) The people of central Alabama had overwhelmingly granted to one of the South's most diehard war Confederates another term.[75]

In the Sixth District, William Parish Chilton weathered an unexpectedly tight race for the seat that he had easily won in 1861. The July battlefield disasters at Gettysburg and Vicksburg, as well as the defeatist propaganda of the Peace Society, had noticeably undermined public confidence in certain parts of the district, especially in Coosa County, with its yeoman majority. Several weeks prior to the election, Chilton returned to Montgomery and commenced a canvass of his district. With official endorsements from the *Montgomery Advertiser* and the *Selma Reporter*, the incumbent endeavored to restore civilian morale. At a political meeting in the state capital, he called on the people "to meet the enemy with hostile arms" and signed resolutions to defend the city "street by street" if necessary. Elsewhere, Chilton delivered similar martial messages, exhorting his listeners at one rally to "drive back the vandal and ruthless foe . . . with a sword in one hand and torch in the other."[76]

To many residents in the Sixth District, Chilton's battle cries smacked of desperate bombast. A growing number of voters preferred the candidacy of M. C. Lane, a lawyer-planter from Butler County (he owned thirty-eight slaves) who touted a platform that called for peace and reconstruction. In 1861, he had decried secession as folly, expressing an unwillingness "to abandon the *old ship*, although now but a miserable wreck, to get upon a *new one*." During the 1863 race, Lane tried to drive a wedge between Chilton and the yeomanry of the district; and the incumbent was certainly vulnerable on a number of issues. Chilton's support of the twenty-slave clause played into the "rich man's war, poor man's fight" rhetoric, as did his refusal to sanction a $4.00 pay raise for enlisted soldiers. On the latter issue, Chilton had tactlessly declared that soldiers should fight for country, not profit, but Lane mocked this supposedly principled stand and believed that it would fall flat with average voters, particularly since congressmen were making $2,760 annually while the common private earned a mere $132 per year. In an effort to swing slaveholders to his side, Lane also highlighted Chilton's support of impressment, including its provision for military usage of slave labor. Chilton responded with a lengthy letter defending his record and clarifying his position on soldier pay. Claiming that he was sick at the time that the House voted on the latter issue, he explained that his main concern was whether the budget could handle a raise. Furthermore, he cited his recommendation that soldiers receive their uniforms and equipment free of charge as proof that he cared about the fighting man. Finally, he highlighted his efforts to have the tax-in-kind suspended in the poorest counties. Acting as Chilton's hatchet man in the campaign, the *Selma Reporter* downplayed the relevance of soldier pay and instead savaged Lane's pacifist platform. "It is sheer madness to talk of reconstruction," this newspaper thundered, "it is too late for this people to look back. They must fight." The choice before the electorate was simple: Chilton and victory, or Lane and defeat.[77]

Chilton ultimately won reelection, but Lane's challenge had been real. The tally was uncomfortably close: 2,941–2,494. Chilton held firm in Montgomery and enjoyed overwhelming support in the Black Belt counties of Dallas and Lowndes, but Lane handily won his home county of Butler and took disgruntled Coosa County by a two-to-one margin. From Rockford in Coosa County, store owner Reuben Mitchell, a member of the Peace Society, jubilantly informed his colleagues in other counties that antiwar candidates had "carried Everything before us." When the challenger also edged out the incumbent in Autauga County, Mitchell prematurely declared Lane the winner in the whole district. A peace Confederate triumph, however, was not to be. The plantation precincts proved the difference. Given Chilton's modest upbringing, his reliance on the slaveholding elites must have privately amused him. The *Montgomery Advertiser*, however, gloated that he had rightfully prevailed over an opponent that it denigrated as a "mediocre place-hunter, operating upon the traitorous feeling of a few, and the ignorance of many." The editors suggested that Lane consider enlisting in the army rather than stir up political trouble at home. The antiwar message, however, had clearly resonated. But it was just as clear that the Sixth District remained loyal to the Confederacy and to its prowar representative. After the election, Lane largely disappeared from the scene, while Chilton resumed his strong advocacy for total war.[78]

Scholarly attention on the election of 1863 tends to focus on the various peace Confederate challenges to the state's war men. Overlooked is the war Confederate challenge to the state's most prominent congressional naysayer, William Russell Smith of the Second District. The quasi war Confederate Smith had weathered a close race in 1861; he would do so again in 1863. Contesting his reelection was William H. Fowler, a newspaperman from Tuscaloosa. Fowler was originally from Greene County, where he edited the *Eutaw Whig* for a number of years, and in 1855 he represented the county in the state House as a Whig. Toward the end of 1860, he accepted invitations to take over both the *Alabama Beacon* and the *Tuscaloosa Monitor*, erstwhile voices for union that in Fowler's hands became propaganda machines for disunion. In January 1861, he served as secretary of the Secession Convention during the early days of heated debate over the issue. No sooner had the majority voted for independence than Fowler resigned as secretary and volunteered for the army, attaining a captaincy in the Fifth Alabama Infantry. Several members of the convention objected to Fowler's abrupt departure, but the new captain left, all the same: "I feel in honor bound to join my company, and with due respect to the Convention I must do so." After serving a year, Fowler organized an artillery battery that bore his name and thereafter deployed to Mobile. He not only guarded that port city but followed political developments in the state. Skeptical of Congressman Smith's dedication to the cause, Fowler decided to run against him. In doing so, the army captain presented himself as one of the state's few war heroes to run for national office. In the end, however, Fowler's bid fell short. Smith won by a comfortable 650-vote margin (1,756–1,108). Of the district's seven counties, only Blount did not go to the incumbent. The results in Winston County appear incomplete, for the records only indicate that Fowler won twelve votes. That county, however, was a bulwark of unionism; its paltry tally for Fowler makes no statistical difference in the outcome. After the war, Smith looked back with great pride on having defeated the forces of secession in both 1861 and 1863. Nonetheless, a relative newcomer to politics had posed a respectable threat to a veteran politico.[79]

EPILOGUE

On January 22, 1864, near the end of the final session of the First Confederate Congress, the lame-duck Jabez Curry read before a packed House chamber a Joint Resolution in Relation to the War. The document was the product of a committee, but it was largely the work of Curry himself, and it thoroughly reflected the war Confederate mindset after three years of struggle. Stressing the cause of "liberty and civilization," Curry declared that "no sacrifice of life or fortune can be too costly." The congressman went on to summarize the reasons for secession (as if that action still needed justification), before heaping praise on the patriotism of the southern people, especially the soldiery. "What we have accomplished, with a population so inferior in numbers and means so vastly disproportionate, has excited the astonishment and admiration of the world." Acknowledging that Congress had enacted harsh and demanding war policies, Curry insisted that the Confederate government was simply reacting to the oppressive policies of the Lincoln administration. It was the Republican-controlled North that had instigated "a cruel war of invasion," that was trying "to convert the South into a San Domingo, by appealing to the cupidity, lusts, ambition, and ferocity of the slave," and that viewed "the heroes of our contest" as traitors deserving of the "guillotine." Under such circumstances, a total war of defiance was absolutely imperative. Calling on the citizenry to persevere for just a little longer, and to trust in God,

Curry promised ultimate victory. "We have passed through great trials of affliction, but suffering and humiliation are the school-masters that lead nations to self-reliance and independence." The words conveyed passion and conviction, and they contained the same nationalistic elements of Lincoln's famous Gettysburg Address, but Curry's message was too verbose and prolix to ever become a popular canticle for freedom. Nevertheless, the resolution was well received by the Confederate Congress, which unanimously endorsed the document and approved its dissemination to the public. For Curry, his presentation before his colleagues constituted a farewell address that betrayed no bitterness over his personal defeat at the polls. It also evinced a feeling of primal honor; the righteous South was holding its own against the wicked North. Confederate politicians of all stripes could take enormous pride in their country's military performance.[80]

Curry's high-profile defeat notwithstanding, the congressional elections in Alabama did not substantially alter the state's commitment to the war. Going into the election, war Confederates held eight of the nine congressional seats (William Smith being the nonconformist). Coming out the election, war Confederates retained six of those seats: Foster, Lyon, Chilton, Clopton, Pugh, and Dickinson (the first three Whigs, the last three Democrats). Dickinson was the newcomer, replacing Dargan in style, but not in substance. Williamson Cobb and Marcus Cruikshank (a Democrat and a Whig) were Alabama's only outspoken peace Confederates in Congress. Several other southern states, notably North Carolina and Georgia, turned out most of their war Confederate incumbents, but Alabama did not.[81]

Alabama's peace Confederates never accomplished much in Richmond. Cobb surprised everyone by refusing even to take his seat when the Second Congress convened its first session in May 1864. The recalcitrant Cobb apparently had no intention of actually serving a government that he despised. It was enough to have denied the hard-liner John Ralls his bid for reelection. Given the peace Confederates' inability to orchestrate any meaningful opposition at the national level, however, Cobb's decision could be considered a mistake. Some twenty-six of the newly elected congressmen were overt peace Confederates, but few of them possessed Cobb's degree of parliamentary experience, not to mention his moral courage in standing up to traditional authority. Had he chosen to do so, Cobb might well have become the leader of a genuine opposition party. Instead, he remained in northeastern Alabama, where he fomented unrest among the unionist community. In March, Cobb called on local residents to withdraw Jackson County from the Confederacy in accordance with Lincoln's Ten Percent Plan. He then began entertaining federal solicitations that he be appointed military governor over the state. Before any of these ideas came to fruition, he died, allegedly assassinated by rebel guerrillas on the first day of November. In contrast to Cobb, Cruikshank regularly attended the sessions of the Second Congress. Although relegated to the less important Printing Committee, he actively promoted peace, voting against every new war measure—particularly renewed suspensions of habeas corpus—and supporting various stillborn proposals for reconstruction. Again, had an opposition party ever materialized, Cruikshank would have made a capable leader within it.[82]

At some point toward the end of 1864, two other Alabamians gravitated into the peace Confederate fold. William Smith, the curmudgeon from Tuscaloosa, did so openly, expressing support for the idea of reconstruction. Whatever talents he might have brought to such a project, however, could never overcome his increasing apathy. Other than showing up to vote against further suspensions of habeas corpus, he was rarely seen in the halls of Congress. Before the conclusion of the final session in 1865, he went home, grumbling about the "mobocratic fanaticism" that had gripped the capital when it was obvious that the war was lost. Thomas Foster was a belated convert; that autumn he began consorting with a North Carolina bloc of antiwar politicos. Consequently, some historians see this Alabamian as "half-hearted" in his dedication to the cause. In fact, shortly after the war, Foster tried to disown his Confederate connection altogether. In seeking a pardon from President Andrew Johnson in 1865, the congressman wrote of his "unabated opposition to secession" and said that he "opposed most earnestly, and vehemently" many of the Confederacy's war policies. Genuine peace Confederates, such as Joseph Bradley of Madison County, questioned this newfound loyalty. "Foster ran against some of the best Union men in the State," Bradley explained in a counter letter to Johnson, "I have no political Confidence in him." Smith and Foster certainly exhibited a reduced enthusiasm for the war toward the end, but their conduct never directly challenged the war socialism of the Rebel government.[83]

One reason for peace Confederate impotency was that, after 1863, Congress no longer exerted any real influence over the course of the war. "The South was one vast military camp," observed an early historian of the Confederacy, "all was being sacrificed to the god of war." The Second Confederate Congress did not even convene its first session until May 1864, less than a year before the rebellion's demise, and most of its legislation merely modified or extended existing war policies. For their part, Alabama's war Confederates could be counted on for continued support. James Pugh called for another suspension of habeas corpus. On December 8, he was joined by Chilton, Dickinson, and Lyon in approving the Confederacy's final exercise of that controversial measure (Clopton, Cruikshank, Foster, and Smith voted against it, though Clopton and Foster had supported earlier versions). James Dickinson recommended doubling the tax-in-kind and pushed for an expansion of the conscription age range. Francis Lyon resumed his efforts to stabilize the country's currency woes. In June, he confessed that his bill to issue hundreds of millions of treasury notes was a "forlorn hope," but he warned that anything less would leave the nation a "financial wreck." Continually thwarted by Secretary Memminger, he spearheaded a call for the treasury secretary to resign. In late 1864, Memminger did indeed leave the Davis administration, but Lyon's dreams of a national currency never came to fruition. All of this, however, seemed anticlimactic after the achievements of the First Confederate Congress. Don E. Fehrenbacher believes that by 1864, the legislators had become "addicted, in many instances, to the exercise of national power," even when their activities would clearly no longer affect the outcome. Adam Ramey claims that the Second Congress developed a "survival response" as legislative deliberation gave way to stoic desperation. Maybe so, but none of the politicians were acting any differently than they had in earlier, more hopeful times.[84]

A form of inertia took over the Confederate Congress in its last two sessions of the war. George C. Rable describes it as a "grim determination to see the war through to its ineluctable end." Few still believed victory possible, but fewer were prepared to admit defeat. "Patriotism," notes Frank E. Vandiver, "could still be found in abundance, though often tempered with a feeling of futility." Searching for something jingoistic to do, congressional war Confederates commenced a purge of disloyal members. In May 1864, William Chilton launched an investigation into Williamson Cobb's questionable allegiance. Six months later, Chilton charged Cobb with treason for having refused to take his seat, for having freely crossed enemy lines, and for having taken an oath of loyalty to the North. Worst of all, according to an affidavit presented by Chilton, Cobb had publicly "embraced and kissed" the flag of the United States. On November 17, 1864, the House expelled Cobb by a 75–0 vote. James Pugh was out sick, otherwise he definitely would have voted for expulsion; Thomas Foster abstained. It is unclear whether the chamber knew that Cobb was already dead. On February 27, 1865, the House moved against the quarrelsome Henry Foote, expelling him in a 73–0 vote. Chilton was on leave at the time, otherwise he likely would have voted for this measure. Not surprisingly, William Smith refused to participate in either expulsion, but more curious was Cruikshank's yea vote both times. He and his peace Confederate brethren were discovering that they had to be careful how they presented themselves—right to the end, the political and public mood was still more prowar than antiwar. Then again, Cruikshank might also have felt that Cobb had abnegated his duty to the electorate, whereas Foote was simply a jackanapes unworthy of his office.[85]

These House purges were in part a response to various ineffectual efforts by peace Confederates to pursue their reconstruction agenda. In late May 1864, the North Carolina delegation submitted a resolution "in favor of peace by negotiation." Cruikshank and Smith supported the proposal, but the other six Alabamians voted with the majority in tabling this measure, 62–21. Similarly, on January 12, 1865, the Foreign Affairs Committee presented a resolution calling on Jefferson Davis to open a dialogue with Abraham Lincoln. The military situation had certainly become more propitious for such an initiative, and Cruikshank and Smith were again on board, but as before their colleagues provided crucial votes in thwarting the measure, 42–38. In any event, President Davis dispatched a three-man commission to entreat with Lincoln at Hampton Roads, Virginia. The interlocutors soon discovered that there was no basis for a mutually acceptable peace; the rebellion would continue. War Confederates were positively elated by the failed talks. As Wilfred Buck Yearns explains, "Congress ended with at least the satisfaction of never having begged for mercy."[86]

The last significant action of the Confederate Congress was its enactment of the controversial law that authorized the recruitment of slaves as soldiers. True to form, Alabama's delegation set aside its self-interest and supported a desperate measure that seemingly undermined the raison d'être of the rebellion. When the bill came up for a final vote on February 20, 1865, Clopton, Dickinson, Foster, Lyon, and Pugh were among the yeas. Clopton had been urging the measure for over a year, while Dickinson served on a "select committee" that strongly recommended the law. Their votes were crucial to its razor-thin passage: 40–37. Cruikshank voted against it, Chilton abstained (though he had voted for an earlier House version), and Smith was absent (though he had voted against an earlier House version). Although the law authorized the enlistment of three hundred thousand slaves for the army, it came much too late to make a difference. But that hardly mattered to the Alabamians who helped pass it; total war demanded that even the craziest ideas be attempted.[87]

Any assessment of Alabama's delegation to the Confederate House of Representatives must conclude that most of its members were zealous patriots who willfully practiced total war. Neither states' rights nor affection for the old Union interfered with their pursuit of independence. The former was compatible with total war, and the latter was discarded in favor of a more exciting political adventure. Though often controversial and unprecedented, every law passed by the Confederate Congress was vital to the war effort, and every one enjoyed constitutional imprimatur. Alabamians played a major role in ensuring that this legislation met both conditions. Had an actual party system emerged, it is not difficult to envisage every delegate from the state (save Smith, and Cruikshank in the Second Congress) forging bipartisan support for hard war policies. After all, there was frequently consensus among them without a party. Based on the performance of Alabama's congressional delegation, a strong case can be made that Alabama was among the most prowar Confederate polities in the entire South.

2
The Gubernatorial Contest

It was a fine hat, a gift from a lady admirer, "not only comfortable but elegant." As he tried it on for the first time in late October 1863, John Gill Shorter perhaps pondered his recent and sudden political demise. Two years before, he had won Alabama's gubernatorial contest with a solid majority over his opponent, Thomas Hill Watts. Yet here he was, having lost to that same rival in August 1863 by almost twenty thousand votes. Shorter had suspected that he might lose his bid for reelection, but he never imagined such a stunning turnabout, particularly since he was proud of his executive record and had the endorsement of most of the state's newspapers. Publicly, he accepted his defeat with dignity. "I shall retire with cheerfulness," the governor informed the legislature in his final message to that body, "and I shall carry with me no other regret than that I have not accomplished more for the good of the State and for her patriotic people." Privately, however, the normally stoic Shorter fumed over his misfortune. To General William Hardee, he wrote in September, "I have been stricken down for holding up the state to its high resolves and crowding the people to the performance of their duty." It must have been especially galling to watch his successor perpetuate many of the same controversial wartime policies that ostensibly cost him his office. Anyway, he did at least have a beautiful new hat.[1]

John Gill Shorter was one of the Confederacy's most devoted war governors (figure 9). During his two years in office, he readily complied with all the directives coming out of Richmond regardless of the strain that they put on Alabama's political economy. His gubernatorial brand of war socialism may well have cost him reelection, but it ensured that Alabama would never shirk its responsibilities to the cause. The editors of the *Clarke County Journal* certainly thought so. A week after the election, they opined, "We honestly think Gov. Shorter deserved better of the people." The man also deserves better of Civil War scholarship. It is not that historians present his tenure unfairly, but that they hardly discuss his tenure at all. The most well-known Confederate war governor is undeniably Joseph Brown, a strident states' rights Democrat who reigned over Georgia for the entirety of the war. Openly defiant of the Davis administration, Brown earned a reputation for obstructionism that has left a terribly misleading and unfortunately enduring impression that south-

Figure 9. John Gill Shorter, studio portrait by Blackshear, Macon, Georgia, 1850s. (Courtesy of Alabama Department of Archives and History)

ern executives undermined Richmond's efforts to prosecute a total war. In actuality, a majority of the twenty-eight men who served as Confederate governors during the conflict were reliable allies of their president. In his dissertation on this topic, Michael Albert Powell dispenses with oversimplified notions of states' rights and instead proffers the idea of "dual federalism," according to which southern leaders typically cooperated with Jefferson Davis, often negotiating the details of policy with their commander in chief, yet rarely refusing to carry out the policy's intent. "The governors recognized that they were subordinate to the Confederate national government," Powell insists, "particularly in the effort to win the war." And no governor understood this hierarchy better than John Gill Shorter.[2]

Shorter was forty-three years old when he became governor in 1861. It was the pinnacle of an active political career. Georgia born and educated (University of Georgia, class of 1837), Shorter accompanied his father to Barbour County, Alabama. There, with his younger brother, Eli, he managed a newly acquired cotton farm and opened a law practice in Eufaula. Shorter exhibited a reserved, gentlemanly charm that enabled him to move easily among the county's high society. In 1843, he married into the wealthy Battle family, gaining additional lands and chattel (he eventually owned one hundred slaves). Shorter's active involvement in the Baptist church further enhanced his image of respectability. A contemporary described his personality as one of "unaffected mildness and simplicity." Beneath this exterior of Christian serenity, however, lay a relentless ambition, one that led Shorter into politics as a Democrat. He served periodically in the state legislature before winning election in 1852 as judge on the circuit court, a position that he held for the rest of the decade. Initially, Shorter conducted himself as a reliable Jacksonian, fighting the good fight against alleged Whig elitism. Soon, however, his political outlook reflected the radicalism of the Eufaula Regency, a bipartisan coterie of prominent Barbour County slaveholders, including Shorter and his brother. In the 1840s, the regency preached states' rights, but by the 1850s, it shifted more pointedly to southern rights, calling for secession in the wake of sectional disputes over the westward extension of slavery.[3]

Threats to slavery brought out the fire-eater in Shorter. Every controversy over the issue—and each year seemed to bring another—convinced him that abolition was an imminent inevitability. He worried about the economic impact of emancipation, and he feared its social ramifications. Like most slaveholders of his day, Shorter accepted the peculiar institution as a positive good, where a natural hierarchy of race legitimated black bondage in the interest of white liberty. Any alteration to this formula guaranteed anarchy. To an audience of planters and yeomen attending the 1852 Southern Rights Convention in Montgomery, Shorter predicted a racial doomsday should abolitionism ever come to fruition. "While the rich would be able to leave a land thus cursed," he voiced his forebodings, "the poor white man would be left in a most lamentable condition . . . reduced to the most abject and degrading servitude." He evidently practiced his convictions from the bench, as well. In 1860, Judge Shorter sentenced to death two slaves found guilty of murdering their master, stipulating that they be publicly hanged in the plantation slave quarters as an example to the rest of the chattel. To be sure, capital punishment may well have been appropriate for what the convicts had done, but coming just months after John Brown's notorious raid on Harpers Ferry, Shorter's action was likely more than stern justice; it was an affirmation of white power. Abraham Lincoln's election later that year elicited further consternation. At a political rally in Clayton, Alabama, one designed to hype the state's forthcoming Secession Convention, Shorter railed against the "black banner of abolition." During the convention itself, he eagerly served as the state's secession commissioner to Georgia. Stressing the urgency of disunion, Shorter warned the residents of his birth state that the incoming Lincoln administration would "usurp the machinery of the Federal Government, and madly attempt to rule, if not to subjugate and ruin, the South." Once the deed of secession was done, Shorter's self-possessed demeanor returned. Organizing and defending the new slaveholders' republic would now require a rational, deliberative approach to governance. To that end, he graciously accepted election as one of Alabama's nine representatives to the Provisional Confederate Congress.[4]

Congressman Shorter was in Richmond when Alabama's voters went to the polls on August 8, 1861, for statewide elections. Attention focused on the gubernatorial race. The incumbent, Andrew B. Moore, had ably steered the state out of the Union and contemplated running again, but having already served two terms he acceded to the traditional limit and stepped aside. As many as five aspirants vied to replace him; or rather, they permitted surrogates to promote their candidacies in a clumsy effort to abide the Confederacy's high-minded experiment in doing away with political parties, along with the vitriolic canvassing. The early front-runner was Robert Jemison Jr., a former Whig from Tuscaloosa. His old political affiliation, however, aroused opposition from former Democrats—no Whig had ever been governor of Alabama—while his cooperationist stance at the Secession Convention clashed with the chauvinistic mood of the times. Jemison soon withdrew in the interest of harmony. Other candidates came under similar, unfavorable scrutiny until former Democrats presented John Gill Shorter to the electorate. Shorter had impeccable Confederate credentials and, according to one historian, "few personal enemies." Furthermore, he enjoyed the endorsement of most of the state's newspapers. On election day, Shorter faced only one other competitor: Thomas Hill Watts, a secessionist Whig from Montgomery. In June, Watts coyly followed Jemison's example, then dramatically reentered the race mere days before the election, apparently after receiving pleas from his supporters. It hardly mattered, for when the polls closed Shorter defeated Watts by a large majority: 37,849–28,121. Curiously, the returns reflected prewar voting patterns more than they did the recent attitudes on secession. Shorter garnered respectable numbers across the state, but his largest tallies came from the hill counties and wiregrass region, areas that had long voted Democrat yet had exhibited reservations about secession. Similarly, Watts dominated Mobile and the Whig-friendly Black Belt counties, which were areas that also demonstrated the strongest support for independence. No one could have known at the time, but this election presaged a rematch between the two men in 1863, one that would produce a strikingly different outcome.[5]

In December, Shorter delivered his inaugural address. It was bellicose in tone, anticipating "an unholy and cruel war," yet optimistic of Confederate victory. The governor proudly cited Alabama's extensive human and material resources, particularly the state's industrial potential, and soberly declared that "the emergency will test the mettle and the nerve of the body politic." Sprinkled throughout the message were statements of pure bombast: "Alabamians will never surrender," "Fight on and fight ever until we conquer a peace," "Who would not be willing to die for Alabama?" As his gubernatorial tenure would demonstrate, Shorter sincerely believed what he was saying, but invocations of patriotism and calls for sacrifice were easy to make in winter 1861–62: Alabama and most of the rest of the South were still untouched by invasion. To be sure, a few Federal warships lurked off the coast of Mobile Bay, but the enemy blockade in 1861 was laughable. In fact, Confederate victory at First Manassas the previous summer seemingly made the whole Union war effort a joke. Nevertheless, the spirit of the inaugural address reflected the governor's basic understanding of how the rebellion would change the South. What Shorter did not yet fully grasp was how the conflict would alter his fundamental understanding of the role of government in a democracy at war.[6]

The paradox of Confederate politics was that every attempt to escape the tyranny of Lincoln and the North resulted in policies that transformed rebel leaders into practitioners of total war. In a provocative study of the Confederacy, Emory M. Thomas exposes the ostensible hypocrisy of such leaders at both the national and state levels. "In the name of independence," he writes, "Southerners reversed or severely undermined virtually every tenet of the way of life they were supposedly defending." This quotation aptly describes the Shorter administration in Alabama. A states' rights Democrat, Shorter came to accept centralized authority, particularly conscription, as an imperative during a time of war. A slaveholder, he displayed little compunction in appropriating private chattel for military purposes. A cash-crop agrarian, he acquiesced to Richmond's crash course in industrialization, even as he exhorted his fellow planters to forgo cotton in favor of corn. In March 1862, only a few months after taking office, the governor called on the people of Alabama "to bury the love of gold and quench out the sordid spirit which values property above liberty, and to plainly cultivate that martyr spirit which will sacrifice every material interest rather than peril the priceless inheritance of freedom." Powell is quick to point out that Shorter was no anomaly in this regard. "Every governor believed in the Confederacy," he explains, but personality and circumstance affected how they went about mobilizing their states. For Shorter, the dichotomy might best be seen as a balancing act between nationalism and liberty, where the governor often had to choose between his country and his constituency. Ideally, the two reinforce one another in pursuit of a cause. In reality, they tend to compete against each other as the stakes rise. Leadership thus became all important in keeping the forces aligned.[7]

Any evaluation of Shorter's administration boils down to his enforcement of war policy. Legislators at the state and national level enacted policy measures, but it was governors such as Shorter who had to carry them out. Thus, responsibility that is collective in theory became individualized in practice. Success or failure—and hence, praise or blame—rested in the person of the chief executive, and Shorter never shied away from this reality. "Let the entire resources and energies of the people be devoted to the one great purpose of war," he proclaimed in early 1862, "war stern and unrelenting, war to the knife, such a war as, in the providence of God, we may be compelled to wage in order to vindicate the inalienable right of self government." To this end, historians give Shorter high marks for his effort. Malcolm C. McMillan describes him as "conscientious and dedicated"; Powell refers to him as an "enthusiastic supporter" of the war. But it was the verdict of the electorate that would ultimately determine the governor's political legacy.[8]

The immediate task confronting Shorter was the mobilization of Alabama's manpower for the common defense. The governor quickly discovered that national demands for soldiers to fight the larger war competed with state demands for local protection and basic law and order. The general call to arms steadily denuded the state of most of its able-bodied men. According to the 1860 census, there were approximately 126,000 white men of military age (fifteen to fifty years old) in the state. At the time of Shorter's inauguration in December 1861, twenty-seven thousand Alabamians were in the ranks of the Confederate army. Within a year, that number had increased to about sixty thousand. And by the time of the election of 1863, the total exceeded seventy thousand. Shorter was proud of his state's military contribution, but he lamented both his lack of control over these troops and their absence on other fronts whenever Alabama itself was threatened. Moreover, his priorities for Alabama did not always mesh with President Davis's priorities for the Confederacy. The state was comparatively isolated from the principal battlefields in Virginia and Tennessee, as well as those along the Mississippi River; consequently, it received much less attention than Shorter felt it deserved. Of particular concern to the governor was the Tennessee River valley and Mobile Bay, important sections of the state that came under increasing enemy duress beginning in 1862, yet that were three hundred miles apart north to south.

The Confederate War Department asserted control over these regions as war zones, but it offered military succor only when doing so comported with its overall strategy of concentrating forces against the main Union armies.[9]

Undeterred, Governor Shorter resorted to the state militia for local defense. Union operations against New Orleans and Pensacola convinced him that Mobile was the next logical target. On March 6, 1862, Shorter issued a proclamation calling forth "a large militia force" from the counties in the southern half of the state with orders to proceed to the bay area for ninety days of service. Over the next several weeks, the governor received more complaints than militiamen; only a few companies formally mustered. Apologetic county officials explained that a majority of their men were already in the Confederate army, and that to comply with the governor's decree would virtually depopulate the land, thereby inhibiting crop production and leaving the slave population inadequately supervised. Incredulous, Shorter reminded these local leaders that militia service was mandatory in a time of crisis. "Must have men at Mobile," he chastised a magistrate in Demopolis, "Shall I abandon Mobile to the Yankees?" The rhetorical question aside, only the port city and its adjacent counties marshaled any significant numbers. Though disappointed by the lackluster militia call out, Shorter correctly believed that there were still plenty of citizens available for military service.[10]

Before the governor could address the deficiencies in the militia system, he had to confront new challenges posed by conscription. In April 1862, the Confederate Congress enacted the first of a series of enrollment acts that essentially made every white man a potential recruit in the rebel army. Those Alabamians who had ignored Shorter's militia proclamation could now be compelled to serve after all, as Confederate soldiers. Though satisfied that conscription was in accord with the various clauses in Section 8 of the Confederate Constitution, the governor could not suppress his distaste for the measure: "If we are to depend upon it to maintain the liberty of the South," he wrote to the War Department in May, "I should almost despair of our ultimate triumph." Nevertheless, Shorter recognized the military necessity of conscription, and a month later he assured Richmond that the central government had his full support: "I deem it important that those who think they can oppose effectual resistance to the law should understand clearly and distinctly that it will be enforced."[11]

Initially, Shorter strove to make conscription as efficient and fair as possible. He thought that state officials, as natives with a better understanding of the local community, could best implement the policy. The War Department seemed amenable to the idea, but when confusion arose over whose budget would pay for such enrolling agents, Richmond authorities thought it best to utilize Confederate officers. Before the end of the summer, the conscription process in Alabama aggravated virtually everyone in the state. As Governor Shorter feared, Confederate agents seemed interested only in filling quotas, press-ganging men throughout the state often without regard for their exemption status. Not surprisingly, draft dodging and desertion escalated, especially in the northern hill counties and the coastal wiregrass region. To combat this nascent lawlessness, the War Department requested that Shorter help crack down. The governor charged county sheriffs to make arrests, but he also remonstrated against the unclear lines of jurisdiction. Privately, he fumed that conscription had become "a humbug and a farce" with enforcement becoming excessively intrusive and needlessly high-handed, even counterproductive, particularly when bureau agents in some instances perversely began using conscripts to hunt down those evading the draft. In a November letter to the president, Shorter apologized that conscription in his state "has been so barren of result," but he insisted that his administration was doing all that it could. Complicating matters was the growing number of "lie outs" and deserters. Shorter publicly denounced the selfishness that was evinced by the various protests and resistance to conscription. In December 1862, he delivered an "Appeal to the People of Alabama," in which he exhorted those with exemptions and those avoiding the draft to follow the patriotic example of the thousands of Alabamians volunteering in the ranks, many of whom had made the ultimate sacrifice. "It is a shame and an iniquity," he declared, "that those two classes of persons should successfully evade the service they owe to their country."[12]

Going into 1863, the governor dropped all pretense of sympathizing with individual liberty and emerged as an unconditional proponent of conscription. According to Kenneth Michael Murray, "Shorter's support for conscription remained greater than that of many other governors." First, he persuaded the state legislature to repeal the exemption for militia officers, thereby turning them over to the Confederate army. In fact, Shorter endeavored to reduce exemptions across the board, producing one of the best conscript-to-exemption ratios in the entire Confederacy. Next, in accordance with congressional amendments to the law, Shorter announced that he would no longer honor the contract with citizens who had purchased substitutes, a decree that made available nearly ten thousand more Alabamians for military service. Finally, he embraced increasingly draconian approaches to rounding up deserters. "Treason to the sacred cause of the Confederacy," the governor intoned to the legislature in an October message, "should be hunted down and visited with condign punishment." To this end, he readily acceded when in January 1863 the Army of Tennessee assumed direct control over conscription. Under General

Gideon Pillow, Confederate cavalry conducted summertime sweeps through Alabama's troublesome counties, ignoring every hue and cry of protest while rounding up hundreds of men for service, whether eligible or not. A manifestly satisfied Governor Shorter expressed his delight to the War Department: "I am thoroughly convinced that the plan of organization recommended by [Pillow] is the only one which promises such timely results as are needed to save the armies."[13]

As it turned out, the greatest casualty of the Confederate policy of conscription was not personal liberty, but the militia system. Governor Shorter frankly informed the legislature in October 1862 that "the whole body of the State militia is absorbed, and we are left with a naked organization." To concerned citizens, Shorter insisted that national law trumped state law whenever the two were in conflict. "It is not for me to make—but to Execute the law," he explained to a Pike County resident in a letter just prior to his bid for reelection in 1863. "If it is unequal, hard, or oppressive, the remedy is not in my hands." That conscription had wrecked the militia system was unfortunate, but it was also unavoidable. "It is my duty to strengthen, & not weaken the hands of the Confederate Government," the governor concluded. For John Gill Shorter, as for most of his fellow war governors, the exigencies of war had turned the exalted ideology of states' rights on its head.[14]

Governor Shorter's increasing deference to Confederate authority over matters of mobilization reflected both his frustration at being shunted aside and his relief at no longer having to suffer that headache. Still, he did not entirely acquiesce to centralized power, instead striving to protect his state in instances when Richmond seemed disinclined to do so. The fate of north Alabama proved especially worrisome to the governor. In spring 1862, Union forces occupied much of the Tennessee River valley, bringing with them the hard hand of war that made the area miserable for the next three years. When not committing depredations themselves, such as sacking the small town of Athens (May 1862), the Yankees facilitated a local civil war between the region's unionist and secessionist communities. In an effort to aid the Confederate population in the valley, Governor Shorter persuaded the state legislature to appropriate $1 million for its defense and authorized the formation of partisan cavalry units, "under the command of bold and discreet leaders," whose task was to harass the invader at every opportunity. Unfortunately for the governor, most of these units were absorbed into the Army of Tennessee, while those that remained (notably Colonel Philip Roddey's constabulary) rarely engaged the enemy in serious fighting. Relief came only when the Confederate army took an interest in the valley: once, in late summer 1862, when Braxton Bragg's Army of Tennessee assembled in the area prior to its offensive into Kentucky, and again, in May 1863, when the South's great cavalry commander Nathan Bedford Forrest foiled Streight's Raid, a Union incursion through the hill counties. After an exciting chase filled with much gunplay, Forrest's troopers bagged the whole enemy force.[15]

Governor Shorter latched onto the Confederate success against Streight's Raid. His reputation as a commander in chief was deficient in the eyes of many northern Alabamians, and the raid made for good propaganda. Back in January 1863, the governor had paid an overdue visit to the war-ravaged valley. After a brief stop in Decatur, however, he was called back to Montgomery, never to return, and he left behind a false perception of indifference. Just a few months later, the valley succumbed to a large-scale Union offensive, of which Streight's Raid was actually a small part. While Forrest won laurels tracking down Streight's band, a separate Union column descended on Florence and Tuscumbia in the northwest corner of the state. This larger force brushed aside Roddey's defending troopers, torched every makeshift factory in the area, and razed huge quantities of stockpiled foodstuffs that were vital to a southern population on the brink of starvation. Christopher Lyle McIlwain astutely observes that coverage of Streight's Raid, both by southern newspapers and in many later scholarly accounts, elides this much more significant Union operation. With the August election mere weeks away, Governor Shorter certainly hoped to divert attention from the disaster, capitalizing on Streight's Raid as a platform to reaffirm his martial credentials. Shortly after the raid, he wrote to the War Department, pointing out that many of the captured Yankee troopers were unionists from Alabama, whom he deemed guilty of "not only levying war against the State but instigating slaves to rebellion and committing deeds of rapine and destruction upon the property of its citizens." His demand that they be handed over for punishment as traitors played well in the state's newspapers. "We greatly admire the spirit of Governor Shorter in this matter," the *Clarke County Journal* crowed, while the *Montgomery Advertiser* prayed that these Alabama "Tories" would face execution for their alleged crimes. Many northern Alabamians, however, remained unmoved by the governor's high dudgeon. Congressman Thomas Jefferson Foster, whose constituency included the residents of Florence and Tuscumbia, preferred to know how the governor intended to respond to the calamity that had befallen his district. Shorter replied in a letter that was shockingly brusque. "Individual-local-and sectional interests however great & important—must be held subordinate to the grand idea of Confederate success," he snarled. "If the Confederacy fails—all is lost." No other statement by Governor Shorter could better articulate the essential truth of Confederate war policy: national survival trumped local needs. For all of his plans to ameliorate the plight of northern Alabama, Shorter ultimately conceded that the valley would be sacrificed on the altar of independence.[16]

In contrast to his ineffectual efforts to protect northern Alabama, Governor Shorter proffered able assistance to the defense of Mobile. To be sure, the city (much like the valley) soon fell under the purview of Confederate authority, but the governor was determined that his state's great port would not become a "mere dependency" of the rebel army. In a bombastic letter to the War Department, he vowed to leave Mobile a "smoking & smouldering ruin" rather than surrender the city to the enemy. Shorter need not have worried, for the Confederacy dedicated a substantial cohort of engineers to strengthening the fortifications all around the bay area. Nevertheless, the governor did his part with remarkable solicitude. When the Confederacy evacuated Pensacola, Florida, in May 1862, Shorter ensured that the artillery that was used to defend that city was redeployed to Mobile. He periodically mustered local militia, albeit with flaccid results, to augment the city's garrison. He also ran interference between military authority and the city's magistrates. For instance, when the army ordered all saloons to be closed for the duration of the war, Shorter successfully petitioned that they be reopened except in times of real emergency. And as he had wanted to do in northern Alabama, the governor paid the city a lengthy visit in autumn 1862. Jefferson Davis was gratified by Shorter's involvement in preparing Mobile for invasion. "Your friendly cooperation," the president wrote to the governor, "which has already been cheerfully rendered, is expected to render valuable aid."[17]

Governor Shorter's greatest contribution to the defense of Mobile was his consistent allocation of impressed slave labor. The Confederate Congress made impressment an official war policy in March 1863, but Alabama had already authorized it at the state level in October 1862. The legislation permitted governmental use of private property for military purposes. Accordingly, Governor Shorter appropriated slaves for a variety of functions, from construction of fortifications to the maintenance of the state's railroad tracks. His efforts only intensified as the war persisted. By summer 1863, Shorter had requisitioned over ten thousand slaves, mostly from the Black Belt counties. "I dislike exceedingly to resort to coercive measures," the governor explained in a public statement, but he insisted that "the occasion fully justifies the exercise of this power." The majority of these laborers worked on the defenses around Mobile or at the salt works in neighboring Clarke County. The term for impressment was not to exceed sixty days, and the slaves were to receive decent treatment, but military commanders routinely abused the system. For instance, General Danville Leadbetter, the chief engineer at Mobile, habitually ignored the time limits, while other Confederate officers apparently regarded the slaves as disposable commodities. Some five hundred slaves died from overwork and "sheer neglect." It should be noted, however, that Leadbetter did provide housing and medical care for his "Mobile Negro Force," and he kept corporal punishment to a minimum, despite numerous instances of malingering.[18]

Shorter came under severe criticism from angry planters seeking redress for real and imagined damage to their chattel. It was bad enough that the governor was enforcing conscription at the expense of individual liberty, but to the state's big slaveholders it was especially disturbing that he would trample property rights by impressing slaves. The governor's correspondence with William Samford, a planter from Macon County, highlights the discord. "I regret to hear of the loss of another one of your negroes, engaged at the defenses at Mobile," Shorter informed Samford in spring 1863. "Quite a number have died," he matter-of-factly added. When Samford raised the question of compensation, Shorter bluntly replied that none was forthcoming because the legislature had made no provision for slaves' getting injured or killed while impressed. Evidently annoyed by all the complaints, the governor dressed down the entire planter class: "If the slaveholders are unwilling to furnish the small amount that is absolutely necessary to give security to their property and protection to their hearthstones, let them not complain if the one is destroyed and the other outraged."[19]

His impatience over impressment notwithstanding, Governor Shorter was not without sympathy for his fellow slaveholders. In various public announcements, he insisted that his administration was striving to minimize abuses, and he assured the citizenry that he was maintaining a record of all impressment grievances so as to reimburse legitimate claims at a later date. Alabama lawmakers subsequently amended the policy and eventually disbursed $1 million in compensation, but this change came too late to salvage Shorter's reputation among the planter class going into the gubernatorial election. "No law, including conscription, was so widely reviled by the Confederate population," asserts Stephanie McCurry in her study of the southern home front. But to war Confederates like Shorter, impressment was vital to the war effort. In her own work on Confederate impressment policy, Jaime Amanda Martinez goes so far as say that its deleterious impact on morale is probably overstated, and the planters' remonstrance overblown. "What is surprising," she argues, "is that slave impressment was often successful," with state and national authorities displaying a "high level of cooperation" in maximizing the use of slaves without unduly upsetting the social fabric. Admittedly, her work focuses on the upper south, but her conclusions seem valid for Alabama. If so, then Shorter deserves high marks for implementing the policy with restrained vigor.[20]

Toward the end of May, in the wake of southern euphoria over Streight's Raid, Shorter announced his candidacy for reelection. "In view, however, of the hard experience gained, and my knowledge of the resources and complications of the State and Confederate Governments," he explained in an acceptance letter, "I ought not to retire from the public service, voluntarily, at the present juncture of affairs." Initial reactions around the state were favorable. Supporters from southern Alabama, particularly in Mobile, cheered the news, as did a politico from Shorter's home county of Barbour who wrote to tell the governor that he "justly merited" reelection. Encouraging words even came from the valley. "The Northern Counties of Ala will support you to a man," averred a resident from Jackson County. The *Montgomery Advertiser*, which espoused political neutrality, conceded that Shorter's leadership would be hard to replace, especially during a time of total war, and so it casually endorsed his campaign.[21]

His manifest support notwithstanding, Shorter did not run unopposed in 1863. In fact, at the time that he announced his bid, other hats were already in the ring. The most notable challenger was Thomas Hill Watts (figure 10), the very man whom Shorter had defeated in 1861. At the start of the Civil War, Watts was among the wealthiest figures in the state, having achieved the South's social trinity: lawyer, planter, and gentleman. Born in Butler County in 1819—the year that Alabama entered the Union—young Tom displayed a lust for learning. Although the eldest of twelve siblings, he converted what would have been a sizeable inheritance in land into college tuition at the University of Virginia. Graduating with honors in 1840, Watts returned to Alabama, started practicing law in Greenville, and then opened his own firm in Montgomery. By the 1850s, Watts and his associates handled cases involving clients from as far away as New England. Like many other young, professional southern men, Watts translated his lucrative law practice into the genteel lifestyle of a cotton planter. In 1860, he owned 179 slaves, who harvested over five hundred bales annually on his Montgomery County plantation.[22]

Watts was known as Big Tom to his many supporters, and his professional success was in many ways an extension of his larger-than-life physique and personality. At six feet two, with the girth to match, he was "gigantic in person." His small, wire-rimmed glasses only accentuated his already large head. Friends and acquaintances often remarked on his "affable and sociable" demeanor and his "unusually happy temperament." Watts was married to Elizabeth Brown Allen, the sister of future Confederate general William W.

Figure 10. Thomas Hill Watts, studio portrait by Shackell, New York, 1860s. (Courtesy of Alabama Department of Archives and History)

Allen, and the husband and wife were among the leading families in Montgomery on the eve of the Civil War. They were also among the leaders of the Baptist community in the capital city.[23]

In politics, Watts was a Whig. He served several terms in the state legislature during the 1840s and early 1850s, espousing the cause of temperance and pushing programs that expedited the development of Alabama's natural resources. With the collapse of the Whig Party in the mid-1850s, Watts briefly endured the political purgatory of the American, or Know-Nothing, Party. Throughout these years, whenever the subject turned toward the sectional crisis, Watts always argued for the preservation of the Union. Everything changed in 1860, however, when the much-despised Republican Party won the presidential election. Delivering a series of public addresses in November, Watts called for immediate secession. "The black flag of abolition dominion and Southern subjection," he declared, "will soon be hoisted at her mast head, and where Washington commanded, a Lincoln will rule." He dismissed those who still urged caution, describing the mere election of Lincoln as an "overt act" of aggression. "They all speak one language and it is uttered in one tone," Watts said of the Republicans, "that there is an irrepressible conflict between free and slave labor; between THEIR institutions and OUR institutions—between THEM and US." Elected to Alabama's Secession Convention in January 1861, Watts brought tremendous stature to the cause of disunion. Moreover, he played a key role as a mediator between the fire-eaters and the cooperationists, two factions that barely disguised their contempt for each other. During one particularly nasty exchange between William Yancey and Robert Jemison Jr., prominent Alabamians in their own right, Watts intervened to soothe the egos: "This is no time for the exhibition of feeling or for the utterance of denunciations." Nevertheless, Watts firmly supported the Ordinance of Secession and helped get it passed in short order.[24]

Following Alabama's entry into the Confederacy, Watts offered his services to his new country. As previously discussed, he lost his gubernatorial bid in August 1861, but soon thereafter he helped raise the Seventeenth Alabama Infantry and became its colonel. Initially stationed around Pensacola, the regiment deployed to Corinth, Mississippi, in March 1862, as part of a larger Confederate effort to thwart Union forces then advancing through West Tennessee. The rank and file seemed to like Watts, but the commanding general, Braxton Bragg, did not. The fastidious Bragg decried what he considered the Seventeenth's "bad state of discipline" and the "imbecility of its officers," particularly Colonel Watts. When Big Tom remonstrated against these harsh accusations, Bragg placed Watts under arrest on preposterous charges of mutiny and treason. The incident marked the beginning of a lifelong antipathy between the two men. Mercifully, toward the end of March, Watts received an appointment as attorney general of the Confederacy. He left on the eve of the great Battle of Shiloh and so missed out on an opportunity to prove his combat mettle. The colonel was there in spirit, however, for at one point during that battle, his former soldiers purportedly shouted "Tom Watts" as they charged into the fray.[25]

On April 9, 1862, Watts commenced his service as attorney general of the Confederate States of America. As an accomplished lawyer, Watts excelled at his new position. He wrote one hundred decisions during his eighteen-month tenure and greatly clarified the rebel government's role in enforcing a wide range of laws. In doing so, Watts and his department emerged as the Confederacy's de facto Supreme Court. To be sure, the attorney general frequently called on Congress to create a national judiciary, but he never shied away from rendering his opinions. More often than not, Watts favored a centralized war effort, his professed respect for states' rights notwithstanding. He proclaimed the conscription acts fully constitutional, insisting that the states wielded limited authority over matters of mobilization and the disposition of human resources. He even included foreigners who owned property in the South, charging that for them conscription was part of their "correlative duty of defending this country." In essence, when it came to prosecuting the war, the needs of the nation and of the armed forces trumped the rights of the states and those of the people. Similarly, Watts upheld the authority of Richmond to suspend the writ of habeas corpus and of the army to impose martial law. He did, however, urge restraint in exercising this extraordinary power. "The common mind," Watts explained, "rarely distinguishes between the *cause* and the *men*, who administer the functions of Power, and hence Liberty may suffer for the sins of the ministers." In other words, Confederate officials needed to demonstrate compassion when implementing policies that were "contrary to the normal theory of Republican Government." These tempering words aside, Attorney General Watts established for himself a deserved reputation as a war Confederate. Certain critics, such as Robert Kean of the War Department, considered him "hardly qualified" and "provincial" in his thinking, but Watts enjoyed the approbation of President Davis, who thanked the Alabamian for his "aid and cooperation" in strengthening the executive branch.[26]

As Alabama's gubernatorial election of 1863 approached, Watts felt the call to run for governor once again. That spring, he received a letter from Levi Lawler, a leading war Confederate from Talladega County, urging Watts to enter the race. In his reply, Watts feigned disinterestedness, but he permitted Lawler to put his name forth. "As a dutiful son I ought to obey her voice," he said of his home state, adding with a touch of patriotic flourish that "whilst there is a hostile foot on Confederate soil, my head, my heart, my hands, my all, shall be devoted to the repulse of the vandal invaders." The formal announcement came in May and with it a mixed reaction from the leading newspapers. The *Clarke County Journal* expressed enthusiasm for Watts. "He is one of the ablest men of our State," declared the editors, "he would make a good governor, we think." Conversely, the *Jacksonville Republican* seemed perplexed: "We can see no good reason why the custom of re-electing a Governor who has done so well should not be followed in this instance." It endorsed the incumbent and recommended that Watts stay in Richmond as the attorney general: "the public good does not require a change." The *Montgomery Advertiser*, wary of a nasty partisan campaign, took a neutral stance and simply urged the people to vote their conscience.[27]

Watts made the biggest splash with his entry, but there were other contenders, most notably two active-duty infantry colonels. In April, soldiers from an all-Alabama brigade that was then defending Vicksburg nominated Isham W. Garrott. A political hard-liner from Perry County, Garrott had served as a secession commissioner before the war and then won accolades during it from officers and men alike for his courage under fire as commander of the Twentieth Alabama Infantry. Watts appears to have viewed Garrott's candidacy as a serious threat. Seeking to get the popular colonel "out of the way," Watts evidently lobbied the president to promote Garrott to brigadier general in the hopes that such a reward would sate his competitor's ambition. Garrott did indeed receive the promotion, but he had actually already begged off a run for the governor's seat, citing devotion to his men as a higher calling. The other colonel, James F. Dowdell, stayed in the race to the end. A prewar Democrat from Chambers County and a prosecession delegate in 1861, Dowdell raised the Thirty-Seventh Alabama Infantry and served with distinction as its commander in the western theater. Unlike Garrott, Dowdell readily accepted a petition from his men (who were also defending Vicksburg) to make a run. Historian Kenneth Michael Murray suggests that Dowdell's candidacy was "chiefly a personal effort to cash in his military laurels." Maybe so, but it also afforded an opportunity to spite an old foe—Big Tom Watts. In 1855, the two had squared off in a grueling congressional campaign, one where Dowdell's surrogates in the press savaged Watts's political integrity en route to a narrow victory at the polls. Dowdell perhaps thought that he could best Watts once again. For his part, Watts most certainly relished the chance at vindication. As it turned out, Dowdell's bid proved delusional and worked against Shorter's prospects for reelection. A few other names, such as Congressman Francis Lyon, were bandied about for governor, but going into its final weeks the contest was really a two-man race: Shorter versus Watts.[28]

In keeping with the Confederacy's official no-party system, none of the gubernatorial candidates canvassed the state. Watts remained in Richmond, where in June he issued a single political statement vowing to serve with fidelity if elected. Shorter remained in Montgomery, where he attended to his full slate of duties as the state's war chief. And Dowdell remained in his home, "too infirm to the see the people." The campaign of 1863 was conducted not through debates, rallies, and orations, but through opinion pieces issued by the "generals of the press." As previously noted, the *Jacksonville Republican* endorsed Shorter, but so did most other newspapers in the state. "Gov. Shorter has shunned no responsibility," proclaimed the *Autauga Citizen*, "he neglected nothing within his reach for the safety and welfare of the state, is always at work, and always moved by the most patriotic determination to thwart the designs of the enemy." The *Alabama Beacon* echoed this high praise: "the interests of the State may be safely confided to him again." Even the *Clarke County Journal* reversed its earlier support for Watts, praising the incumbent for his efforts "to defend the state against Yankee invasion and to harmonize our people and our State government with the complex governmental machinery of the Confederates States." All these newspapers justified the incumbent's authoritarian style of command on the grounds of military necessity.[29]

Watts may have lagged behind in press coverage, but he enjoyed an active base that circulated numerous petitions on his behalf as "the peoples favorite." One petition contended that the state needed a fresh start, that Shorter was burned out, and that Watts was the ideal replacement. A letter authored by "Earnest Alabamians" praised the challenger's trifold experience in law, politics, and the military. Another, going by the moniker "Montrose," emphasized Watts's character: "With a head and heart like his, cool, calm and well-poised, liberal, generous and upright, he would guide with unerring judgment the ship of state . . . The People of Alabama are determined to have him." The *Selma Reporter* published many of these petitions and, ultimately, endorsed Watts. As the one newspaper most devoted to his candidacy, it spent much of the summer debunking rumors that Watts had ties to the Peace Society or that he was an advocate of reconstruction (i.e., a negotiated cease-fire followed by conditional reunification). In actuality, few people seriously believed that Watts favored a reunion with the North (the *Sumter Independent* described him as a "man of extreme war feelings"), but his neglect in denying these aspersions outright apparently suggested to the peace crowd that he might be receptive to such a plan once in office. In any event, the *Selma Reporter* wedded martial bombast to its endorsement in an effort to assure its readers that its man was good on the war: "Better to die in the moment covered with glory, and join the procession of brave ones who have gone before us than to linger like cowards and waste by piece-meal in the chains that will clank upon our free arms and fester through the infamy of years."[30]

During the first week of July, less than a month before Alabamians went to the polls, the Confederacy suffered twin defeats at Gettysburg and Vicksburg. Several state newspapers tried to downplay the significance of these losses, but Shorter understood their harmful impact on both the home-front morale and his chances for reelection. On July 13, he issued a lengthy statement defending his record. He cited his various efforts at augmenting security in Mobile and northern Alabama, and he justified his resort to impressment. Of probably the greatest interest to the electorate, however, was his summation of how he was addressing the economic hardships of the average citizen. Impressment, coupled with the recent tax-in-kind law (April 1863), both frequently abused by unethical local agents, hit Alabamians hard, particularly the yeoman class, whose menfolk were away in the army. A government survey completed in the spring discovered that nearly a third of all families in Alabama were indigent; the state was in the grip of a "salt famine," and the roads were trafficked by "corn women" begging for food. The governor honestly contended that indigent relief was one of his top priorities. He distributed large quantities of food and salt (thanks in part to generous legislative funding); he urged planters to shift from cotton to grain; and he cracked down on illicit distilleries that were wasting much-needed corn on whiskey production. Shorter closed his address with an acknowledgment that many were unhappy with his administration, but—in a nod toward the election—he also expressed faith in "an inward approval, which the popular verdict shall neither give nor take away."[31]

Two topics that were left out of Shorter's public vita were the Confederacy's takeover of state industry and the suspension of habeas corpus in matters related to conscription. The governor would have been hard pressed to present either as an example of his strong leadership. First, through a practice described by historian Michael Brem Bonner as "expedient corporatism," the War Department steadily assumed control over the South's industrial economy, either through direct contracts with southern businessmen or through the forced sale of installations deemed vital to the war effort. In the case of Alabama, this practice amounted to de facto Confederate ownership of the state's ironworks and supervisory oversight of Selma as a national arsenal. Governor Shorter readily acceded to Richmond's management of Alabama's manufacturing capacity, ignoring this significant breach in states' rights. Second, military authorities had increasingly suspended the writ of habeas corpus in their efforts to round up draft dodgers. As Michael Albert Powell notes, the outcry by most southern governors against this violation of civil liberty "was rather muted." This was certainly Governor Shorter's attitude. As previously discussed, he had long ago lost any desire to protect the rights of citizens who refused the call to arms. Happily for the governor, and for the War Department, Alabama's supreme court ruled that the writ of habeas corpus was no defense against compulsory military service. Beginning in January 1863, the three-man court tossed aside every legal challenge. "Let us not weaken or destroy our Confederate power," remarked Justice George Stone, "by embarrassing that government in the manly exercise of those functions with which the States themselves have clothed it." Judicial imprimatur notwithstanding, Shorter wisely avoided the issue in his July address. The court's proceedings would not be published until September, well after the election.[32]

On the whole, Shorter's address appears to have persuaded some Alabamians that his policies were essential, albeit unpleasant. Evidently moved by its message of shared sacrifice, William C. Bibb of Montgomery called on planters to make available more slaves for military impressment. "I am willing as a slaveholder to contribute one fourth or more of my fellow force," he personally pledged toward the end of July. Similarly emboldened was the *Montgomery Advertiser*, which complemented the governor's words with its own appeal to press on with the rebellion: "All that is needed to win independence for all time to come, is the patriotic determination which we know burns now as brightly as ever in the hearts of our army and people." If women had held the franchise in 1863, then perhaps they would have appreciated the governor's sincere attempts to alleviate their hardships and voted for him. In any event, Shorter's statement stands as a detailed encapsulation of what a war state all over looked like in 1863. Had the Confederacy been clearly winning that year, then Shorter's draconian performance might have come across as heroic, and his record might have propelled him to a landslide at the polls. But victory seemed far away after Vicksburg, and the governor had still more demands to impose on his people.[33]

One of those demands was the broken-record call for additional manpower. On June 5, President Davis issued a peremptory request for the states to furnish fifty thousand men for local defense under Confederate aegis. Alabama's portion of this figure was seven thousand. The only way that the governor could fulfill this quota was through increased conscription, which invariably fomented discontent, or through the militia, which at least offered a patina of patriotism. Conscription, however, had largely become the purview of the Confederate army, while the militia system had become a punch line. On June 17, Shorter ordered county authorities to commence drafting men into service, but he fretted privately over how to go about this latest mobilization. When he explained to Richmond that even if he could recruit more men they would be without any equipment, an unsympathetic War Department retorted, "can you not adopt measures to induce the array of all your arms-bearing population for defense?" Fortunately, the governor received genuine encouragement from prowar Alabamians who implored him to scrape the barrel, and to do so through a fully activated militia. William Brooks, the former president of the Secession Convention, recommended that the governor instigate the equivalent of a *levée en masse* for everyone between the ages of "16 and 60," with a ban on all exemptions and substitutions. James P. Tarry of Perry County agreed with this sweeping course and beseeched Shorter to enlist "every man phisically able to perform military duty."[34]

Desperate to comply with Richmond's demands and emboldened by his political allies at home, Governor Shorter issued a proclamation on July 20, calling for a special session of the legislature. The purpose of this session, scheduled for August 17, was to resurrect the state militia in order "to clothe [the] Executive with larger powers for the Public defense." The press cheered the governor's decision. "Our armies need more men to resist the invader," the *Clarke County Journal* intoned, "All will be wanted . . . and none need expect to escape." The *Montgomery Advertiser* tried to shame those who had yet to shoulder a musket. "The men who are now at home engaged in private business must go and fight," its editors cried, "Better to die and leave all behind a blank uncertainty, than to live ignobly and leave a heritage of beggary, slavery and disgrace." The *Mobile Register* resorted to gendered peer pressure: "We call upon the women to do their duty and shove every masculine friend or relative to the front." Bellicose editorials aside, the South did need men and Alabama still had bodies, but Shorter's proclamation was ill timed politically. Coming just two weeks before the election (and two weeks after Vicksburg), it threatened to alarm citizens and turn away their votes. Furthermore, the special session, scheduled for after the election, would undoubtedly comprise many new legislators whose commitment to the war was as yet unknown. The current legislature, however, had proved timid in militia matters, so Shorter's calculation that some turnover (other than his own) might actually be helpful was a sensible gamble. As the governor explained to a concerned citizen, "it is the people themselves who must be aroused to meet the crisis which is upon us, with manliness and courage."[35]

Historian Malcolm C. McMillan suggests that Shorter was surprised by his eventual defeat, that he never saw it coming, largely because he incorrectly gauged the real "mood of the electorate." Going into August, however, Shorter did have reason for optimism. Most papers backed him, including the *Mobile Register*, which endorsed him at the eleventh hour, and he received several letters from political friends wishing him victory. But Shorter also received two letters, both from staunch supporters, that cut through the newspaper propaganda and presented the governor with a more honest, albeit ominous, assessment of the political climate. On July 22, John Clisby of Coosa County informed Shorter that antigovernment sentiment was "open, bold and defiant" in many parts of the Coosa River valley. He spoke of a "secret organization" (i.e., the Peace Society) that was "not for independence but reunion," and he said that it was both protecting army deserters and encouraging them to vote illegally. He warned that if the governor did not immediately dispatch a contingent of trustworthy soldiers to police the precincts, then peace candidates would prevail and "proscribe every secessionist in the land." On July 26, Z. L. Nabors of Pickens County praised Shorter for "the very excellent manner in which you have discharged the duties of Executive," but he frankly considered reelection to be "a dull prospect." He pointed out that Pickens and the surrounding counties were crawling with "*speculators*" and "*substitute men*" along with a great many planters "who love their negroes more than their country." Nabors never hinted at anything like a "secret organization" at work, but he clearly lamented the dearth of true war Confederates in his district. Governor Shorter likely appreciated these candid insights, but it was too late in the race to rectify the defeatism that was highlighted in these two letters. Having done what he felt was his best in a trying time, Shorter could now only resign himself to the will of the people.[36]

On August 3, the election passed without incident. The returns, however, soon confirmed a smashing victory for Watts (table 2). The challenger won by twenty thousand votes—28,960 to 9,265—including majorities in forty-five of the state's fifty-two counties. The virtually forgotten third candidate, James Dowdell, polled 1,475 votes, mostly from the eastern counties around his home in Chambers. There are some discrepancies in the returns. For St. Clair County, the *House Journal* inexplicably recorded the gubernatorial figures for 1861, when Shorter won the county 1,103–79. The real numbers, as corroborated by multiple newspapers, are Watts, 634; Shorter, 119. This outcome is more consistent with that county's reputation as a haven for deserters and members of the Peace Society. Furthermore, the assembly rejected the returns for Limestone, Marshall, and Winston Counties, citing improper reporting by the registrars. (Oddly, this invalidation apparently only applied to the gubernatorial race; the returns for the congressional and legislative races in those counties were all counted as legitimate.) Taking these adjustments into account, the actual outcome is Watts, 28,756; Shorter, 8,680; Dowdell, 1,471.[37]

The face of the returns demonstrates that Watts performed only slightly better than when he ran in 1861, whereas Shorter's popularity dropped dramatically. The incumbent was down almost thirty thousand votes; an astounding electoral shift in just two years. Clearly, Shorter's supporters abandoned him in 1863. Closer scrutiny, however, reveals some curious developments, qualifies Watts's landslide, and offers some solace to the loser. In the northern half of the state (districts 1 through 4) and the wiregrass region (district 8), Watts picked up over six thousand more votes than in 1861. He trounced Shorter in the very region that John Clisby had described as inundated with traitors—Coosa, Talladega, and Tallapoosa Counties. Alabama's yeomanry had typically voted Democrat before the war but now supported an erstwhile Whig. Moreover, many Alabamians in these districts had displayed reluctance on the question of secession and yet seen their lands ravaged by enemy occupation and raids. Shorter personified this unhappy fate and paid for it at the polls. Still, it is worth noting that the incumbent won five northern counties

Table 2. Alabama's Gubernatorial Returns—1863 versus 1861 (by District)

	1863 Returns			1861 Returns		
County	Watts	Shorter	Dowdell	Watts	Shorter	Misc.
District 1						
Franklin	607	266	2	0	1,717	0
Lauderdale	214	207	0	95	462	0
Lawrence	378	103	12	0	0	0
Limestone[a]	1	275	0	795	145	0
Madison	111	283	3	37	1,985	9
Morgan	275	182	0	836	117	0
Total	**1,586**	**1,316**	**17**	**1,763**	**4,426**	**9**
District 2						
Blount	242	168	3	304	948	0
Fayette	421	162	22	134	1,032	31
Jefferson	501	89	27	141	983	7
Marion	140	158	7	0	770	0
Tuscaloosa	848	187	0	496	1,274	0
Walker	272	62	32	1	936	0
Winston[a]	64	27	4	0	71	16
Total	**2,488**	**853**	**95**	**1,076**	**6,014**	**54**
District 3						
Cherokee	639	383	28	21	1,500	0
DeKalb	331	272	0	19	809	29
Jackson	128	213	2	152	1,454	0
Marshall[a]	139	283	0	23	1,363	3
St. Clair	634	119	0	79	1,103	0
Total	**1,871**	**1,270**	**30**	**294**	**6,229**	**32**
District 4						
Calhoun	745	574	45	98	2,098	0
Randolph	949	402	57	95	1,318	27
Shelby	977	55	8	1,206	228	0
Talladega	1,528	152	29	1,223	461	0
Total	**4,199**	**1,183**	**139**	**2,622**	**4,105**	**27**
District 5						
Bibb	616	32	1	656	535	0
Choctaw	495	39	0	557	418	35

Table 2. *Continued*

	1863 Returns			1861 Returns		
County	Watts	Shorter	Dowdell	Watts	Shorter	Misc.
Greene	529	149	5	452	641	0
Marengo	525	130	6	728	209	11
Perry	680	184	0	984	374	0
Pickens	622	130	0	189	1,416	0
Sumter	399	101	1	379	546	0
Total	**3,866**	**765**	**13**	**3,945**	**4,139**	**46**
District 6						
Autauga	526	70	32	924	129	0
Butler	797	42	61	1,311	390	0
Coosa	1,169	88	46	825	936	0
Dallas	863	107	6	1,115	150	0
Lowndes	555	103	23	909	279	0
Monty	1,116	313	104	1,843	434	0
Total	**5,026**	**723**	**272**	**6,927**	**2,318**	**0**
District 7						
Chambers	702	210	178	1,290	502	0
Macon	919	193	114	1,391	388	0
Russell	625	276	34	725	636	3
Tallapoosa	1,037	85	251	1,745	600	0
Total	**3,283**	**764**	**577**	**5,151**	**2,126**	**3**
District 8						
Barbour	826	447	3	373	1,524	3
Coffee	507	73	31	81	778	0
Covington	438	40	19	365	309	0
Dale	434	115	89	51	1,255	0
Henry	422	227	0	49	1,152	3
Pike	966	229	139	893	1,380	0
Total	**3,593**	**1,131**	**281**	**1,812**	**6,398**	**6**
District 9						
Baldwin	150	67	2	192	73	8
Clarke	512	70	0	448	693	0
Conecuh	388	62	13	671	194	0
Mobile	959	857	0	1,736	464	0

Continued on the next page

Table 2. *Continued*

	1863 Returns			1861 Returns		
County	Watts	Shorter	Dowdell	Watts	Shorter	Misc.
Monroe	453	33	28	748	215	0
Washington	109	65	0	86	117	0
Wilcox	477	106	8	650	302	0
Total	**3,048**	**1,260**	**51**	**4,531**	**2,058**	**8**
Statewide Totals						
Gross	28,960	9,265	1,475			
Invalid[a]	204	585	4			
Official	28,756	8,680	1,471	28,121	37,813	185

[a] The returns from Limestone, Winston, and Marshall Counties were ruled invalid by the secretary of state due to unstated irregularities in the voting.

Sources: Alabama Legislature, *House Journal,* 1862, 117–18; 1863, 110–11.

(Jackson, Madison, and Marion, officially; and Limestone and Marshall, unofficially). So there were diehards in the Tennessee River valley who applauded the outgoing governor's tough approach to waging the war.

In the Black Belt and bay areas (congressional districts 5, 6, 7, and 9), Watts was actually down more than five thousand votes from his 1861 performance. The Black Belt enjoyed a strong Whig presence among the planter class before the war, yet the slaveholders did not flock to the former Whig's standard during it. Shorter assumed that he lost the planter vote because of his enforcement of impressment (and he continued to receive complaints well after the election), but those same planters appear to have expected little meaningful change under a Watts administration. Rather than vote, most of them appear to have stayed home. Interestingly, the electorate in the big plantation counties comfortably reelected to Congress Francis Lyon and William Chilton, both of whom were former Whigs who voted for impressment at the national level. The results in Mobile are similarly noteworthy. Whereas Watts easily won this county in 1861, he barely edged out Shorter in 1863. Mobilians had come to appreciate Shorter's genuine efforts to protect the region from enemy incursions. These mitigating observations in no way diminish the fact that Watts utterly crushed Shorter (the incumbent trailed badly even in his home county of Barbour), but they do indicate that election outcomes are never as straightforward as the simple returns might suggest.[38]

While few were surprised by Shorter's defeat, the huge margin was unexpected. "Gov. Shorter took the time to do his duty and did not take the time to play the demagogue," noted the *Mobile Register*, "Why then has he been voted out of his chair by so large a majority?" Answers to that question run the gamut—secession, conscription, impressment, inflation, invasion, starvation—and if not the policies themselves, then Shorter's maladroit implementation, which often came across to an exhausted citizenry as insensitive and unjust. In the words of one historian, the governor "had reluctantly overseen the greatest expansion of state government in Alabama history." Anyone orchestrating such a top-down revolution would have encountered fierce popular resistance. Undoubtedly, personality was also a factor in Shorter's demise. He was officious, humorless, and patronizing; but mostly he was a true believer who was intolerant of anything less than a total commitment. To Shorter, the war was an act of faith. "The spirit of martyrdom," he declared at one point, "must characterize this Contest, or we will be overwhelmed by the huge power arrayed against us." Shorter sometimes complained about directives coming out of Richmond, but in the end he always complied. He expected no less from the people, who were free to grumble but were ultimately compelled to obey. If that meant that Alabama was to become more like an imperial province and less like a sovereign state, then so be it—only independence achieved by the sword could bring back prosperity and freedom. For good reason did President Davis describe Shorter as "zealous in the cause." In rejecting the incumbent at the ballot box, Alabamians never deluded themselves about an end to wartime hardships; they simply hoped that Watts—Big Tom—would display less fanaticism and more sympathy, and perhaps restore a semblance of states' rights autonomy. Nevertheless, historians such as Malcolm C. McMillan rightly give the outgoing governor high marks for his assiduous performance: "The Confederacy possessed too few men of the quality of Shorter." Whatever his faults, John Gill Shorter transformed Alabama into arguably the most ardent state in the rebellion.[39]

Executive war powers would soon transfer to Thomas Hill Watts. It must have been thoroughly satisfying for him to bury the combined tallies of his two great political rivals. In his resignation letter to President Davis, Watts exulted, "the people of Alabama, by an almost unanimous voice, through the ballot box, have elected me to the Chief Magistracy of that State." He thanked the president for entrusting him with the responsibilities of the attorney general and promised to provide "cordial support" as governor. Back in Alabama, newspapers that formerly endorsed Shorter speedily rallied around the governor-elect. The *Autauga Citizen* conceded that "we have the consolation of knowing that we shall have an able man at the head of our affairs." "Col. Watts will make you an able and popular Governor," the *Clarke County*

Journal similarly declared to its readers, going so far as to add "and [he will] be deserving of your support for reelection to a second term." Clearly, a fresh feeling of optimism pervaded Alabama's political landscape, but it was contingent on everyone's persevering in the war effort. The "generals of the press" united in their efforts to silence renewed whispers about reconstruction and various "twaddle about an honorable peace." Branding those who espoused such ideas as "cowardly croakers" and "submissionists," the newspapers called for ever-greater service and sacrifice from the citizenry. They also looked to Watts to carry the revolution forward. "If anyone unacquainted with the facts," intoned the *Montgomery Advertiser,* "should infer from the recent election in Alabama that Col. Watts would, in any contingency, compromise the independence of the Confederate States, he would do great injustice to the position which this distinguished gentleman has long occupied on the question at issue in this contest." The Peace Society was on notice.[40]

Watts was determined to establish himself as a "war man all over." In a widely circulated public letter dated September 12, Watts denounced "a thousand times" the idea of reconstruction and proclaimed his unwavering patriotism. "If I had the power, I would build up a *wall of fire* between Yankeedom and the Confederate States, there to burn, for ages, as a monument of the folly, wickedness, and vandalism of the puritanic race!" This was not empty rhetoric, for his teenage son, John Wade Watts had recently enlisted in the Seventh Alabama Cavalry and thereby become one of the flames in that wall of fire. In late October, the governor-elect embarked on a tour of the state, one designed both to introduce himself to the people and to reassure them that all was not lost. To crowds in Butler and Dallas Counties, he declared that the state's resources were "greater today than when the war commenced" and that "not many days would elapse before the power of Lincoln would be effectually broken." In Talladega County the new governor vowed to sustain the president, whom he considered to be a man of "genius and moral worth." In a pointed rebuke of the Peace Society, Watts also insisted that secession was fully justified, that reconstruction was an "absurdity," and that he would "see *every man and woman perish in one grand carnival of blood*" before he would accept defeat. Alabamians may well have believed Big Tom's stirring words, uttered just one month after the Confederate Army of Tennessee finally won a major battle—the slugfest at Chickamauga in northern Georgia. According to correspondents who accompanied him, "Mr. Watts found the reported disaffection in certain localities greatly exaggerated." His "conversational style," "unflagging energy," and "buoyant hopefulness" seemingly won over audiences that had grown weary of Shorter's sanctimonious proclamations. In substance, however, he was not much different from the man whom he was replacing.[41]

While Watts conducted his parade through the counties, Shorter continued his executive duties as diligently as ever. The lame-duck governor had until December, and he very much wanted to hand over an administration that was well positioned to carry on the war. On August 17, the state legislature convened its special session to address the governor's request for a stronger militia organization. "Alabama will be invaded," he warned those gathered in the capital, "before many weeks the guns of the enemy will be heard on her borders." And so he implored the assembly to create a reliable militia force that he could deploy throughout the state. This plan meant drafting just about every able-bodied man not already in the Confederate army, but as the governor stated, "Alabama has ever cheerfully and promptly responded to the uttermost of every demand which has been made upon her." A fuller discussion of the legislature's enactment of the militia law is contained in chapter 3, but in essence most of the remaining manpower in the state was drafted into so-called county reserves, whose deployment was restricted to their local communities. "It was the best I could get," Shorter commented afterward.[42]

For the last weeks of his term, Shorter faded into the background. He continued to impress slaves and provide indigent relief, but in purely military matters he entirely deferred to Confederate authority. With the governor's tacit approval, General Gideon Pillow intensified his crackdown on deserters and draft dodgers. In October and November, cavalry forces swept across northern Alabama, forcibly recruiting men and, in some instances, killing those who resisted. Any refusal to serve now came to be seen as outright treason. These flying squadrons hanged two women in Talladega County for helping their husbands evade the draft, and they did the same to a man named James Wood for organizing a "secret Union League" in Coosa and Tallapoosa Counties. In Pike County, Confederate authorities arrested a local judge for issuing a writ of habeas corpus to a man claiming an exemption. An anonymous letter to the *Selma Morning Dispatch* mocked the governor for his indirect culpability in these travesties. Criticizing Shorter for having elevated duty above liberty, the writer opined that "lawyers need no longer turn over aged and dusty volumes of law to find out the rights of clients." Martial law was the new order. To be sure, the governor petitioned the War Department for clemency in the case of the Pike County judge; and when General Pillow eventually released him, Shorter publicly applauded the decision as a triumph for civil liberty. It is likely, however, that Shorter would have remained silent had Pillow opted to maintain the incarceration. He certainly said nothing about the summary executions.[43]

Alabama's gubernatorial transfer of power occurred in Montgomery on December 1, 1863. Despite the privations of a long war, the inauguration was a gala event. At noon, Thomas Hill Watts, dressed in a "plain suit of homespun," entered the state House walking abreast with John Gill Shorter, who was perhaps wearing his new hat. The hall was lavishly decorated and crowded with politicians and many "fair daughters of Alabama." Walter Crenshaw, the Speaker of the House, administered the oath of office, and then Watts delivered his address. It was a long speech, one that presented a superfluous history of the Revolution, statehood, and the sectional crisis of the 1850s, but one that also offered a moving summary of Alabama's suffering up to that point. Though he intimated some modifications to his predecessor's approach, Watts vowed to maintain an all-out war effort. "Let us renew our faith to the Southern cause," the new governor exhorted toward the end, "should we be conquered, everything worth living for will be gone." An evening reception filled with band music and "abundant refreshments" completed the ceremony. State senator Edward Moren found the closing festivities amusing. "It was clear that provisions was scarce," he later informed his wife, "for in all my life I never saw such a manifest desire to devour everything as was exhibited by the Gov's guests when supper was announced." The executive branch now belonged to Big Tom.[44]

Had he known what was coming in 1864, Governor Watts might well have preferred to let Shorter win another term. All the problems that his predecessor had confronted in the first half of the war seemed compounded tenfold during the second half. Impressment and the tax-in-kind intensified dramatically in the opening months of 1864. Confederate agents appropriated beasts of burden wherever they could be found, yet they compensated the owners at market values that did not take into account runaway inflation. Similarly, they made off with bacon and corn and other foodstuffs that yeoman families could ill afford to do without. Watts lodged numerous complaints with the War Department, deprecating the "odious" manner by which the government collected these items. "Many impressing officers care neither for God nor man," he fumed in one letter. No matter his anger, Watts still complied with national law. He did, however, do what he could to alleviate the suffering of Alabamians, such as pushing for more indigent relief and suspending state taxes in selected counties hardest hit by these war policies.[45]

The omnipresent need for manpower also beset Governor Watts. Here was an issue that would put the governor at odds with both his president and his legislature. Mere weeks after he took office, Watts became embroiled in a running fight with Confederate military authorities over conscription, one that would last most of the year. In February 1864, Congress expanded the draft to include all white men between the ages of 17 and 50, and it eliminated most exemptions. The new law basically torpedoed Alabama's 1863 Militia Act, which had placed old men and teenagers—the "sires and striplings" of the state—into the local units known as county reserves. Now, the Confederate army would also have them. Publicly, Watts encouraged war-weary Alabamians to turn out: "shall we at home be laggards in the race for glory?" he asked at one point. "We need more men!" he shouted at another. But behind the scenes the governor protested this latest demand on his state. At first he explained the dangers of denuding the home front of militia, namely a spike in lawlessness by deserters and bandits. He then ordered all foreigners in Alabama to enlist or leave, hoping that might appease Confederate authorities. When army commanders in the region, however, ignored the governor's pleas to stop press-ganging state employees, Watts became more strident. "The States have some rights left," he lectured the War Department in May, "the laws of Alabama must be executed and I must have some troops at my command to execute them." His missive falling on deaf ears, the governor later spoke of a looming "conflict between Confederate and State authorities." What exactly Watts meant by that was unclear, but Jefferson Davis finally intervened on behalf of the governor. Toward the end of 1864, the president instructed the conscription bureau to honor certificates of exemption that were signed by the state executive, a decision that protected over ten thousand Alabamians. Janet E. Kaufman contends that disputes over conscription wrecked the relationship between Montgomery and Richmond. Although Watts had been "aglow with patriotic ardor" at the start of his tenure, she says, he ended it as an opponent of the commander in chief. Perhaps so, but Malcolm C. McMillan contends that the two men remained on friendly terms, each respecting their mutual political pressures.[46]

Watts objected to never-ending conscription not because he opposed the policy, but because he thought that his state's remaining pool of manpower could better serve the cause through local defense. Like Shorter before him, Watts successfully shielded the Corps of Cadets at the University of Alabama; these cadets were young men whom the regular army very much wanted. Furthermore, he retained control over such irregular units as James Clanton's brigade in southern Alabama and Philip Roddey's cavalry in the Tennessee River valley, forces that Shorter had employed as internal troubleshooters. These forces, augmented at times by the county reserves, tried in vain to stop a Union cavalry raid in July 1864. Led by Major General Lovell Rousseau, Yankee troopers slashed their way through eastern Alabama, burning foundries and tearing up railroads. State forces offered laughably ineffectual resistance. From this disaster, Watts concluded that what he really needed was a stronger militia system. Conscription notwithstanding, the governor estimated that there were still some thirty thousand men available for duty.

Unfortunately, they were all in the county reserves, which restricted their deployment. "The militia laws as they now stand are almost worthless," the governor opined in August 1864. The apparent remedy was to call on the legislature once again to address the matter. The assembly's peace Confederates had acceded to a militia overhaul in 1863, but they were in no mood to do so again. Even war Confederates balked at the governor's eleventh hour squeeze. When the issue came before the state Senate in September, it passed a bill that granted the governor unrestricted command of the militia, but the House tabled the measure. Peace Confederates contended that Alabama was already enthralled to the military; therefore, a new militia law was pointless. Instead, in light of Sherman's capture of Atlanta, which portended an eventual Union triumph, they took the opportunity to promote a plan for reconstruction. Watts would have none of it. He considered such talk a betrayal of the South's heroic soldiery and insisted that there was "no alternative but to fight on, fight ever until liberty and independence shall crown our efforts." The militia system would never be revised, and thereafter local defense in Alabama became virtually nonexistent.[47]

Watts was unhappy that the legislature failed to come through on the militia issue, but his outrage over the reconstructionist agenda confirmed that he remained a war Confederate to the end. In fact, as enemy forces encroached deeper into Alabama, the governor delivered some speeches befitting the most diehard propaganda. When Mobile came under attack in late 1864, Watts exhorted the people "to share in the glory of defending the state." He included himself: "I will go with you to the battle field and there await the fate no brave man fears. Alabama *must*, Alabama *shall* be defended." Similarly, in February 1865, as powerful Union columns prepared to carve up the entire state, Watts gave a rambling address that combined delusion, bunkum, and melodrama. "We hold more territory now, than we did twelve months ago," he explained to a stupefied audience in Montgomery, adding that "our armies are, perhaps, not as strong in actual numbers as they were, but they are stronger now, compared with the enemy, than ever before." Predicting an imminent victory, he thundered that "subjugation is impossible." Watts followed with praise for President Davis and took perverse satisfaction is saying that 150,000 Yankees "sleep on [southern] soil the sleep that knows no waking." "Are we dogs!" he then shouted rhetorically at those who might entertain reconstruction, "that we are ready to lick that hand that smites us?" Watts closed his remarkable performance with a rendition of Patrick Henry's fiery speech during the Revolution: "Give me liberty, or give me Death!" When the end actually did come, mere weeks later, the governor received neither. Big Tom fled the state capital in early April, vowing to maintain the rebellion from an office in Eufaula. He was captured by Union cavalry on May 1, 1865.[48]

Final defeat notwithstanding, Confederate Alabama was ably served by its two principal war governors. Technically, three men held the position of governor during the Civil War; Andrew Moore's last year overlapped with the Confederacy's first year. Nevertheless, it was the administrations of Shorter and Watts that guided the state through the most difficult stages of the conflict. Historian Malcolm C. McMillan aptly describes the former as "conscientious and dedicated" and the latter as "possessed of superior intellect." Shorter's reign—December 1861–December 1863—was the more hopeful, for these were the years when the South had a real chance to win. In pushing Alabamians toward total war, Governor Shorter did his part to make victory possible. Conscription and impressment, among other war measures, came to fruition during his tenure. As a result, the Confederacy received vital human and material resources that enabled its armies to stave off the northern invader. Watts's reign—December 1863–April 1865—was the more desperate, for the unremitting pressure of renewed enemy offensives finally brought the war to Alabama itself. Watts steadfastly enforced the war policies of his predecessor, but the unstated objective had become simple survival. Mounting external factors, namely the unstoppable Union army, exacerbated growing internal problems, such as desertion and economic collapse, all of which reached the point where even Big Tom could not turn things around.[49]

In his study of the Confederate command system, Frank E. Vandiver observes that the necessities of war produced centralizing tendencies at both the national and state level. The authoritarian nature of President Davis is well understood, but as this Alabama case study demonstrates, Confederate war governors could be just as assertive. "To prevent strong government, they resorted to it," Vandiver states. But this generalization mischaracterizes Alabama's chief executives. Shorter and Watts exercised power not so much as a reaction to a supposedly despotic president, but out of a belief that they could more efficiently extract the requisite war effort from their citizens. Using Michael Albert Powell's scale of dual federalism within the Confederacy, Shorter leaned toward cooperation with national authority, Watts toward negotiation, but the leaders in Montgomery and Richmond pursued the same goal—independence. Given their genuine devotion to the rebel cause, Shorter and Watts would likely have implemented war socialism regardless of the directives that were issued by their president. After all, as E. Merton Coulter notes, "Alabama became less excited over the controversial issues of the war than did some of her sister states." Compared to the constant political drama between Jefferson Davis and his counterparts in Georgia and North Carolina, the absence of any serious discord from Alabama is a form of proof that Shorter and Watts developed and enjoyed a much healthier relationship with their president. To be sure, of the two, the Davis administration preferred Shorter. "I cannot refrain," secretary of war James Seddon said of Shorter's leadership in December 1862, "from once more acknowledging with grateful appreciation the zeal and liberality manifested by your State in sustaining the common cause of the Confederacy." The secretary's subsequent interaction with Watts was more strained, particularly over matters of conscription. McMillan may be going too far in describing Watts as an "obstructionist," but he certainly received no flattery from Richmond.[50]

In the final analysis, the gubernatorial election of 1863 was not a protest vote against an incumbent who supposedly plunged the state into wartime ruin. Rather, it was a respectful plea for different leadership. Shorter lost not because of the policies that he espoused, but because of his imperious enforcement of them. The voters grudgingly accepted the reality of total war, but they apparently wanted a governor who showed more compassion. It was very much a matter of style, not substance; the dour Shorter versus the gregarious Watts. Regardless of personality, both men were strong, effective, and dedicated heads of state. Anyone ranking Alabama's governors over the course of the state's history would do well to include these two individuals near the top of the list. Thomas Hill Watts may have garnered the sobriquet "war man all over," but the appellation equally describes John Gill Shorter. Together, they helped transform the polity of Confederate Alabama into a war state all over.

3

Of Senators and Legislators

IF ALABAMA'S HOUSE DELEGATION TO the First Confederate Congress was prowar, then its senators were doubly so. William Lowndes Yancey and Clement Claiborne Clay were two of the state's most famous politicians. Yancey was the great prophet of secession, having called for a southern nation since the late 1840s. Clay was the son of Clement Comer Clay, a popular former governor of the state during its formative years. Both men clamored for secession in 1861, and both men advocated a total war path to independence. They also exited the political stage in 1863; Yancey by his untimely death in July, and Clay by his failed bid for reelection in November. Their replacements in the Confederate Senate were respectively Robert Jemison Jr. and Richard Walker, former Whigs who had displayed little enthusiasm for secession. Like the congressional and gubernatorial outcomes, the ascent of these two men has become part of the scholarly narrative that suggests that Alabama was sliding into defeatism in 1863. Kenneth C. Martis, for instance, describes these developments as "the most abrupt turnabout in Confederate congressional history." A breakdown of the actual voting, however, shows that a majority of war Confederates supported both Jemison and Walker. As with the other contests in the state that year, a deeper assessment of the senatorial elections (as well as the new senators themselves) reveals a polity that was still committed to victory, albeit one that was a bit more sober in its expectations after two years of revolutionary struggle.[1]

In accordance with the Confederate constitution, senators were elected by state legislatures. So, any examination of Alabama's senatorial elections invariably brings the preceding legislative races under scrutiny; the winners in the latter determined the winners of the former. Confederate state legislative history remains a ripe field in need of better harvesting, but local lawmakers seemed just as dedicated to the cause as any other southerner. In one of the few studies of this history, May Spencer Ringold rightly contends that the southern war effort "would have gotten off to a slow start" had state politicians "failed to support Confederate policies and programs." Alabama's general assembly certainly leaned prowar most of the time. In 1862, it acceded to the imperatives of conscription by subordinating the militia system to Confederate service. It also enacted (on October 31) an aggressive policy of impressment several months before that practice became national law. On the eve of the August 1863 elections, however, the war was not going well. Military defeats coupled with home-front privation spawned a political atmosphere that was weary of Confederate jingoism. It is perhaps telling that less than one-third of Alabama's lawmakers sought reelection at this time of crisis. The state's furtive Peace Society hoped to exploit the ostensible disillusion of these legislators and the perceived disaffection among the voters. "Change is the cry and many valuable mens experience will be lost to the country," opined James Mallory, an aged planter from Talladega County who decried those who sued for peace "even if it took us back to union with our enemies." Running a behind-the-scenes canvass in counties that had opposed immediate secession, peace Confederates won a substantial number of contests. This coterie then arrived in Montgomery intent on steering Alabama toward a policy of reconstruction. The upcoming senatorial elections offered an ideal opportunity to further this goal. But in the end, a reconstructionist agenda never materialized because peace Confederates never established dominance over the assembly, let alone over state government more broadly.[2]

Analyzing the legislative contests in Alabama is no easy task. The 1863 campaign involved approximately 230 candidates from the state's fifty-two counties, vying for the sixteen seats (out of thirty-three) in the Senate that were subject to election, and all one hundred in the House (table 3). Identifying a candidate's political stance is not always possible, particularly in the absence of an official party structure. Wartime constraints on movement, which inhibited any real canvass, further cloud the picture. Some individuals announced their candidacies through the newspapers, but they offered few insights into their political minds beyond boilerplate patriotism. To be sure, local voters certainly knew who was who in their community, but their unrecorded familiarity is of little help to historians. Happily, subsequent legislative voting records, especially in the election of senators (to be discussed later in the chapter), help tremendously in distinguishing the war men from the peace advocates. Vagaries in political affiliation notwithstanding, the House witnessed astonishing turnover; 86 percent of the incoming members were freshmen. Only fourteen incumbents (out of twenty-three who ran) retained their seats. The sizeable presence of peace Confederates in the new House was especially noticeable. In contrast, the state Senate remained a stable bastion of Confederate nationalism. Five incumbents won, only two lost, and the chamber proved overwhelmingly prowar in its politics. Looking over the field of 133 lawmakers, however, one newspaper correspondent identified just fifteen who possessed "ability of a high order," evenly divided between both chambers. These men he dubbed "the artillery" of the legislature; everyone else was merely the "musketry." Another observer was less clever and more

Table 3. Alabama's Legislative Returns—1863 (by District and County)

District 1	Chamber	Candidate	Total	
Franklin	Senate	**William M. Jackson (I)**	497	
		Arthur H. Kellar	252	
	House	**Anderson Orr**	272	
		Samuel K. Oates Jr.	247	died in Oct. 1863
		Joshua "Burns" Moore	210	
		John A. Steele	207	
		Thomas Thorn	162	
		Jeremiah Dailey	147	
		Wesley M. Smith	116	
		David R. Lindsay	110	
		F. LeBaron Goodwin	84	
		James H. Thompkins	76	
		Abner W. Ligon	n/a	replaced Oates
Lauderdale	Senate	**James W. Stewart**	419	
	House	**Tolliver L. Chisholm**	323	
		Alex M. McAlexander	268	
		William R. Chisholm	118	
		Stephen J. Matthews	107	
		John S. Kennedy	54	
Lawrence	Senate	**[James A. Hill (I)]**	n/a	also represents Walker and Winston (dist. 2)
	House	**James S. Clark**	377	
		Francis W. Sykes (I)	267	
		Hodge L. Stephenson	264	
		Alexander W. Bently	198	
		Thomas M. McGehee	17	
Limestone	Senate	**[Joshua P. Coman (I)]**	n/a	also represents Morgan (dist. 1)
	House	***John B. McClellan***	264	
		James W. S. Donnell	224	
		William H. Walker	150	
		Ike Beauchamp	78	
Madison	Senate	**[Ferd. L. Hammond (I)]**	n/a	
	House	**Joseph C. Bradley**	428	
		John W. Scruggs	424	
Morgan	Senate	**[Joshua P. Coman (I)]**	n/a	also represents Limestone (dist. 1)

Continued on the next page

Table 3. *Continued*

District 1	Chamber	Candidate	Total	
	House	**George P. Charlton**	258	
		John C. Orr (I)	157	
		A. J. Garrison	124	

District 2	Chamber	Candidate	Total	
Blount	Senate	**Curtis G. Beeson**	107	also represents St. Clair (dist. 3)
		William N. Crump (I)	287	
	House	***Reuben Ellis (I)***	nvr	
		A. M. Gibson	nvr	
Fayette	Senate	**[A. J. Coleman (I)]**	n/a	also represents Marion (dist. 2)
	House	**Alexander Cobb (I)**	596	
		Jeptha Seay	389	
		E. W. Lawrence	354	
		H. H. Read	106	
		John R. Cooper	90	
		Asbury Burks	57	
Jefferson	Senate	***Mitchell T. Porter***	nvr	also represents Shelby (dist. 4)
	House	***John C. Morrow***	nvr	
Marion	Senate	**[A. J. Coleman (I)]**	n/a	also represents Fayette (dist. 2)
	House	***Daniel G. W. Hollis***	277	
		Micajah L. Davis (I)	154	
		Miles J. Taylor	136	
		Lang C. Allen	97	
		John Y. Caldwell	29	
Tuscaloosa	Senate	**[Robert Jemison (I)]**	n/a	elected to CSA Senate in Aug. 1863
		Ezekiel A. Powell	372	replaced Jemison in Oct. 1863 after special election
		John R. Blocker	270	
		Newbern H. Browne	133	
	House	**Thomas P. Lewis (I)**	nvr	
		William A. Bishop	nvr	
Walker	Senate	**[J. Albert Hill (I)]**	n/a	also represents Lawrence and Winston (dist. 1 and 2)
	House	**John Manasco**	289	
		Frances A. Musgrove	187	

Table 3. *Continued*

District 2	Chamber	Candidate	Total	
Winston	Senate	**[J. Albert Hill (I)]**	n/a	also represents Lawrence and Walker (dist. 1 and 2)
	House	**Zach White**	269	
		James M. Wooten	58	

District 3	Chamber	Candidate	Total	
Cherokee	Senate	**[Frizell M. Hardwick (I)]**	n/a	
	House	**Thomas B. Cooper**	741	
		John W. Brandon	697	
		William A. Vincent	626	
		George W. Howell	558	
		Arnold Shamblin	472	
		Samuel L. Russell	440	
		Robert B. Kyle	375	
DeKalb	Senate	**James Critcher**	400	also represents Marshall (dist. 3)
		Seabird Cowan	278	
	House	***Jeptha Edwards***	639	
		George W. Malone (I)	598	
		Levi W. Lynch (I)	173	
Jackson	Senate	***[Francisco Rice (I)]***	n/a	
	House	**P. Brown**	188	
		James W. Young	180	
		William H. Robinson	137	
Marshall	Senate	**James Critcher**	317	also represents DeKalb (dist. 3)
		Seabird Cowan	142	
	House	**Arthur C. Beard**	nvr	
		John J. Sibley	nvr	
St. Clair	Senate	**Curtis G. Beeson**	558	also represents Blount (dist. 2)
		William N. Crump (I)	188	
	House	**George W. Ashe**	576	
		Howard R. Buchanan	188	

District 4	Chamber	Candidate	Total
Calhoun	Senate	**Thomas A. Walker (I)**	669
		Gideon C. Ellis	631

Continued on the next page

Table 3. *Continued*

District 4	Chamber	Candidate	Total	
	House	***William M. Hames***	803	
		Edwin T. Read	730	
		Daniel T. Ryan	686	
		William B. Martin (I)	568	
		J. G. Bryan	408	
		William B. Ferguson	273	
		William J. Borden	236	
Randolph	Senate	***William T. Wood***	1,259	
	House	**Henry W. Armstrong**	814	
		Augustus A. West	788	
		Milton D. Barron	787	
		William E. White	589	
		Peter M. Howle	570	
		Jonah Green	543	
		Joel T. Morrison	64	
Shelby	Senate	***Mitchell T. Porter***	453	also represents Jefferson (dist. 2)
		Sylvester Steel	488	
		Edward C. Seale	33	
	House	**John Keenan**	488	
		Samuel Leeper	471	
		Major Sherrell	358	
		John P. Morgan	251	
		Burwell B. Lewis	149	
		N. P. Rives	138	
		Alexander Nelson	91	
		Wylie H. Horton	41	
		J. Pierce	16	
Talladega	Senate	**[Benton W. Groce (I)]**	n/a	
	House	**Lewis E. Parsons**	1,157	
		Henry Sims	869	
		Levi W. Lawler (I)	828	
		Isham Steed	522	
		Joseph H. Johnson	494	
		John Henderson	419	
		Augustus Moss	275	
		William C. Brown	225	

Table 3. *Continued*

District 5	Chamber	Candidate	Total	
Bibb	Senate	*[Edward H. Moren (I)]*	n/a	also represents Perry (dist. 5)
	House	**James W. Davis**	nvr	
Choctaw	Senate	**[Turner Reavis (I)]**	n/a	also represents Sumter and Washington (dist. 5 and 9)
	House	**James S. Evans**	299	
		John T. Foster (I)	276	
		John B. Coleman	176	
		John P. Cook	157	
		J. B. Turner	34	
Greene	Senate	**[William E. Clarke (I)]**	n/a	also represents Marengo (dist. 5)
	House	**Wiley Coleman (I)**	414	
		Augustus Benners (I)	375	
		Thomas C. Clark	210	
		James R. Evans	145	
		Henry F. Evans	97	
		Algernon S. Jeffries	10	
		Samuel Morrow	7	
Marengo	Senate	**[William E. Clarke (I)]**	n/a	also represents Greene (dist. 5)
	House	**William B. Modawell**	322	
		Levi W. Reeves	303	
		Walter E. Winn	38	
Perry	Senate	*[Edward H. Moren (I)]*	n/a	also represents Bibb (dist. 5)
	House	**John H. Chapman**	548	
		James L. Price	461	
		John N. Walthall (I)	420	
Pickens	Senate	**John J. W. Payne**	474	
		Absolum L. Neal	255	
	House	**James T. Gardner**	474	
		Benjamin Atkinson	429	
		James Nuner	300	
		Henry Stith	283	
		John N. Collier	60	

Continued on the next page

Table 3. *Continued*

District 5	Chamber	Candidate	Total	
Sumter	Senate	**[Turner Reavis (I)]**	n/a	also represents Choctaw and Washington (dist. 5 and 9)
	House	**John D. McInnis**	323	

District 6	Chamber	Candidate	Total	
Autauga	Senate	**[Samuel F. Rice (I)]**	n/a	also represents Montgomery (dist. 6)
	House	**Leonidas Howard**	316	
		Thomas A. Davis	252	
		Daniel Wadsworth	58	
		Bolling Hall	1	
Butler	Senate	**[Edmund Harrison (I)]**	n/a	also represents Lowndes (dist. 6)
	House	**Walter H. Crenshaw (I)**	539	
		Stephen F. Gafford	387	
		Thomas J. Burnett (I)	269	
		Alexander McKellar	254	
		H. B. T. Montgomery	167	
		T. H. Hampton	37	
Coosa	Senate	**William Garrett**	847	
		Leander Bryant	432	
	House	**Thomas U. T. McCain**	873	
		James Vansandt	795	
		Eli S. C. Parker	786	
		McKinney Thomas	512	
		John B. Leonard	441	
		John H. Clisby	380	
Dallas	Senate	***Robert H. Ervin***	879	also represents Wilcox (dist. 9)
		James M. Calhoun (I)	0	
	House	***Nathaniel H. R. Dawson***	529	
		Elijah Bell	461	
		Thomas J. Goldsby	390	
		Washington M. Smith	360	
		M. S. Cleveland	150	
Lowndes	Senate	**[Edmund Harrison (I)]**	n/a	also represents Butler (dist. 6)
	House	**William S. May**	412	
		Peyton T. Graves	360	

Table 3. *Continued*

District 6	Chamber	Candidate	Total	
		Russell P. McCord	285	
		C. "Ed" Crenshaw	149	
Montgomery	Senate	**[Samuel F. Rice (I)]**	n/a	also represents Autauga (dist. 6)
	House	***William H. Ogbourne***	688	
		Tristram B. Bethea	586	
		William H. Rives (I)	539	
		Thomas J. Mitchell	419	
		Peter B. Mastin	281	
		William Falconer	251	

District 7	Chamber	Candidate	Total	
Chambers	Senate	**[William H. Barnes (I)]**	n/a	
	House	**James J. McLemore**	nvr	
		John C. Towles	nvr	
Macon	Senate	***Robert F. Ligon (I)***	1,064	
	House	**Augustus B. Fannin**	766	
		Joseph C. Head	639	
		Charles J. Bryan	567	
		Richard H. Powell	535	
Russell	Senate	**[John A. Lewis (I)]**	n/a	
	House	**David B. Mitchell**	422	
		Frank A. Nisbet	323	
		Theophilus White	306	
		William E. Godwin	218	
		William G. Flake	211	
		Leander F. McCoy	194	
		John Fred Tate	30	
		Lyman W. Martin	1	
Tallapoosa	Senate	**[Willis D. Matthews (I)]**	n/a	resigned in early 1864
		Michael J. Bulger	n/a	replaced Matthews in Aug. 1864
	House	**A. A. Dent**	1,102	
		Robert T. Ashurst	1,057	
		Early Greathouse	892	
		James A. J. Phillips	357	

Continued on the next page

Table 3. *Continued*

District 7	Chamber	Candidate	Total	
		Joseph Lindsay	309	
		Isaac B. McCaffy	198	
		Williamson R. Berry (I)	187	
		William McCord	187	
		L. W. J. Pool	152	
		Wesley Burton	35	

District 8	Chamber	Candidate	Total	
Barbour	Senate	**[Lewis L. Cato (I)]**	n/a	
	House	**Caspar W. Jones**	701	
		William H. Chambers	606	
		Cader A. Parker (I)	575	
		John F. Treutlen	559	
		A. D. Campbell	553	
		Gardner H. Davis	511	
		J. C. Wilson	4	
Coffee	Senate	**[DeWitt C. Davis (I)]**	n/a	also represents Covington and Conecuh (dist. 8 and 9)
	House	**John G. Moore**	484	
		Joseph E. P. Flournoy	73	
Covington	Senate	**[DeWitt C. Davis (I)]**	n/a	also represents Coffee and Conecuh (dist. 8 and 9)
	House	**Alfred Holley**	259	
		James M. K. Little	210	
Dale	Senate	**Reddick P. Peacock**	341	also represents Henry (dist. 8)
		Joseph R. Breare	168	
	House	**Q. L. C. Franklin**	nvr	
		H. I. M. Kennon	nvr	
Henry	Senate	**[Reddick P. Peacock]**	n/a	also represents Dale (dist. 8)
	House	**George W. Williams**	446	
		Levi Parish (I)	347	
		James Tye	313	
Pike	Senate	**Daniel A. McCall**	784	
		David B. Smedley	450	
	House	**Jacob R. Brooks**	833	

Table 3. *Continued*

District 8	Chamber	Candidate	Total	
		William R. Cox	727	
		Green W. Carlisle	508	
		James W. Jackson	413	
		John S. Carter	313	
		W. F. Ross	259	
		Joel H. Rainer (I)	148	
		Eli N. Ford	143	

District 9	Chamber	Candidate	Total	
Baldwin	Senate	**Robert W. Brodnax**	2	also represents Clarke and Monroe (dist. 9)
		J. H. Hastie	213	
		Joseph Hall	12	
		William P. Leslie	4	
	House	**R. B. Bryers**	nvr	
Clarke	Senate	**Robert W. Brodnax**	427	also represents Baldwin and Monroe (dist. 9)
		William P. Leslie	72	
		J. H. Hastie	49	
		Joseph Hall	5	
	House	***John Y. Kilpatrick***	nvr	
Conecuh	Senate	**[DeWitt C. Davis (I)]**	n/a	also represents Coffee and Covington (dist. 8)
	House	**William Greene**	257	
		William A. Ashley (I)	193	
Mobile	Senate	**Theophilus Toulmin (I)**	1,416	
	House	**Samuel Wolff (I)**	1,361	
		John T. Taylor	992	
		Jacob Magee	972	
		Cleveland F. Moulton	860	
		C. S. Smith	388	
		Cary W. Butt	361	
		Amos R. Manning	285	
		John A. Winston	258	
		W. B. Hamilton	138	
		Misc.	74	

Continued on the next page

Table 3. *Continued*

District 9	Chamber	Candidate	Total	
Monroe	Senate	**Robert W. Brodnax**	243	also represents Baldwin and Clarke (dist. 9)
		William P. Leslie	261	
		J. H. Hastie	37	
		Joseph Hall	1	
	House	***Samuel J. Cumming***	354	
		Benjamin F. Stallworth	239	
Washington	Senate	**[Turner Reavis (I)]**	n/a	also represents Choctaw and Sumter (dist. 5)
	House	***Thomas P. Ashe***	68	
		John D. Starke	42	
		D. M. Cato	30	
		Monroe Riley	3	
Wilcox	Senate	**Robert H. Ervin**	467	also represents Dallas (dist. 6)
		James M. Calhoun (I)	13	
	House	**John Moore**	464	
		John A. Jackson	18	

Note: Incumbents indicated with (I); winners are in bold; Confederate veterans are in italics; staggered Senate seats not up for reelection are indicated with the name in brackets and with vote tally n/a; "nvr" signifies that no vote was recorded.
Source: Election Files of the Alabama Secretary of State, folders 12 and 13, SG002475, Alabama Department of Archives and History.

pessimistic in predicting that the new assembly would amount to a "regular demagogical reign."[3]

The House experienced the most change, and it was there that the Peace Society would exert its greatest influence over state affairs. Peace Confederates won every race for that chamber in eighteen counties and split the representation with war men in eleven others; they obtained thirty-seven seats in total. Their regional strength was similar to the vote on secession: the Tennessee River valley, the northern hill counties, and portions of the wiregrass. Various confidential correspondence and military reports confirm the identities of some of them as "unconditional Union Men" and others as active members in the Peace Society. Emerging as the chieftain of the peace Confederates in the House was Lewis E. Parsons. A wealthy lawyer and former Whig from Talladega County, Parsons was a longtime political foe of Jabez

Curry and took great delight in not only winning a landslide at the polls for himself, but helping fellow peace Confederate Marcus Cruikshank take the district's congressional seat. "What do the last dollar and last drop of blood men think of such results?" one of Parsons's friends rhetorically queried in the election's aftermath. Allied with Parsons were several able politicos from north Alabama, including Joseph C. Bradley, a lawyer from Madison County who had been touting reconstruction from the moment that secession became a reality; James S. Clark, a cooperationist delegate from Lawrence County; and George W. Malone, a middling farmer from DeKalb County and one of the few incumbents who ran and won. From the wiregrass came Alfred Holley, an outspoken unionist from Covington County.[4]

Peace Confederates may have enjoyed a semblance of quasi party order, but they were outnumbered by hard-liners who possessed greater parliamentary experience. War Confederates swept the legislative races in twenty-three counties and split in eleven others, amassing fifty-one seats. Foremost among them was Walter H. Crenshaw. A planter-lawyer and former Whig from Butler County, Crenshaw supported secession, easily won election to the legislature, and served as Speaker of the House for the entirety of the war (the only southern Speaker to do so). He was the principal architect of the state's impressment law, particularly those provisions that required the planter class to furnish foodstuffs and livestock to the army for "adequate compensation." Historian Jon L. Wakelyn describes Crenshaw "as a tower of support for the war effort." He was joined by two other victorious incumbents: Augustus Benners, a large planter (over eighty slaves) from Greene County, and Levi W. Lawler of Talladega County, also a big planter (over ninety slaves). Benners strongly urged secession in 1861, but by 1863 he had grown uneasy about the course of events. "We are all distressingly anxious for the war to close," he wrote in June, "but there seems now no prospect of such a desirable event—The South cant stop & the North wont." His worries aside, Benners was committed to the cause and comfortably won reelection to his assembly seat: "I want to do my duty to my state & country." Lawler had both openly promoted the candidacy of Thomas Watts for governor and denied the peace Confederates a sweep in Talladega. A leading member in the House (serving on both the Military Committee and the Ways and Means Committee), he worked hard to get the state's impressment bill "passed forthwith." One other noteworthy war Confederate was Captain Nathaniel H. R. Dawson of Dallas County. Dawson was yet another big planter (eighty slaves), but his stature derived mostly from his participation in the Battle of First Manassas as a company commander in the Fourth Alabama Infantry. He was a fresh face in politics, but he brought the gravitas of a war hero to his seat in the legislature.[5]

In the state Senate, the situation was more straightforward; war Confederates dominated. The "artillery" here consisted of Lewis L. Cato, a longtime leader in the fire-eating Eufaula Regency of Barbour County; Turner Reavis, a close friend of Governor Shorter's and a huge planter (nearly one hundred slaves) from Sumter County; Samuel F. Rice, a former chief justice of the state supreme court from Montgomery; and Thomas A. Walker, a planter and railroad man from Calhoun County. Interestingly, despite his incumbency and social standing, Walker barely weathered a serious challenge (669–631) from a virtual unknown, a former private in the disbanded Second Alabama Infantry named Gideon C. Ellis. It is unclear where Ellis stood on the war or whether he received backing from the Peace Society, but he came within forty votes of what would have been a significant upset. Elsewhere, peace Confederates did win some Senate seats. The most prominent was William Garrett, a respected farmer and amateur scholar from Coosa County. According to John H. Clisby, a war Confederate who lost his race for the House, Garrett publicly disavowed any connection to the Peace Society, "but is for an entire change in our State Government from Gov. down." Garrett soundly defeated his opponent Leander Bryant, about whom little is known, and then assumed a similar role in the Senate as that of Parsons in the House. Notable among his peace colleagues was Curtis G. Beeson, a small slaveholder from St. Clair County. In what was likely a fierce contest for a seat that represented two counties (Blount and St. Clair), Beeson defeated the incumbent William N. Crump, 695–475. Crump was a secessionist from Blount who served over a year with the Forty-Ninth Alabama Infantry before resigning in early 1863 at the rank of lieutenant colonel. Beeson's victory over a high-ranking war man must have been especially gratifying. Beeson lost on Crump's home turf, but he buried his rival on his own, aided in no small measure by the activities of the Peace Society and various deserter bands that not only roamed the backcountry of St. Clair, but apparently voted as well. One such band calling itself "Old Abe's Men" later tried to kill Crump, wounding the colonel in an assassination attempt shortly after the election. Another peace Confederate worth mentioning is Robert F. Ligon of Macon County. Ligon was a former captain in the Twelfth Alabama Infantry; his military credentials helped offset the prevalent notion that the soldiery always favored total war politicians.[6]

Peace Confederates might have achieved a greater presence in the Alabama Senate had more seats in their regions of strength been up for election. Six prowar senators, five from northern Alabama (A. J. Coleman, Benton W. Groce, Frizell M. Hardwick, J. Albert Hill, and Francisco Rice) and one from the wiregrass (Dewitt C. Davis) did not face reelection, yet these men represented districts that peace Confederates swept in the races for the House. Therefore, it is not far-fetched to suppose that all six might have lost in 1863. But by way of qualification, staunch war Confederates such as William M. Jackson, a secessionist planter from Franklin County, and Mitchell T. Porter, a lieutenant colonel in the Twentieth Alabama Infantry (newly paroled from Vicksburg) from Jefferson County, prevailed in races where the House seats all went for peace candidates. As always, factors beyond the obvious ones are at play in any political contest. In any event, peace Confederates in the Senate numbered no more than five or six, a pittance compared to the bloc that operated in the House. Conversely, war Confederates in the Senate numbered at least twenty-one, a powerful supermajority.

A common denominator in both political camps was slaveholding (table 4). Sixty-two war Confederates owned slaves, thirty-two as members of the planter class (i.e., twenty or more slaves), while twenty-seven peace Confederates owned slaves, seven as planters. Fifteen other members, whose political alignment is unclear and who include four planters, also owned slaves. The combined chattel in the Alabama general assembly numbered about 2,650. Thirteen members, nine of them peace Confederates and just one war Confederate, owned no slaves. Data for fifteen other members is unknown. Given that secession was motivated in large part as a defense of slavery, it is not surprising that war Confederates dominate the slaveholders' ranks. Nevertheless, peace Confederates were also clearly vested in the peculiar institution. For instance, big planters such as James W. S. Donnell (seventy-two slaves) and Francis W. Sykes (forty-seven slaves), both from counties in the ravaged Tennessee River valley, actually saw reconstruction with the North as a possible means of retaining their human assets. Donnell was especially desirous of peace, having personally witnessed Union forces plunder his estate outside Athens, Alabama, in May 1862. He very much hated the Yankees, yet he blamed the secessionists for plunging the South into an unwinnable war.[7]

An uncommon denominator in both political camps was military service. In the decades after the Civil War, having worn the butternut and gray would be almost mandatory for holding office, but not so during that conflict. A mere twenty-two incoming legislators—six in the Senate and sixteen in the House—had extant service records in the Confederate army. Three out of every four of these men were war Confederates, a ratio that reinforces the thesis that the South's fighting men wanted their government to pursue total victory. At least four had suffered combat wounds, three (including Nathaniel H. R. Dawson) had served in the renowned Fourth Alabama Infantry, and one, Captain John Y. Kilpatrick of Clarke County, made a point of wearing his

Table 4. Roster of Alabama Legislators, 1863–1865

Senator	County	Birth Year	Profession
Barnes, William H.	Chambers	1824	Lawyer
Beeson, Curtis G.	St. Clair	1802	Planter
Brodnax, Robert W.	Clarke	1790	Planter
Bulger, Michael J.	Tallapoosa	1806	Planter
Cato, Lewis L.	Barbour	1822	Planter-Lawyer
Clarke, William E.	Marengo	1815	Lawyer
Coleman, A. J.	Fayette	1818	Farmer
Coman, Joshua P.	Limestone	1812	Physician
Critcher, James	Marshall	1811	Miller
Davis, DeWitt C.	Covington	1830	Lawyer
Ervin, Robert H.	Wilcox	1822	Physician
Garrett, William	Coosa	1809	Planter-Merchant
Groce, Benton W.	Talladega	1820	Physician
Hammond, Ferd. L.	Madison	1814	Farmer
Hardwick, Frizell M.	Cherokee	1806	Farmer
Harrison, Edmund	Lowndes	1805	Planter-Merchant
Hill, James A.	Walker	1820	Minister
Jackson, William M.	Franklin	1824	Planter
Jemison, Robert	Tuscaloosa	1802	Planter-Merchant
Lewis, John A.	Russell	1826	Lawyer
Ligon, Robert F.	Macon	1823	Lawyer
Matthews, Willis D.	Tallapoosa	1804	Minister
McCall, Daniel A.	Pike	1816	Planter-Merchant
Moren, Edward H.	Bibb	1825	Physician
Payne, John J. W.	Pickens	1820	Physician
Peacock, Reddick P.	Dale	1812	Merchant
Porter, Mitchell T.	Jefferson	1825	Lawyer
Powell, Ezekiel A.	Tuscaloosa	1817	Politician
Reavis, Turner	Sumter	1812	Planter-Lawyer
Rice, Francisco	Jackson	1822	Physician
Rice, Samuel F.	Montgomery	1816	Lawyer
Stewart, James W.	Lauderdale	1806	Physician
Toulmin, Theophilus	Mobile	1796	Planter
Walker, Thomas A.	Calhoun	1811	Planter-Lawyer
Wood, William T.	Randolph	1826	Farmer

House Representative	County	Birth Year	Profession
Armstrong, Henry W.	Randolph	1819	Farmer
Ashe, George W.	St. Clair	1821	Farmer

Slaves	Prewar Party	Denomination	CSA Service	War or Peace
6	Democrat	Methodist		WC
13				PC
12	Whig			WC
21	Democrat	Presbyterian	47th AL Inf.	PC[b]
47				WC[b]
22	Democrat			WC
9		Baptist		WC
18				?
21				PC
37				WC
110	Democrat	Baptist	7th AL Inf.	WC
15	Democrat	Methodist		PC
26	Whig	Episcopalian		WC
3	Democrat			PC
6				WC
79	Democrat	Episcopalian		WC
?		Baptist		WC
60	Whig-Democrat			WC
178	Whig	Methodist		WC[b]
12				?
33	Democrat	Methodist	12th AL Inf.	PC
0		Methodist		PC
15				WC
4	Whig	Presbyterian	29th AL Inf.	WC
18	Know-Nothing			WC
1				?
14		Episcopalian	20th AL Inf.	WC
2	Whig-Democrat	Methodist		PC[a]
98	Whig			WC
7	Democrat	Baptist	4th TN Cav.	WC
23	Know-Nothing	Methodist		WC
19	Democrat	Methodist		?
77	Democrat	Episcopalian		WC
102	Democrat			WC
8	Democrat		30th AL Inf.	WC
Slaves	Prewar Party	Denomination	CSA Service	War or Peace
0	Democrat			PC
11				PC

Continued on the next page

Table 4. *Continued*

House Representative	County	Birth Year	Profession
Ashe, Thomas P.	Washington	1830	Planter
Ashurst, Robert T.	Tallapoosa	1816	Planter
Atkinson, Benjamin	Pickens	1837	Farmer
Barron, Milton D.	Randolph	1817	Farmer
Beard, Arthur C.	Marshall	1810	Planter-Merchant
Bell, Elijah	Dallas	1820	Minister
Benners, Augustus	Greene	1818	Planter-Lawyer
Bethea, Tristram B.	Montgomery	1810	Planter-Lawyer
Bishop, William A.	Tuscaloosa	1820	Farmer
Bradley, Joseph C.	Madison	1813	Lawyer
Brandon, John W.	Cherokee	1838	Farmer
Brooks, Jacob R.	Pike	1806	Farmer
Brown, P.	Jackson	?	
Bryan, Charles J.	Macon	1836	Farmer
Bryers, R. B.	Baldwin	1822	Overseer
Carlisle, Green W.	Pike	1810	Farmer
Chambers, William H.	Barbour	1827	Planter-Lawyer
Chapman, John H.	Perry	1822	
Charlton, George P.	Morgan	1822	Farmer
Chisholm, Tolliver L.	Lauderdale	1817	
Clark, James S.	Lawrence	1830	Lawyer
Cobb, Alexander	Fayette	1820	Merchant
Coleman, Wiley	Greene	1819	Planter
Cooper, Thomas B.	Cherokee	1807	Merchant
Cox, William. R.	Pike	1838	Teacher
Crenshaw, Walter H.	Butler	1817	Planter-Lawyer
Cumming, Samuel J.	Monroe	1822	Lawyer
Davis, James W.	Bibb	1806	Farmer
Davis, Micajah L.	Marion	1825	Farmer
Dawson, Nathaniel H. R.	Dallas	1829	Lawyer
Dent, A. A.	Tallapoosa	1822	Merchant
Donnell, James W. S.	Limestone	1820	Farmer
Edwards, Jeptha	DeKalb	1828	Merchant
Ellis, Reuben	Blount	1813	Merchant
Evans, James S.	Choctaw	1825	Physician
Fannin, Augustus B.	Macon	1821	Merchant
Foster, John T.	Choctaw	1807	Physician
Franklin, Q. L. C.	Dale	1797	Clerk
Gafford, Stephen F.	Butler	1822	Farmer

Slaves	Prewar Party	Denomination	CSA Service	War or Peace
12		Episcopalian	32nd AL Inf.	WC
20				PC
47				WC
3	Democrat			PC
24	Whig	Methodist		?
39		Baptist		PC[a]
88	Whig			WC
39	Know-Nothing			WC
26	Know-Nothing	Baptist		?
?	Democrat			PC
0				PC
2				WC
1				WC
44			3rd AL Inf.	WC
?				WC
18				WC
84	Democrat	Methodist		WC
4				WC
?				WC
0				PC[a]
1				PC
0	Democrat			PC
70	Democrat			WC
10	Whig-Democrat			PC
0			46th AL Inf.	WC
33	Whig	Presbyterian		WC
9		Presbyterian	17th AL Inf.	WC
0	Democrat			PC
?				WC
80	Democrat		4th AL Inf.	WC
3				PC
72		Presbyterian		PC
1			49th AL Inf.	?
1			48th AL Inf.	WC
18				PC[a]
30	Whig			WC
13				WC
?				WC
23				WC

Continued on the next page

Table 4. *Continued*

House Representative	County	Birth Year	Profession
Gardner, James T.	Pickens	1817	Distiller
Gibson, A. M.	Blount	1823	Horticulturalist
Graves, Peyton T.	Lowndes	1823	Farmer
Greathouse, Early	Tallapoosa	1810	Minister
Greene, William	Conecuh	?	
Hames, William M.	Calhoun	1826	Lawyer
Head, Joseph C.	Macon	1818	Farmer
Holley, Alfred	Covington	1811	Farmer
Hollis, Daniel G. W.	Marion	1837	Clerk
Howard, Leonidas	Autauga	1816	Planter
Howell, George W.	Cherokee	1820	Merchant
Jones, Caspar W.	Barbour	1826	Farmer
Keenan, John	Shelby	?	
Kennon, H. I. M.	Dale	?	Minister
Kilpatrick, John Y.	Clarke	1835	Lawyer
Lawler, Levi W.	Talladega	1816	Railroads
Leeper, Samuel	Shelby	1801	Teacher
Lewis, Thomas P.	Tuscaloosa	1819	Jeweler
Ligon, Abner W.	Franklin	1821	Justice of the Peace
Magee, Jacob	Mobile	1811	Merchant
Malone, George W.	DeKalb	1818	Farmer
Manasco, John	Walker	1801	Farmer
May, William S.	Lowndes	1816	Farmer
McAlexander, Alex M.	Lauderdale	1838	Lawyer
McCain, Thomas U. T.	Coosa	1804	Farmer
McClellan, John B.	Limestone	1836	Teacher
McInnis, John D.	Sumter	1809	Farmer
McLemore, James J.	Chambers	1831	Editor
Mitchell, David B.	Russell	1824	Planter
Modawell, William B.	Marengo	1819	Lawyer
Moore, John	Wilcox	1825	Farmer
Moore, John G.	Coffee	1822	Physician
Morrow, John C.	Jefferson	1833	Lawyer
Moulton, Cleveland F.	Mobile	1837	Lawyer
Nisbet, Frank A.	Russell	1815	Planter-Lawyer
Oates, Samuel K., Jr.	Franklin	1830	Merchant
Ogbourne, William H.	Montgomery	1820	Sheriff
Orr, Anderson	Franklin	1819	Farmer
Parish, Levi	Henry	1814	Farmer

Slaves	Prewar Party	Denomination	CSA Service	War or Peace
2				WC
2			19th AL Inf.	?
35				WC
12		Baptist		PC
?				PC
?		Presbyterian	51st AL Cav.	WC
0				PC
12	Whig			PC
10				WC
45		Methodist		PC
2				PC
26				WC
14				WC
2				?
?	Democrat	Presbyterian	Adams Cav.	WC
91	Democrat	Baptist		WC
?	Whig	Presbyterian		PC
9	Know-Nothing			WC[a]
?				PC
8				PC
10				PC
3	Democrat	Baptist		PC
44				WC
6			4th AL Inf.	WC
0				PC
18			50th AL Inf.	PC[a]
42				WC
4				PC
5				WC
8				WC
21				WC
?				WC
4			28th AL Inf.	PC
0				?
42	Democrat	Methodist		WC
?				?
46	Whig	Methodist	18th AL Inf.	PC[a]
3				PC
5				WC

Continued on the next page

Table 4. *Continued*

House Representative	County	Birth Year	Profession
Parker, Cader A.	Barbour	1819	Minister
Parker, Eli S. C.	Coosa	1823	Physician
Parsons, Lewis E.	Talladega	1817	Lawyer
Price, James L.	Perry	1811	Planter-Merchant
Read, Edwin T.	Calhoun	1810	Minister
Robinson, William H.	Jackson	1833	Lawyer
Ryan, Daniel T.	Calhoun	?	
Scruggs, John W.	Madison	1818	Merchant
Seay, Jeptha	Fayette	?	
Sibley, John J.	Marshall	1825	Clerk
Sims, Henry	Talladega	1804	Railroads
Sykes, Francis W.	Lawrence	1816	Physician
Taylor, John T.	Mobile	1815	Lawyer
Towles, John C.	Chambers	1814	Farmer
Vansandt, James	Coosa	1805	Minister
Vincent, William A.	Cherokee	1810	
West, Augustus A.	Randolph	1837	Farmer
White, Zach	Winston	1793	Farmer
Williams, George W.	Henry	1808	Planter
Wolff, Samuel	Mobile	1823	Merchant
Young, James W.	Jackson	1831	Saddler

[a] Qualified status due to some peculiarities in the vote for Confederate senator.
[b] Supposition based on other political factors.
Note: Ezekiel A. Powell replaced Robert Jemison Jr. when the latter won election to the Confederate States Senate in August 1863; Michael J. Bulger replaced Willis D.

cavalry uniform to every legislative session. Among their four peace Confederate comrades was John B. McClellan of Limestone County, who sacrificed an arm to the cause that he now opposed.[8]

Significantly, nearly fifty other veterans lost their legislative races. Their political views can only be guessed at, but presumably most of them would have been war Confederates. Captain Robert Kyle, for example, the conscription agent for the northeastern part of the state, was definitely a war man; he succumbed to the peace Confederate sweep in Cherokee County. Another was Captain Thomas Davis of the Sixth Alabama Infantry, a physician who entered the race for Autauga County once he learned that the prowar incumbent Daniel Pratt had decided to retire from politics. His rival, the peace Confederate Leonidas Howard, had the advantage of canvassing the precincts,

Slaves	Prewar Party	Denomination	CSA Service	War or Peace
17		Baptist		WC
5				PC
16	Whig	Presbyterian		PC
95	Whig			WC
18		Baptist		WC
?			4th AL Inf.	WC
15				WC
32	Democrat			WC
0	Whig			PC
0				PC
25	Whig			PC
47	Whig	Methodist		PC
41				WC
25				WC
0		Methodist		PC
?				PC
2	Democrat		31st AL Inf.	PC
?				PC[b]
21	Whig-Democrat	Baptist		WC
10				WC
6				

Matthews when the latter resigned after the December 1863 session; Abner W. Ligon replaced Samuel K. Oates Jr. when the latter died in October 1863.
PC: Peace Confederate.
WC: War Confederate.

while Davis remained with his regiment. Howard acknowledged that Davis was a "formidable opponent," but he also observed "considerable dissatisfaction to Dr. Davis" among the voters. Be that as it may, Davis still came close to winning in absentia, garnering 252 votes to Howard's 316. And, of course, there was Lieutenant Colonel William Crump's previously mentioned loss in a high-profile Senate race. These outcomes might well have turned out differently had soldiers been allowed to vote (a topic to be discussed more fully in chapter four). This dearth of direct military experience, however, hardly disqualified the assembly from enacting war policy; a majority had kin in the ranks, and they endured the anxiety of all home-front families that constantly feared the worst. For instance, Cader Parker, a war Confederate from Barbour County, grieved the loss of a son, mortally wounded at Gettysburg, while John Manasco, a peace Confederate from Walker County, had lost a son of his own the previous year at Shiloh.[9]

An irrelevant denominator is the past political affiliation of the legislators. Of fifty-three members whose prewar party label can be identified, twenty-seven were Democrats, sixteen were Whigs, five were Whigs who became Democrats, and five were Know-Nothings (i.e., the American Party). Respectively, the war Confederate–peace Confederate divide, where known, is 15–11 among Democrats, 9–6 among Whigs, 2–3 among Whigs-to-Democrats, and 4–1 among Know-Nothings. Overall, the numbers favor the war Confederate mindset, 30–21, but the ratios are so close for each former party that definitive conclusions are impossible. Therefore, the persistent notion that Whigs opposed the war while Democrats supported it cannot be sustained by the data, at least from Alabama. As has been said previously, the former politics of Alabama's lawmakers is a poor predictor of their stance on the rebellion. A similarly inconclusive measure of the assembly's commitment is the religious faith of each legislator. Of forty-one members whose Christian denomination can be identified, twelve were Baptists, five were Episcopalians, fifteen were Methodists, and nine were Presbyterians. The war Confederate–peace Confederate divide here, where known, is 8–3 among Baptists, 5–0 among Episcopalians, 5–8 among Methodists, and 5–4 among Presbyterians. Again, the numbers favor the war Confederate outlook, 23–15, but again, the individual ratios are too close (and the sample too small) to draw any meaningful conclusion, except perhaps that the Episcopal Church was somehow more diehard for the cause than the others.[10]

The new legislature convened on August 17, a typically hot, late-summer day in the Deep South. The small talk among the gathering politicians included the usual gripes about mosquitos and bedbugs. But there were also complaints about the course of the war, as well as probing murmurs about reconstruction. Dr. Edward H. Moren, an incumbent senator from Bibb County, was impressed by the "goodly number" of members in the House who "were opposed to this thing in the first place." According to Moren, these peace Confederates entered the capitol as self-styled "new councillors" ready to displace the secessionists, who, they proclaimed, "have nearly had their day for a while at least." The war Confederates, however, moved swiftly to affirm their dominance. In the Senate, William H. Barnes of Chambers County presented a resolution that called on the people to "pledge the entire resources of the State to the last dollar, and the last man, to the successful prosecution of the war now being waged." Peace Confederates realized that the passage of such a bellicose statement could undermine any plan for reconstruction. William Garrett attempted a series of stalling tactics, moving to refer the resolution to committee or at least delay a vote until a later date. Before the day ended, however, Barnes's prowar resolution was adopted, 26–1. The lone dissenting vote came from James Critcher of Marshall County. Even Garrett voted yea, lest he be branded a defeatist.[11]

Any significant opposition to the Confederate war effort was going to have to come from the House. Yet the "goodly number" of peace men in that chamber pursued a curious path. On the second day of the session, Lewis E. Parsons proffered his own war resolution. It began with an unexpected panegyric about the "patriotism and ability of President Davis" and a vow to sustain the "good labors" of the commander in chief with "unabated" and "hearty" and "candid" support. (William Garrett presented a similarly worded addendum about Davis in the Senate.) Parsons went on to recommend a pay raise for enlisted men, but there was nary a hint of reconstruction or cease-fire, let alone any criticism of hard war policies, all mainstays of the Peace Society. Following a brief, inconclusive discussion about just how much army privates should actually be making, the Parsons Resolution was adopted. Unfortunately, the House secretary did not record the actual vote. Surely, many peace Confederates disapproved of the flattering endorsement of Jefferson Davis. Why Parsons went over the top with his martial rhetoric is unclear. Perhaps he was trying to lull the war crowd into accepting his followers as loyal Alabamians until a more opportune time when they could show their true colors without fear of retribution. This is how Alexander White, a peace Confederate from Selma, Alabama, saw the matter. He considered Parsons's words to be "a telling refutation of [the] unfounded calumnies" that had been heaped on the peace Confederates by prowar "extremists." If so, then it was a risky gamble in reverse psychology.[12]

For over a week the two chambers wrangled over the precise wording of a joint resolution on the war. In the Senate, Garrett had second thoughts and tried in vain to toss the laudatory references to Jefferson Davis. But on August 29, the legislature finally passed a joint resolution that strongly reflected the sentiments expressed in the original Senate version. Pledging "all the resources of the State," it called for a full-scale war effort: "Our oft repeated purpose never to submit to abolition rule remains unshaken." It further declared that "the paramount duty of every citizen" was to support the armed forces and abide by the laws of the Confederacy. Finally, in a not so subtle denunciation of the Peace Society, it condemned any action to "dishearten the people and the soldiers at a period like this." With this resolution, any potential antiwar movement in the legislature had been seemingly quashed.[13]

Dr. Edward H. Moren was bemused by the resolution's hyperpatriotism. The good doctor was a dedicated Confederate, but he was under no illusions about the South's prospects. As the former surgeon of the Twenty-Ninth Alabama Infantry and as an inspector of the state's hospital facilities, Moren was witness to the actual carnage of war. The chest thumping of the war Confederates annoyed him, and so he abstained from voting on Barnes's resolution. The timidity of the peace Confederates, however, nonplussed him. That group had marched into Montgomery intent on changing the course of the war and had instead added their verbal complicity to furthering its totality. "It is future security, future prosperity, future liberty and independence," Moren surmised, "that causes a people uncomplainingly to Endure all this." Two years into the struggle, the rebel nation remained an elusive dream, but one apparently still worth pursuing.[14]

The peace Confederates may have acquiesced in the war resolutions, but those were mostly boastful words designed to placate the fanatics. The more important goal was replacing the state's war Confederate senators with men of their stripe. On July 27, one week before the state elections and three weeks before the called legislative session, the great William Yancey died of a kidney infection. The fire-eater had played an instrumental role in Alabama's secession. And as a prowar senator at the national level, Yancey had set aside his states' rights philosophy and voted in favor of conscription and impressment. There were expressions of grief all across the South, but Yancey's demise was a political windfall to the peace Confederates; a coveted seat in the Confederate Senate had just become available. One of the first names to be bandied about as a possible replacement was Jabez Curry, a prospect that horrified the peace Confederates. The man whom they had in mind was state senator Robert Jemison Jr. of Tuscaloosa (figure 11). A former Whig, Jemison had ably led the cooperationists in 1861, denouncing the secessionists as "restless, rash, and reckless politicians." His gubernatorial bid in 1861, one that promised a more prudent style of leadership, foundered against the tide of secessionist euphoria. The climate was more subdued in 1863, however, and peace Confederates saw in Jemison someone who might modulate the total war extremism coming out of Richmond. For unspecified reasons, Curry begged off despite encouragement from many friends who were convinced he could win. Perhaps the firebrand from Talladega did not want to risk a second political defeat in less than a month. The only other serious contender was John A. Winston, a former governor known for his prewar Jacksonian politics and the erstwhile colonel of the Eighth Alabama Infantry, a regiment that he helped raise in 1861. On August 22, Jemison easily won election on the first ballot: 97–12.[15]

The peace Confederates were elated by Jemison's victory, with Joseph C. Bradley going so far as to claim that the new senator was "elected by union

Figure 11. Robert Jemison, portrait by Samuel Hoffman, 1903. (Courtesy of Alabama Department of Archives and History)

men." Nevertheless, it is hard to see this outcome as an endorsement of a reconstruction agenda. After all, a majority of war Confederates also voted for the man. Sixty-one years old at the time, Jemison commanded near universal respect that transcended his politics. He was one of the wealthiest people in the whole Confederacy, having made a fortune in business and farming. He managed several mills and a stagecoach company, and he had investments in iron foundries and railroads; he amassed over ten thousand acres of land, divided among six plantations, and owned 178 slaves. Since 1840, he had regularly served in the general assembly, and at the time of his election to the Confederate Senate he was serving as president of the Alabama Senate. He had, indeed, vigorously opposed secession, going so far as to castigate William Yancey at the convention when the latter insinuated that cooperationism was akin to treason. Yet he was also a proud southerner who urged Alabamians to rally together after secession: "public welfare demanded unity of action." He later signed the very Ordinance of Secession that he had voted against. As a state senator, he voted for impressment and even supported a failed effort to abolish Winston County, a notorious haven for unionists. Jemison also tied his financial fate to his new country, serving as a government agent tasked with selling long-term cotton bonds and promoting the use of Confederate treasury notes. He purchased many bonds himself, knowing full well that their later cash value would only be honored by a Confederate treasury department, making military victory all the more imperative. Knowing all of this about the man, war Confederates had no hesitation electing Jemison to the Confederate Senate.[16]

Alabama's peace Confederates apparently ignored the new senator's prowar bona fides. Instead, they deluded themselves into thinking that Jemison was a crypto-reconstructionist, the same faulty assumption that they had made about Governor Watts. The honeymoon ended before it began. In a farewell address to the general assembly, Jemison referred to the rebellion as "a holy cause." "It matters not whether our separation was right or wrong, wise or unwise," he explained, "the alternative now presented to us is to press forward, arms in hand, until we shall have achieved an honorable and glorious independence." In a thinly veiled rebuke of reconstructionist thinking, Jemison reminded his listeners that slavery was also at stake, that emancipation had become a fundamental condition of any reunification with the North. "If there is any man in the land who would accept peace on these terms," Jemison intoned, "he deserves a traitor's doom." The *Montgomery Advertiser* exclaimed that Jemison and his speech "cannot but be hailed with satisfaction by the true patriots of the country." Peace Confederates, particularly Joseph Bradley, maintained cordial relations with Jemison, but they were likely disappointed by his fiery language. They could perhaps derive some comfort from knowing that they had at least denied the likes of Jabez Curry a continued place in the government.[17]

As a Confederate senator, Robert Jemison Jr. expressed prowar sympathies, though his voting record was erratic. During the first session of the Second Confederate Congress, he urged that the age range for conscription be further expanded to sixteen–sixty, and he supported legislation that repealed substitution for military service. He also appears to have backed calls for further increases in the government's power to impress private property. In February 1864, however, when President Davis requested yet another suspension of habeas corpus, Jemison voted against it. Beyond war policy, Jemison immersed himself in fiscal policy, serving on the Senate Finance Committee, where he quickly discovered that the Confederacy's currency woes were an incurable disaster. Jemison made no flowery speeches on the Senate floor as his predecessor was wont to do, but in the words of historian Wilfred Buck Yearns, "he continued in a quieter fashion" a similar philosophy of total war. The only complaint that anyone made about Jemison came from his boardinghouse mate Congressman William Russell Smith, who opined that his fellow Alabamian "snored liked a steamboat." Curiously, when the second (and final) session of the Second Congress convened in November 1864, Jemison declined to partake. The purported reason was his need to attend to "private business" back in Tuscaloosa, but Christopher Lyle McIlwain speculates that the senator's erstwhile doubts about secession and rebellion had returned. Perhaps, but Jemison did join a local chapter of the Society of Loyal Confederates, a statewide organization that pledged continued resistance and raised funds for indigent relief. Jemison's "unionist Whig" background notwithstanding, his overall service to the cause classifies him as a Confederate patriot.[18]

Peace Confederates had one more chance in 1863 to impose their agenda on Alabama's political landscape—the election to fill the Confederate Senate seat of Clement Clay, whose term was expiring. In late November, three months after electing Jemison, legislators gathered again for their regular session. The military backdrop was one of nervous optimism. The Army of Tennessee had recently won a bloodbath at Chickamauga and currently had Union forces besieged in Chattanooga. Decisive action of some sort was brewing. Alabama's politicos held their breath as they awaited the outcome; success might well wash away the discontent over Vicksburg and Gettysburg. The situation in East Tennessee seemed to add a sense of urgency to the senatorial election, especially for the peace Confederates, who desperately needed a political victory. But they would need to unseat an experienced politico who wanted to retain his office. Back in September, the *Montgomery Advertiser* presented a strong endorsement for the incumbent, highlighting his "honor and patriotism." The newspaper insisted that "Mr. Clay makes us a better Senator than any one we can send in his place."[19]

Forty-six years old in 1863, Clement Claiborne Clay had been a fire-eater for almost two decades (figure 12). He grew up in Huntsville, enjoying all the privileges of a prominent slaveholding family. His father was Clement Comer Clay, the Democratic governor of the state in the late 1830s, and he was a distant cousin to the great Henry Clay of Kentucky. The younger Clement possessed a sharp mind but suffered from chronic respiratory maladies that left him "frail and thin in appearance." His poor constitution may have contributed to an irritable personality that did not respond well to professional setbacks. In 1843, Clay married Virginia Tunstall, by all accounts a pretty and delightful woman whose vivacious personality contrasted with his petulant

Figure 12. Clement Claiborne Clay, daguerreotype by Matthew B. Brady, 1850s (Courtesy of Library of Congress)

nature. At parties, she would gossip; he would argue. "Heavens! He knows how to quarrel!" observed Mary Chestnut at a social gathering in Richmond during the war.[20]

Clay greatly admired his father and followed him into politics. He initially espoused the Jacksonian views of his father, but the emerging sectional crisis of the 1850s pushed Clay steadily into the southern rights wing of the Democrats, where he formed strong political associations with William Yancey and Jabez Curry. In 1853, he lost a congressional race to Williamson Cobb, that quintessential Jacksonian known for his common-man drawl and imperfect banjo tunes. Clay and Virginia could barely disguise their contempt for Cobb. Before the year was out, however, Clay surprisingly won election to the US

Senate. According to Mills Thornton, Alabama's political community increasingly began to see the state's Whig party as a puppet of northern interests, and the Jacksonian wing of the Democrats as demagogues of the uneducated masses. Therefore, the time was ripe for new men such as Clay to enter the political arena, "in order to save the people from themselves." This elitist outlook permeated the entire secessionist movement. As a senator, Clay vigorously defended the institution of slavery (he had eighty-eight slaves of his own). He supported southern access to Kansas and blamed Republicans for the violence in that territory. In doing so, he developed a reputation as an "abolitionist baiter" who goaded his Senate colleagues from New England with calls to reopen the African slave trade.[21]

In the volatile years leading up to secession, Clay suffered spates of ill health that inhibited a more active involvement in the political maneuverings of the time. Nevertheless, he kept himself on stage with powerful speeches that upheld the honor of the South. In September 1859, before a crowd in Huntsville, Clay explained to his listeners that Alabama was "one of thirty three free, sovereign and independent States, composing a confederation, not a consolidation, a union, not a nation." He went on to emphasize that slavery was fundamentally a matter of property rights. "To protect and preserve it, is the chief end of every government," Clay averred, "when protection ceases, allegiance ceases." Back in the Senate, in the wake of John Brown's raid on Harpers Ferry, the Alabamian glared at the Republican delegates and openly accused them of creating a "chasm between the North and the South so deep and wide that it can never be bridged over." When Alabama finally seceded, Clay resigned his seat, but not before delivering a final, fire-eating farewell: "Not a decade, nor scarce a lustrum, has elapsed, since [Alabama's] birth, that has not been strongly marked by proofs of the growth and power of that antislavery spirit of the northern people which seeks the overthrow of that domestic institution of the South, which is not only the chief source of her prosperity, but the very basis of her social order and State polity."[22]

Clement Clay was too old and infirm to fight in the army, but he was more than eager to serve his new country in a political capacity. The position of Confederate senator especially appealed to him, being a continuation of what he had already been doing for the past eight years. In autumn 1861, Clay did indeed win election to the Confederate Senate, but not without some serious opposition. The legislature had elected William Yancey without much fuss, but political moderates did not want fire-eaters holding both Senate slots; they preferred Thomas Hill Watts. So, instead of receiving an acclamation, Clay had to sweat ten ballots before garnering a relatively small majority: 66–53. Rather than celebrate, Clay pouted about the length of the process and the closeness of the final vote. He contemplated a grand refusal of the seat, but his political friends salved his ego and persuaded him to ignore the tally. Clay's wife also seems to have played a role in convincing him to buck up. Virginia had always encouraged her husband's career, often hosting important dinner engagements to win over potential patrons, but she also very much wanted to experience the high society of Richmond. Clement was going to be a senator.[23]

Senator Clay produced a prowar record in the Confederate Congress. In 1862, he voted with the majority on conscription and its subsequent amendments, but he failed in his efforts to include alien residents in the dragnet. Most senators feared that drafting foreigners would undermine Confederate diplomacy, but Clay thought it only fair that noncitizen immigrants who had established domicile in the South should share the burden of fighting. He did, however, thwart a proposal to create new regiments that comprised mostly conscripts, arguing that replenishing existing regiments was the smarter approach. Clay also strongly supported the tax-in-kind, urging a 12.5 percent levy on farm produce, though he acceded to the 10 percent figure in the final version that passed in April 1863. Virginia Clay applauded her husband's stance: "The more [the majority] recognized that only in increased taxation lay the prolonging of our national life." Clay also approved presidential requests to suspend habeas corpus. He voted against impressment, however. Most states, including Alabama, had already enacted that measure, and so further legislation seemed superfluous. But Clay also spoke from personal experience when he complained that impressment aggravated civil-military relations. In January 1863, military authorities had appropriated some of his wagons and teams for several weeks yet refused to offer fair compensation. The senator also suffered the loss of eleven slaves who escaped to enemy lines while impressed as laborers in the niter works of northern Alabama. Evidently, their supervision had been negligent, and Clay was not pleased.[24]

Clay was a dutiful war Confederate, but he never emerged as a driving force in the Senate. At various times, he served on three committees—commerce, military, and navy—but he does not appear to have done much real work on any of them. In October 1862, he did usher through a bill that sought to rectify the rampant problem of counterfeit banknotes, especially the so-called invasion money that was allegedly being distributed by Union soldiers. "We must suppress it by severe and summary punishment," he declared at the end of a floor speech on the topic. The Confederate mint honored the senator's efforts on behalf of monetary probity by putting his image on a one-dollar treasury bill, several million of which were in circulation by the end of the war. Clay also played a key role in preventing the creation of a Confederate Supreme Court. Recalling their old Jacksonian suspicions of a centralized judiciary, former Democrats derailed the proposal at every opportunity. For his part, Clay successfully moved to deny the high court any appellate jurisdiction, thereby denying it the all-important power of judicial review. Thus modified, it passed the Senate only to be stillborn, as expected, in the House. Other than these moments of triumph, Clay was mostly just another senator in the chamber, one who was all too often irritated whenever his colleagues disagreed with his suggested wording for whatever bill was on the floor.[25]

Regardless of how one assesses Clay's performance as a senator, he was unique among Confederate politicians in forging a genuine bond with President Jefferson Davis. "Unless it be Clay of Alabama," remarked the wife of a fellow senator, "that Davis has not a personal friend." The Confederate president may have been respected for his intellect and devotion to the cause, but he was widely reviled for his arrogance and lack of compassion. It seemed that the man was always at loggerheads with one prominent leader or another, including engaging in some nasty exchanges with William Yancey; yet he never spoke a bad word about Clement Clay. The Clays were frequent guests of the Davises, and sometimes the only guests, even though the wives were usually cool toward each other. Senator Clay often accompanied Davis on morning rides, and they shared many a meal. "I dined with the President," the Alabamian happily recalled of one such meeting in 1863, "on beef soup, beef stew, meat pie, potatoes, coffee, and bread." The details of their conversations are hearsay, but it appears that Davis did most of the talking, though Clay did run interference between the president and William Yancey when those two came to verbal blows over military appointments and postmaster jobs. "He is a strange compound which I cannot analyze," Clay confided to Yancey in April 1863; "I have tried harder than I ever did with any other man to be his friend." This special relationship with Jefferson Davis might well be Clay's greatest contribution to the Confederacy. The Alabama senator sometimes feigned his cordiality, but he also seemed to realize that Davis needed a confidante, someone with whom to commiserate without embarrassment. By simply being an indulgent listener, Clay brought peace of mind to his president, however transitory the mood. The two men would remain close for the rest of their lives.[26]

Clay yearned for his own peace of mind, too. In spring 1863, he betrayed noticeable disillusion with the war. "A general gloom prevails here [in Richmond] because of the scarcity and high price of food," he related to his wife. With a touch of guilt over his "simple fare" luncheons with the president, he expressed a "wish that the army in the field had more to eat." When Vicksburg fell later that summer, Clay grumbled that "the war will continue for years" (he predicted that it would last until 1865). News from northern Alabama only further disheartened him. For much of 1862, Union troops occupied Huntsville and vast swaths of the surrounding valley. They plundered the senator's estate, among other depredations, and they briefly arrested Clay's father. "I feel humiliated that I am not doing something," Clay opined at one point. On a visit home in October (after Confederate forces had temporarily cleared the valley), Clay observed rampant lawlessness, which he attributed to Lincoln's Emancipation Proclamation. "The disloyal stand in open defiance of constitutional authority," he wrote to the War Department, "there is a general feeling among such that the Confederate government is too weak." The senator believed that only a large, permanent garrison could restore order, if for no other reason than to regain control of an unruly slave population (Clay lost twenty-seven more of his chattel as runaways). Clay's mother tried to mollify her son's distress: "The negro is more to be pitied than blamed. They are ignorant & grasping, as we are, for a happier future!" Conversely, Clay's wife compounded his anxiety. Despite mounting financial difficulties, which included a hefty $115 per month on room and board, Virginia continued to spend extravagantly on parties and gifts. Moreover, she refused to engage in the duties that were expected of a southern woman, such as visiting the soldier hospitals or knitting clothing for the troops. The couple argued more frequently, with Clement at one point accusing the always flirtatious Virginia of "beau-catching." With these many travails on his mind, Clay pursued his reelection with diminished enthusiasm.[27]

In mid-November, "a number of notabilities" arrived in Montgomery. They included Clement Clay, Jabez Curry, ex-governor and ex-US senator Benjamin Fitzpatrick, and John Jacob Seibels. The first two were well-known war Confederates. Fitzpatrick had been a cooperationist on secession, reluctantly resigned his seat in Washington, and thereafter leaned toward peace. Seibels was a former colonel in the Sixth Alabama Infantry and a principal leader in the Peace Society; he was a favorite among the peace Confederates in the legislature. These men were in town to make known their willingness to serve if elected to the Confederate Senate. Despite their obvious intentions, a correspondent for the *Mobile Register* claimed "to see no evidences of an undignified scramble for office," and went on to predict that the assembly would make its selection "without a contest." The prediction was dead wrong; the stakes were too high for a nonpartisan affair. At least ten other prominent names were thrown into the mix, but the race boiled down to the four individuals who were physically present. The *Selma Morning Dispatch* considered Curry to be the "most formidable aspirant" and urged Clay's supporters to unite behind the fire-eater from Talladega. The *Mobile Tribune* countered that Clay was the better candidate because of the incumbent's "superior" experience:

"In times like the present, it is better to retain tried, faithful public servants." The *Montgomery Advertiser* had leaned toward Clay earlier in the fall but now refused to endorse anyone, insisting only that the next senator be a man of "unimpeachable fidelity to the Confederate Government; one who by his record is known to be unchangeably opposed to any policy or act that savors of reunion with the North." This newspaper never mentioned Seibels by name, but it was clearly urging the war Confederates to unite behind one of their candidates, lest a reconstructionist prevail.[28]

Unity within the ranks of the war Confederates posed a problem. Curry and Clay each had strong followings in the legislature; each expected the other to bow out. George Walden, a former representative from Talladega County, contacted sitting legislators to urge them to back Curry. "I know him well, and know him to be a pure man, as well as a man of brilliant talents," Walden vouched. Conversely, state senator John J. W. Payne, a slaveholding physician from Pickens County, openly endorsed Clay as a politician who was "sound upon the present issues" and saw no reason to abandon the incumbent. But there *was* a reason, one that Curry's surrogates brought to the fore just prior to the election. In April 1863, Clay voted against an army pay raise in the Senate, whereas Curry voted for one in the House. Clay's position was principled but unpopular. (As a US senator, he had voted against a pension bill for Mexican War veterans, and so he was only being consistent in his fiscal parsimony.) To him, a pay raise would add to the debt, fuel inflation, and not really help the common soldiers, who—as Clay dubiously claimed—"do not need or desire any increase of their pay." Clay's vote was no secret, but the fact that it had become a heated topic of discussion bothered the incumbent. On November 14, Clay confronted Curry outside the capitol and accused his rival of seeking to exploit the story for political gain. Curry mumbled a denial that Clay found unconvincing. It was an ill-timed rift between the state's two leading war Confederates.[29]

The peace Confederates salivated over the Curry-Clay dispute. The split seemed to guarantee that any candidate of their choice would win. Benjamin Fitzpatrick had statewide name recognition, but he was old and out of touch with current affairs. John Jacob Seibels, however, was the total package. A former newspaper editor from Montgomery, he had supported Stephen Douglas in 1860 and had, the following year, denounced secession "with all his might." During the war, he openly criticized the Impressment Act and then became deeply involved with the Peace Society. He also possessed solid military credentials, having raised the Sixth Alabama Infantry and led it into action at First Manassas. The fact that Seibels had been a longtime political enemy of the late fire-eater William Yancey only strengthened his appeal. Finally, Seibels was in contact with the peace movement outside of Alabama, most notably in Georgia, so he would presumably make an excellent liaison for any coordinated effort at reconstruction. The only reservation that peace Confederates might have had with the colonel was his apparent willingness to accept some form of emancipation as a precondition for reunion. Nonetheless, John Jacob Seibels was their strongest option, and so the peace Confederates entered the balloting with a united front.[30]

The senatorial election in November 1863 is a Rosetta stone for determining the political stance of Alabama's legislators during the Civil War (tables 5 and 6). The differences between the candidates were as stark as possible. Anyone who voted consistently for Curry or Clay (or for any of the hawkish fringe candidates) must be considered a war Confederate. The reverse goes for those who voted for Seibels; they are properly labeled as peace Confederates. On the morning of November 20, Benton W. Groce of Talladega County formally nominated Curry. William M. Jackson of Franklin County did the same for Clay, as did William H. Ogbourne of Montgomery for Seibels. Thereafter, the balloting commenced with the goal being a simple majority of the total votes cast. The first ballot established a pattern that persisted through the next ten. Curry and Clay each garnered vote tallies in the mid- to low thirties, while Seibels regularly accrued numbers in the mid-forties. A handful of legislators voted for two outliers: Robert Hardy Smith, a respected Mobilian who was generally prowar, and John Cochran, a fire-eater from the Eufaula Regency. A couple of war Confederates switched back and forth between Curry and Clay, but otherwise virtually no one budged through the first eleven ballots. Consequently, no one was elected.[31]

This deadlock offers an instructive case study in the importance of party politics. The war Confederates had the numbers, decisively in the Senate and marginally in the House, but they lacked the unity of a party structure. In multiballot elections, it is acceptable for politicians to vote for favorite sons on the first round or two, but thereafter they are expected to rally around their party's strongest candidate. But Alabama had no parties in 1863; it had factions that were oriented around personalities. Leaders within the war Confederate camp might have acted like political whips, but they too were divided. Walter H. Crenshaw, the Speaker of the House, voted for Clay each time, while Thomas A. Walker, the president of the Senate, stood unwaveringly for Curry. "I would not be astonished if neither Clay nor Curry were elected," the editor of the *Mobile Tribune* observed, "it will be very difficult to bring about a reconciliation between the friends of these two gentlemen." Conversely, the peace Confederates from both chambers displayed remarkable solidarity, a testament to the political skills of Garrett and Parsons. Un-

Table 5. Alabama's Senatorial Election—November 1863 (by Ballot)

Ballot	Curry	Clay	Seibels	Fitzpatrick	Smith	Cochran	Pettus	Brooks	Watts	Walker	Others	Total
Nov. 20												
1	35	34	44		4	1						118
2	35	32	44		4	1						116
3	34	33	46		3	1						117
4	33	34	45		3	1						116
5	32	35	45		3	1						116
6	32	34	45		3	1						115
7	33	30	45		3	2						113
Nov. 21												
8	31	32	44		5	2						114
9	33	31	42		5	2					1	114
10	36	29	41		5	2					1	114
11	36	26	41		4	2					2	111
12	40		32	20	3	9	7					111
13	40			48	6	8	9					111
14	41			51	3	6	7					108
15	50			52	2	1		4				109
16	51			52	2	0		3				108
Nov. 23												
17	26	19		44	0	1			10	4		104
18	24	20		45	4	1			11	2		107
19	24	17		46	3	1			10	5		106
Nov. 24												
20				47	5	1				61		114

Source: Alabama Legislature, *Senate Journal*, 1863, 138–65.

Table 6. Alabama's Senatorial Election—November 1863 (by Ballot for Each Legislator)

Senator	Curry	Clay	Seibels	Fitzpatrick	Brooks	Cochran	Pettus	Smith	Watts	Walker	Others
Barnes		1–11								20	
Beeson			1–12	13–20							
Brodnax	12–17	1–11, 18–19								20	
Clarke, W.		1–11		12–19						20	
Coleman, A.	4–7, 12–16, 18–19	8–9								20	10–11
Coman	3										
Critcher			1–12	13–16, 20					17–19		
Davis, D.		1–11			15–16	12–14					
Ervin	1–19									20	
Garrett			1–12	13–20							
Groce	1–19									20	
Hammond			1–12	13–16, 18–20						17	
Hardwick	1–19									20	
Harrison	1–16								17–19	20	
Hill	1–6, 12–17, 19	7–11							18	20	
Jackson		1–11, 17–19		12–16						20	
Lewis, J.										20	
Ligon			1–12				13–14			20	
McCall	15–16	1–11, 17–19				12–14				20	
Moren				15–19			14	1–13, 20			
Payne	15	1–11, 17–19			16		12–14			20	
Peacock										20	
Porter	1–11, 14–19						12–13				

Powell	1–2		3–7, 10–11	12–17, 20				8–9, 18–19			
Reavis	15	1–11, 17–19			16		12–14			20	
Rice, F.	12–16	1–11, 17–19								20	
Rice, S.	1–16								17–19	20	
Toulmin	1–11			12–20							
Walker	1–19									20	
Wood	1–19									20	
House Representative	**Curry**	**Clay**	**Seibels**	**Fitzpatrick**	**Brooks**	**Cochran**	**Pettus**	**Smith**	**Watts**	**Walker**	**Others**
Armstrong			1–11	12–20							
Ashe, G.			1–11	12–20							
Ashe, T.	12–16	1–11, 17–18								19–20	
Ashurst			1–6, 8–12	13–17, 19–20					18		
Atkinson	1–19									20	
Barron			1–12	13–20							
Bell	10, 15–16		1–9, 11				12–14	20			
Benners	11–13, 15–16	1–10, 17–19		20							
Bethea	1–11			12–19						20	
Bradley			1–11	12–20							
Brandon			1–12	13–20							
Brooks, J.	1–3, 15–19	4–5				7–14					
Brown	1–16										
Bryan	1–3, 5–7, 9–16	4, 8								20	
Bryers	12–14, 16				15					20	
Carlisle	1–6, 17–19									20	

Continued on the next page

Table 6. *Continued*

House Representative	Curry	Clay	Seibels	Fitzpatrick	Brooks	Cochran	Pettus	Smith	Watts	Walker	Others
Chambers	15–16	1–11, 17–19				12–14				20	
Chapman		1–11		12–20							
Charlton	1–16									17–20	
Chisholm	10–11		1–9	12–16						17–20	
Clark, J.			1–12	13–20							
Cobb			1–8, 10, 12	13–20							9, 11
Coleman, W.	11–13, 15–16	1–10, 17–19		14						20	
Cooper			1–12	13–20							
Cox	1–11			12–16, 20					17–19		
Crenshaw		1–11		12–16, 20					17–19		
Cumming		1–10									
Davis, J.			1–12	13–20							
Davis, M.	14–16	1–11		17–19			12–13			20	
Dawson	15–16	1–11, 17–19					12–14			20	
Dent			1–8								
Donnell			7–12	13–20							
Ellis	12–16			18–19						20	
Evans	9–11		1–8	12–20							
Fannin	4	1–3, 5–9				12	13–14	10–11		20	
Foster	1–17							18–20			
Franklin	16	1–11, 17–19		15		12–14				20	
Gafford	1–3, 7–10	4–6							17–19	20	
Gardner	1–19									20	
Graves	1–18									19–20	

Greathouse			1–12	13–20							
Greene			1–10	20							
Hames	1–19									20	
Head	13		1–12	14–20							
Holley			1–12	13–20							
Hollis	14–16	1–11, 17–19					12–13			20	
Howard			1–11	12–20							
Howell			1–11	12–20							
Jones	1–2, 7–11, 15–16	3–6				12–13			17–19	20	
Keenan	1–19									20	
Kilpatrick	12–14, 16	1–11			15						
Lawler								1–16, 18–19		20	
Leeper			1, 3–12	13–20							
Lewis, T.	15		3, 7, 11–12	14, 16				1–2, 8–10, 13, 18, 20	17, 19		
Ligon			1–12	13–20							
Magee			1–11	12–20							
Malone			1–12	13–20							
Manasco			1–12	13–20							
May	12–19	1–11								20	
McAlexander	1–19									20	
McCain			1–12	13–20							
McClellan	10–11		1–9	12–16, 18–19						17, 20	
McInnis	1–19									20	
McLemore			1–6								
Mitchell								1–16, 20	17–19		

Continued on the next page

Table 6. *Continued*

House Representative	Curry	Clay	Seibels	Fitzpatrick	Brooks	Cochran	Pettus	Smith	Watts	Walker	Others
Modawell	12–14, 16	1–11, 17–19			15					20	
Moore, J.	1–19									20	
Moore, J. G.				16		1–15, 17					
Morrow			1–12	15–20				13–14			
Nisbet		1–11, 17–19		12–16						20	
Ogbourne	14–16		1–12	20				13	17–19		
Orr			1–12	13–20							
Parish	1–19									20	
Parker, C.	15–16	1–11, 17–19				12–14				20	
Parker, E.			1–12	13–20							
Parsons			1–12	13–20							
Price	12	1–11, 17–19		13–16						20	
Read	1–19									20	
Robinson	12–16	1–11, 18								19–20	
Ryan	1–19									20	
Scruggs	1–19									20	
Seay			1–12	13–20							
Sibley			1–12	13–20							
Sims			7–12	13–20							
Sykes			1–11	12–20							
Taylor	1–19									20	
Towles		1–6								20	

Vansandt			1–12	13–20							
Vincent			1–11	12–20							
West			1–12	13–20							
White				17–20							
Williams	4, 7–16	1–3, 5–6, 17								20	
Wolff	1–19									20	

Note: Twenty rounds of ballots were cast. The numbers in each column indicate which ballots the legislator cast for that candidate. Congressman Wolff, for example, voted for Curry for the first nineteen ballots and then switched to Walker.

Absent from the Senate: Cato, Matthews, and Stewart.

Absent from the House: Beard, Bishop, Edwards, Gibson, Kennon, Moulton, and Young.

Source: Alabama Legislature, *Senate Journal*, 1863, 138–65.

fortunately, they peaked at forty-six votes, a number that made up just under 40 percent of the legislative body, coincidentally a figure that was nearly identical to the delegate vote against secession in 1861.[32]

A significant development in the senatorial election occurred on the afternoon of November 21. Prior to the twelfth ballot, Clay's name was withdrawn, evidently with his permission. The incumbent had been privately fuming about the whole process, critical of the "new men, who had never been in office before & of whom I had never heard." Clay expected to lose. "On the whole my opinion is, that the Leg. will elect a Douglas or anti-secession Dem. or Curry, to succeed me." His removal seemingly cleared the path for Curry, but the politics of personality persisted. Theophilus Toulmin of Mobile, who had voted for Curry on the first eleven ballots, inexplicably nominated Benjamin Fitzpatrick. Toulmin and Fitzpatrick were both elderly and so perhaps were comrades in their earlier political lives, but Toulmin's action made no sense in the moment. To be sure, Fitzpatrick's candidacy would siphon some votes from Seibels, but it mostly complicated the war Confederates' prospects. Turner Reavis, a Clay supporter, further muddied the waters by nominating General Edmund Pettus, a secessionist and an active duty war hero from Dallas County. Happily for the war Confederates, the twelfth ballot finished Seibels. The peace Confederates began sidling over to Fitzpatrick, and the colonel's name was withdrawn. A sufficient majority of war Confederates, however, still could not bring themselves to vote for Curry. On the next few rounds of voting, the former congressman did pick up a few Clay men, but the prowar outliers Smith, Cochran, and (now) Pettus collectively garnered some twenty votes, a tally that would have put Curry over the top had it gone for him.[33]

The critical moment in the election came with the fifteenth and sixteenth ballots. Sensing the shift in momentum, the peace Confederates fully backed Fitzpatrick. He was not as reliable as Seibels, but he was better than Curry. Similarly, the war Confederates finally seemed to have gotten their act together. The names of Cochran and Pettus were dropped, a tacit nod in favor of Curry. But then, DeWitt C. Davis, a Clay supporter from Covington County, abruptly nominated William Brooks, a hard-liner from Perry County. A majority of Clay's followers still threw their weight behind Curry, enabling him to crack the fifty-vote threshold and come to within a nose of winning, but the nomination of Brooks hurt Curry. It only amounted to a few votes, but these votes came from men who had shown support for Curry on earlier ballots. Counterfactually speaking, Curry should have won on either of these ballots, but there was no official war party to pressure its disgruntled members to work together. Besides those who voted for Brooks at this crucial stage, five

Clay supporters abstained (Barnes, Cumming, Fannin, Gafford, and Towles). Loyalty to their man appears to have trumped all other considerations; the venomous contretemps between Curry and Clay had proven catastrophic to the war Confederates. As a result, Fitzpatrick also came within a whisker of winning, thanks to an unlikely coalition of peace Confederates and disaffected Clay voters. He, too, might have won, had four peace Confederates not also abstained at this juncture (Ligon, Dent, Greene, and McLemore). Robert F. Ligon, a veteran who voted for Seibels and Pettus, and only for those two, apparently wanted to elect a military officer irrespective of politics. It should also be pointed out that ten legislators (three from the Senate and seven from the House) were not present for the election. Other than Lewis L. Cato, a fire-eater from Barbour County who likely would have supported Curry, and Willis D. Matthews, a nonslaveholding pacifist minister from Tallapoosa County who likely would have voted with the peace Confederates, the missing legislators' possible actions cannot be known. Regardless, neither the war men nor the peace men gained satisfaction on the fifteenth and sixteenth ballots.[34]

After a pause for the Sabbath, the senatorial election resumed on November 23. Curry's shortfall seems to have convinced Clay's supporters that their man was the better choice all along. The incumbent was renominated, along with two new candidates: governor-elect Thomas Hill Watts and state supreme court justice Richard Wilde Walker. Needless to say, with so many big names in the ring, the balloting was predictably inconclusive. For three consecutive rounds (the seventeenth, eighteenth, and nineteenth), the distribution closely replicated the first eleven; Curry ran slightly ahead of Clay, and Fitzpatrick polled Seibels's old numbers. Watts garnered a respectable ten votes from a curious mix of prowar and antiwar men. Walker finished among the now standard outliers Robert Smith and John Cochran. In exasperation, the assembly adjourned for the day. When it reconvened at noon on November 24, the mood was all compromise, at least among the war Confederates. The prowar factions conceded that they were not going to elect a hard-liner and so withdrew the names of Curry and Clay, as well as Watts. Most of them then united behind Walker and elected him on the twentieth ballot: 61–47. A large majority of peace Confederates (about forty), along with a few breakaway war Confederates, stood by Fitzpatrick, but Alabama finally had its new senator. Augustus Benners, one of those breakaways, considered the result to be a stale ending to "a very hurried and unsatisfactory session."[35]

Richard Wilde Walker, a forty-year-old planter from Madison County, was a true dark horse. Wilfred Buck Yearns describes him as "a unionist Whig," but both terms are inaccurate. He was no secessionist zealot like his older brother LeRoy Pope Walker, who later briefly served as the Confederate secretary of war, but Richard was not averse to disunion and proved a loyal Confederate. Early in his political career he was a Whig, but in the mid-1850s he made the journey into Alabama's democracy by way of the Know-Nothings. Walker was an associate justice on Alabama's supreme court when the war broke out. After serving in the Provisional Congress, he resumed his judicial duties. Walker's opinions on various war policies reflect the mind of a man who generally agreed that governing authorities during wartime were entitled to expanded power. With his colleagues on the bench, he upheld the constitutionality of impressment and conscription, though he balked when it came to the suspension of habeas corpus. As for the rebellion itself, Walker was more for it than against it.[36]

The Alabama press took a few days to digest the unexpected results of the election. Most newspapers voiced confidence in Walker, and several were noticeably pleased that Seibels with his "squints at reconstruction" had been thwarted, but they were also generally disappointed with the outcome. The *Huntsville Confederate* went so far as to describe Clay's defeat in particular as "a public calamity," one brought about by a needless altercation over soldier pay. The *Clarke County Journal* blamed the legislature's failure to elect a hard-liner on the "existence of the party spirit," when in fact it was arguably the *absence* of a party system that hurt the war Confederates. The *Montgomery Advertiser* similarly deplored the fates of Clay and Curry, but it ultimately sighed its approval: "Judge Walker will perhaps give more general satisfaction than would that of any other man at this time." For his part, Clement Clay found some schadenfreude in his loss. Neither he nor his wife liked Fitzpatrick personally, and the lame-duck senator forever after believed that Curry had stabbed him in the back over the issue of soldier pay. His stalwarts in the legislature had helped deny both foes the prize. The reaction of the peace Confederates to Walker's victory is unknown, but given that most did not vote for him they were surely unhappy. To have elected Seibels as senator would have signaled a powerful rebuke of the whole war. Even a Fitzpatrick win would have sent a message that Alabama was losing its patience with Richmond. Instead, the peace Confederates got Walker, who did nothing to advance their manifesto for reconstruction.[37]

Richard Walker's career as a Confederate senator was brief and undistinguished. In keeping with his judicial record, he approved legislation that strengthened Richmond's power to impress and conscript (although he did vote to retain exemptions for war-related professions), but he opposed any measure that suspended habeas corpus. He also appears to have supported the recruitment of slaves as soldiers, to include their emancipation as a reward for dutiful service, though he ultimately abstained when the issue came to a formal vote in March 1865. It may be too much to brand Walker an outright war Confederate, but he was definitely not a reconstructionist. Therefore, any scholarly interpretation that presents Walker as an opponent of the cause misreads the historical record. War Confederates may not have been thrilled by the man, but Walker's elevation to the Senate was really a setback for the peace Confederates. In fact, both of Alabama's newly elected national senators were faithful Confederate politicians who never agreed to peace without independence.[38]

THE MILITIA ACT OF 1863

Besides electing two senators, the Alabama assembly of 1863 passed a comprehensive militia bill. Enacted on August 29, it was the most significant piece of legislation to come out of Montgomery in the last half of the war. In reorganizing the militia system, Alabama's lawmakers took a final step toward total war. It was not the *levée en masse* of French Revolution repute, but it did complete the mobilization of the state's manpower. In addition to bolstering the number of volunteers and conscripts, the new militia system ensured that every man was assigned a specific role in providing for the South's common defense.

Prior to the state elections—prior to his own defeat—Governor John Gill Shorter called the incoming legislature into a special session to address the militia issue. As discussed elsewhere, previous gubernatorial attempts to put the militia on a proper war footing foundered on legislative lethargy and indifference; both chambers tabled the matter in December 1862. By summer 1863, however, the war had reached a point of crisis. In his message to the called session, Governor Shorter stressed the "present emergency" as a sufficient, if not obvious, reason for a strong militia. "I invoke the wisdom and unfaltering patriotism of the General Assembly to combine the remaining military power of the State, and devote it to the great and paramount object of public defense." Shorter insisted that a well-organized militia would constitute "an insuperable barrier against incursions and raids." In contrast to their prior dereliction of duty, lawmakers now took seriously the governor's urgent request for an effective militia.[39]

Like the election of senators, the proceedings on the militia topic reveal the political outlook of many of Alabama's lawmakers. There is also ambiguity, for politicians can be inconsistent in how they vote. Fortunately, the senatorial election in November 1863 places war Confederates and peace Confederates in stark relief. The voting patterns on display then are not only invaluable for an analysis of the militia debates that took place three months earlier, but they help clear up some scholarly misperceptions. The historian Malcolm

C. McMillan contends that the militia issue exposed the face of defeatism in many parts of Alabama. The August election, according to McMillan, created a legislature that was "inclined to sue for peace and [was] ready to sabotage the war efforts of the Alabama governors." Consequently, the Militia Act proved "useless" and "totally inadequate" to the needs of the state. Christopher Lyle McIlwain disagrees. Acknowledging that many of the political newcomers were reconstructionists, he nevertheless stresses that their influence was limited, at least for the time being. "If the majority of this legislature had actually been committed to peace," McIlwain states, "it would not have passed any militia bill at all." Based on the ensuing legislation, McIlwain's observation can actually be inverted. A majority was committed to war.[40]

A close examination of the militia debates and voting patterns shows a legislative branch engaging in thoughtful and earnest discourse over how best to utilize its most precious resource—the citizenry—in a war that most still wanted to win, but that most understood was not going well. The arguments also highlight the difference of opinion that is inherent in democratic politics. In general, the war Confederates wanted a functional militia system that could police the interior, as well as serve as a force multiplier for the army against enemy invasion. Conversely, the peace Confederates preferred a less active militia. To them, the unfavorable war situation demanded a termination of the struggle, not its prolongation as augured by a revamped militia system. Still, neither side was dogmatic. War Confederates had no intention of granting the governor unlimited military power, and peace Confederates conceded that a responsible militia organization might prove indispensable in maintaining order during a postwar transition.

The first day of the called session—August 17—was consumed by administrative details, the drafting of war resolutions, and a reading of the governor's long message, but lawmakers soon went to work on the militia. Early the next morning, Senator William H. Barnes, a war Confederate from Chambers County, formally introduced the militia bill. To expedite the process, both chambers agreed to form a Joint Committee on Military Affairs, one with sixteen members (seven from the Senate and nine from the House). War Confederates dominated with twelve, including Augustus Benners, who had strived in vain to push militia legislation the previous year. Robert F. Ligon and Lewis E. Parsons represented the interests of the peace faction. Outside observers hoped that the assembly would move with alacrity. Henry F. Coyne, the editor of the *Montgomery Mail*, preemptively chastised the legislators: "We hope that no useless time will be spent in irrelevant discussions," he said in one issue. "It cannot, surely, take more than a day or two to perfect a military bill which shall meet the present exigency," he said in another. Coyne need not have worried. The joint committee took about a week to draft a bill. The Senate then deliberated for two days, while the larger House took four days.[41]

Much of the bill's wording was fairly straightforward and typical of any militia organization, but two sections proved controversial and elicited extensive discussion. Section 2 stipulated that every man between the ages of sixteen and sixty would serve in some capacity as militiamen. In the House, James S. Clark and Jeptha Seay, peace Confederates from Lawrence and Fayette Counties respectively, tried to raise the minimum age to eighteen, but their motion was defeated, 52–34. The majority vote heavily reflected the war Confederate faction, which successfully preserved the broader age range. A similar debate occurred in the Senate, with a similar result.[42]

Section 3 pertained to the composition of the militia and proved to be the most complicated portion of the entire bill. The legislature decided to create two classes. Class 1, known as the county reserves, consisted of everyone under seventeen or over forty-five, the physically unfit, and those holding public office from all three branches of government. John Y. Kilpatrick, a war Confederate and active-duty cavalry captain from Clarke County, emphasized this last group as proof of the state's commitment to shared sacrifice. In raw numbers, this class amounted to about 28,800 Alabamians, but as per Section 11, Class 1 militiamen could not be deployed beyond their county of origin. Class 2 encompassed everyone else, those whom the governor could send anywhere in the state at any time. Setting aside the usual exemptions, such as physicians, teachers whose jobs predated the war, ministers of active congregations, and those in war-related occupations, approximately 14,900 Alabamians fell into this category. War Confederates led by Frizell M. Hardwick of Cherokee in the Senate and Cader A. Parker of Barbour in the House offered motions to modify the age constraints in Class 1 so as to shift more men into Class 2, but just enough of their colleagues voted with the peace Confederates to kill both efforts. In an encouraging display of bipartisan cooperation, both chambers agreed to waive the Class 1 requirement for residents in the Tennessee River valley, counties that were essentially under enemy occupation. Disharmony returned, however, when state senator James A. Hill, a war Confederate from Walker County, moved to expand the jurisdiction of Class 1 militiamen to "adjoining counties," thereby giving the governor greater flexibility in conducting local defense. The amendment carried 20–10, with seventeen war Confederates voting with the majority. (William Garrett notably led the minority in its opposition.) The House evidently refused to accept the Senate's amendment, for the final law explicitly confined the county reserves to their respective locales. Unfortunately, because Speaker Crenshaw pressed the chamber to vote on the matter, there are neither minutes of any discussion nor a tally of any votes, "the clerk not being able to record them under an order from the House."[43]

On August 27, the Alabama legislature passed the militia bill and sent it to the governor, who signed it two days later. The final vote in the Senate was not recorded, but in the House the math was overwhelming: 69–11. At least forty-one war Confederates joined with twenty-five peace Confederates to enact a war measure that was long overdue. Among the majority was Lewis E. Parsons, putative leader of the peace Confederate faction, who also voted against his colleagues' efforts to narrow the act's age range. Therefore, it would seem that even had peace Confederates enjoyed greater strength in the legislature, a new militia law would still have been enacted. Another curiosity was the erratic voting behavior of Lewis L. Cato, a hard-line war Confederate from Barbour County. In keeping with his radicalism, he proposed that officeholders be included in the Class 2 category and that the county reserves be compelled to operate in adjacent counties. But he also displayed a less strident side, supporting efforts to raise the minimum militia age to eighteen and trying to eliminate gubernatorial control over the University of Alabama's Cadet Corps. The conduct of Parsons and Cato is a reminder that political labels are generalizations that cannot account for every individual decision. In any event, state lawmakers had done their duty. Daniel T. Ryan, a war Confederate from Calhoun County, took pride in what he had wrought. "I felt somewhat fearful that we would have a discordant Legislature," he explained to his constituents back home, but instead he encountered "perfect harmony of feeling and concert of action." Augustus Benners was less upbeat, even though he too voted for the militia bill. Upon his return to Greene County, Benners laconically recorded in his diary, "had a disagreeable session of two weeks." The exhausted war Confederate had nothing more to say about one of Alabama's most important wartime laws.[44]

State newspapers were generally pleased with the Militia Act, in addition to a supplementary law that empowered local authorities to round up deserters. The *Clarke County Journal* was confident that Alabama now had everything that it needed to persevere in the struggle. "Let us teach the enemy," this organ declared, "that he has not only to conquer our great armies, but must 'wipe out' the *militia* . . . before he can find a secure resting place." Governor Shorter was less enthused. He was certainly glad to have a formal militia structure at last, but he was disappointed by both the size of Class 1 and its tight restrictions on deployment. Moreover, like his successor, Thomas Hill Watts, he was never able to muster more than five thousand of the supposed fifteen thousand Class 2 militiamen. Watts evidently considered even those who turned out as "not worth much as soldiers." Regardless of their abilities, Alabama's militiamen augmented Confederate efforts to defend the state. They fought ineffectually against Rousseau's Raid in 1864 and Wilson's Raid in 1865, but they proved to be invaluable in carrying out expeditions against deserter bands and unionist guerrillas. In autumn 1863, for instance, militia forces in Coffee County wiped out Ward's Raiders, "a group of outlaws who . . . terrorized the defenseless women and old people" of the Pea River region. And as Stephen V. Ash explains, the militia all across the South played an important role in policing an increasingly restless slave population.[45]

The day before it adjourned, the state assembly passed a joint resolution urging the Confederate Congress to formulate a national policy about how best to incorporate those very slaves into the rebel army. This important, though generally overlooked, action is another telling indicator of Alabama's embrace of total war. To be sure, slaves had been impressed for military purposes, such as construction of fortifications, but none had ever been assigned to regular army units in the field, at least not in any official capacity. The impetus for a more radical usage of slaves came from the citizenry itself. On August 15, residents of Greene County held a series of public forums in which they demanded that slaves be recruited into the Confederate army. "The North having armed a portion of our slaves to fight against us, we, in turn, should arm enough of them to at least counterbalance the force of the insurgent blacks arrayed against us." Benjamin H. Micou, a planter from Tallapoosa County and the president of the Tallassee Armory, agreed. "The people are clamoring," he notified authorities in Richmond, "for the Slaves to be brought into service for defence of our rights and liberties." The incongruity of these statements foreshadowed the war Confederate attitude in the last half of the war, when the goal of independence supplanted rational thinking about the peculiar institution and its inherent theories about white supremacy.[46]

The Alabama House took the lead in addressing this controversial topic. On August 25, the Committee on Confederate Relations, which comprised six war Confederates and two peace Confederates, presented a draft resolution that proved far more radical than the final version. It called for the immediate enlistment of slaves into the army as teamsters, sappers, nurses, cooks, and any other roles requiring physical labor of the noncombat variety. "It is a matter of serious regret," noted the committee, "that a measure of such obvious policy had not been adopted by our armies from the beginning." The resolution then proposed arming the slaves and putting them in the ranks, not only to offset the North's enrollment of freedmen into its own armies, but to prevent a "war of extermination" between the races. "This people—our domestic servants," the committee insisted, "must be employed for us or against us." Anticipating objections from colleagues, the committee stressed the slaves' supposed "fidelity and obedience," and said that with "proper military training" virtually any slave could be made into "an efficient soldier." When Chairman Tristam B. Bethea of Montgomery delivered the report, he did so with the unanimous backing of the entire committee.[47]

Debate on the House floor was testy but brief. James S. Clark, a peace Confederate from Lawrence County, questioned the reliability of slaves as soldiers. He predicted that "they would desert in the hour of danger and difficulty." Bethea brushed aside these misgivings, reiterating his belief in the "faithfulness and devotion of the negroes to their masters." Levi W. Lawler fully agreed that slaves should be used in the army for fatigue duty and accepted the resolution's wording to that effect. He was not keen, however, about arming them. Lawler suggested that the assembly avoid explicitly endorsing the idea of slave soldiers, and instead urge the politicians in Richmond to develop a "policy of using in some effective way a certain percentage of the male slave population . . . to perform such services as Congress may by law direct." The language was less provocative, but the inference was clear. So amended, the resolution passed by a surprisingly large majority: 67–13. True to form, James S. Clark voted with the House minority, along with three other peace Confederates, including the big planters James W. S. Donnell and Leonidas Howard. Eight war Confederates also voted against the resolution, most notably Walter H. Crenshaw and Augustus Benners, men who usually supported extreme war measures. Benners in particular believed that once slaves were elevated above their subservient status, which military service would certainly do, then the peculiar institution could not be maintained. He would later condemn as a "Nigger bill" an 1865 law authorizing the use of slaves as soldiers. The majority of legislators, however, came together in another instance of prowar, bipartisan cooperation. Alabama was willing to give this racial "experiment" a try.[48]

Public reaction to the resolution, which was innocuously titled, "To Increase the Army of the Confederate States," was varied. There was consensus on using slaves as work details in the armies, but disagreement about also putting them in uniform. One newspaper editor curtly dismissed as "repugnant" the idea of slaves as soldiers. Another was more receptive: "in case of pressing need, these negroes could be used as a fighting force, and made to do good service." The whole discussion, whether in the press or the legislature, reflected the arrogance of a deluded master race. At no point did anyone broach the subject of emancipating those slaves who served. There were some concerns about "a practical acknowledgement of equality," but nary a hint at bestowing freedom as a reward to slaves who fought under the rebel banner. Rather, there was a presumption that most slaves would obey orders to attack their liberators and then return to a life of bondage. Furthermore, in the context of states' rights, the resolution was remarkable for its deference to the central government. Prior to the war, Alabamians had jealously guarded their control over slavery. During it, they became more and more willing to surrender that power to the leaders in Richmond. Congress, not the state legislatures, would decide what to do with the slaves. Hypocrisy aside, the fact that any debate of this type was occurring at all is astonishing. As the first southern polity to promote the militarization of slavery, Alabama was, indeed, a war state all over.[49]

As 1863 came to a close, the much rumored reconstructionist agenda had yet to manifest itself in any significant way. Instead of denouncing the war, peace Confederates were sometimes its loudest cheerleaders. Instead of opposing further mobilizations of Alabama's manhood, whether white or black, most peace Confederates threw their votes behind the militia bill and the resolution calling for slaves in the army. Instead of sending antiwar senators to Richmond, they helped elect one, Robert Jemison, whose commitment to the cause was never in doubt, and failed to stop another, Richard Wilde Walker, who expressed no interest in reconstruction. In fact, without the voting data from the second senatorial election, a historian would be hard pressed to substantiate the existence of a peace movement at all in the legislature. War Confederates were taken aback by their opponents' supine behavior. Jabez Curry, in particular, had feared the worst after his defeat. In an unbridled letter to Robert Jemison, he contended that "the Douglas faction [i.e., peace Confederates] retains more party hatred and done more to produce disaffection, if not disloyalty, to the government than all other agencies combined." Curry singled out Lewis E. Parsons as the principal villain in the story. Describing him as a man of "mean passions," Curry worried about Parsons's "premeditated efforts to dispirit and lower the tone of our people and prepare them to make or accept unacceptable propositions for peace." Yet Curry's fears were not realized, at least not during the two legislative sessions of 1863. Parsons and his followers made no real attempt to redirect Alabama's course in the war.[50]

As Alabama's lawmakers prepared to leave Montgomery for the Christmas season, Speaker Walter H. Crenshaw praised his legislative peers for their hard work in trying times: "I take it for granted that there are none on this floor who would willingly submit to the power of the Northern despotism. Then if we are in earnest in our determination to make this great revolution successful, if we are resolved that the blood of our sons and brothers that have already fallen in this contest, shall not be spilled in vain, we must forget all our past differences, and as a band of brothers advance to the breach and contribute all in our power to promote the success of the glorious cause." In just a few sentences, the Speaker conveyed a nationalistic sentiment that cut across partisan lines. War Confederates absolutely agreed with Crenshaw's words, but even most peace Confederates assented. Like their rivals across the aisle, peace Confederates loathed the Yankee invasion and hated the thought of disgracing the legacy of those who had already died. As long as victory remained a possibility, Alabama's polity would stand by the war. The state elections of 1863 had produced a whiff of defeatism (at least in the House), but that odor had seemingly passed. The assembly was not scheduled to meet again in regular session for another eleven months. Any peace platform would have to wait until then, a painfully long time at a critical juncture in the conflict. As a result, war Confederates would control Alabama's destiny going into the final year of the rebellion.[51]

4

Alabama's Soldiery and the Elections

On July 2, 1863, Major Robert Sands of the Third Alabama Infantry witnessed a curious incident. The Battle of Gettysburg was well into its second day of carnage, and the men in his regiment were enduring a heavy Union cannonade from Culp's Hill. Leaning against a tree for protection, Sands observed a nearby private cursing loudly and flailing about on the ground. During a subsequent lull in the firing, the major queried the frantic soldier and learned that the man had accidentally unearthed a hive of yellow jackets. Asked why he did not get away, the private blurted out, "You see them Yanks, up yonder? They Shoot. You see them yaller jackets there? They sting. Bullets kill; but yaller jackets don't. I tuk the yaller jackets."[1]

Humor aside, this anecdote serves as a political metaphor for Alabamians in 1863. In fighting for their new nation on faraway battlefields against an obvious and hated enemy, the "Yanks," Alabama's soldiers suffered unexpected stings from the home front, where peace Confederates (i.e., "yaller jackets") betrayed the frontline sacrifice with manifestos to end the war short of victory. In his study of Civil War soldiers, Joseph Allan Frank points out that men on both sides "understood that the war had a political dimension," one that as voting citizens they could influence so as to ensure that politicians back home pushed for total victory. In effect, "the ballot was a political bullet" to be fired at anyone threatening to call it quits. While Frank's thesis is valid for soldiers in most states, technicalities in Alabama's constitution prevented its volunteers from participating in the state elections that August. Thus, Alabama soldiers fought the war with plenty of bullets, but with nary a ballot. As stalwart champions of Confederate independence, they would most certainly have voted in large numbers for war Confederate candidates had they been able. Instead, Alabama's citizen-soldiers could only figuratively swat in vain at political developments beyond their control.[2]

In most revolutionary wars, the heart and soul of the cause is the patriotism of the army in rebellion. When it comes to the American Civil War, many historians conclude that Johnny Reb very much wanted to win and put forth a prodigious effort. "Soldiers rightly saw themselves in the vanguard of the struggle for independence," Gary W. Gallagher asserts in his study of Confederate nationalism. Consequently, they made the ultimate sacrifice at a frighteningly high level. "No other white Americans," Gallagher further elaborates, "have lost such a huge percentage of their young men killed or maimed." In accounting for this willingness to die, Jason Phillips speaks of a "resilient ethos or culture of invincibility" that pervaded the ranks of the Confederate army. According to Phillips, rebels utterly despised the Yankees and refused to believe that people from the North could ever conquer the mighty South. The ordeal of combat, regardless of a particular battle's outcome, intensified this determination to drive the invader from southern soil. Even after terrible defeats at Gettysburg and Vicksburg, Phillips maintains that Confederate soldiers "persevered and remained hopeful." Charles Royster agrees, writing in his examination of the war's destructiveness that despite the defeats of 1863, "soldiers still had the capacity both to repel the enemy and to embody the South's aspirations to cultural and political independence." In effect, the Confederate fighting man had become the face of his nation—and he knew it.[3]

Reinforcing this notion of a martial Confederate ideology is the scholarship of James M. McPherson, Reid Mitchell, and Joseph Allen Frank, who contend that inchoate nationalism greatly helped sustain rebel soldiers at the front, particularly from 1863 onward. McPherson identifies a symbiotic connection between love of liberty and love of country as a persistent factor in southern perseverance. "Such words as *glory, honor, courage, sacrifice, valor,* and *sacred,*" he insists, were not just empty platitudes or romantic abstractions, but serious descriptors of genuine southern nationalism. "How smugly can we sneer at their expressions of a willingness to die for those beliefs," McPherson concludes, "when we know that they did precisely that?" Mitchell elaborates on Confederate ideology, describing it as a combination of "white supremacy, economic opportunity, and resistance to governmental interference," with the soldier seeing himself as "a defender of a democratic and virtuous society." Despite military reversals at the front and deteriorating conditions back home, the rebel fighting man generally remained loyal. In fact, Mitchell says of the soldier that "his suffering proved his patriotism and thus raised his self-esteem." Frank presents Confederate ideology at its extreme, arguing that most rebel soldiers displayed an outright mania for victory. "Reflecting a morally intransigent view of the war," he explains, "Southerners swore never to make peace with the invader [and] vowed to kill Northerners without compunction." Consequently, soldiers became the militant personification of nationalism; their vision for the South—absolute independence through a sanguinary triumph over the hated Yankee—became the only objective that they could accept from their political leaders.[4]

Of course, not every southern soldier was a Confederate nationalist. In his study of military culture during the Civil War, Randall C. Jimerson asserts that while "most [Confederate] soldiers wanted peace only with victory, an increasing number favored peace at any price." Exceptions to the notion of a diehard rebel soldiery include conscripts who often deserted, malcontents infected by the defeatism of the Peace Society, and the "later enlisters," men who joined the army well after the martial romance of the war's first year had dissolved into a grim struggle for survival. According to Kenneth W. Noe, later enlisters fought more out of a sense of civic duty than enthusiasm for the cause, though he finds that Alabamians among this group "clearly were more motivated politically" than those from other states. In a recent case study on Alabama, Kristopher A. Teters observes that while slaveholding soldiers were zealous, yeomen in the ranks tended to be less chauvinistic about Confederate independence. Significantly, however, Noe and Teters note that both later enlisters and yeomen in general proved to be reliable and loyal soldiers. Even Bell I. Wiley, whose study of the common soldier is skeptical of rebel fanaticism, concedes that "the morale of soldiers seems always to have been better than that of civilians."[5]

This is not to say that Rebel soldiers were happy; they rarely were. Much like their Yankee counterparts, they complained about virtually everything when it came to life in the army. "To anyone that has been in or about camp," observed an Alabama newspaper correspondent, "*grumbling* is the chief characteristic." Soldiers grumbled about campground drill, they opined about incompetent officers, they protested delays in payroll, they howled about the poor quality and quantity of mess—which all too often took the form of the infamous pork grease and cornmeal concoction known as "Cush"—they mourned fallen comrades, and they displayed homesickness. In a letter to his wife, Private Thomas Warrick of the Thirty-Fourth Alabama Infantry pithily summed up these manifold tribulations: "Such is the fate of a Confederate soldier." But none of this should suggest that southerners in the ranks were ever ready to surrender. The extant letters and diaries of Confederate soldiers, particularly those from Alabama, do not often refer to the cause, but when they do a resolve to win is unmistakable, the innumerable other irritations with army life notwithstanding. It is natural for men in arms to gripe and carp about hardships, and to miss their homes and loved ones; these complaints are universal to all armies throughout history.[6]

To be fair, a small portion of Alabama's soldiery did briefly yield to the siren call of defeatism. In summer 1863, for example, officers from the Fifty-Ninth and Sixtieth Alabama Infantry Regiments (both formerly part of Hilliard's Legion) reported instances of disaffection in the ranks stemming from the circulation of Peace Society propaganda while the units were stationed in Knoxville, Tennessee. One such item predicted that "the Yankees will whip our Rumps by Christmas." Nothing deleterious came of it, however, and unit commanders evidently restored morale, in some cases through participation in a prowar soldiers' club known as the Comrades of the Southern Cross, which organized within the Army of Tennessee in August 1863. A more serious incident involving the Peace Society occurred at Pollard, Alabama. From December 1863 through January 1864, upwards of one hundred men, mostly conscripts, from the Fifty-Seventh and Sixty-First Alabama Infantry Regiments went on strike, refusing to participate further in the war. The Confederate government ignored calls to have these so-called mutineers shot and instead transferred the regiments to the front, where they actually performed with noteworthy courage. So, if we set aside the various exceptions and dismiss the ubiquitous grousing within the ranks, the fighting men discussed in this study constitute the dependable combat power of the field armies, those who could be counted on to be present when actual fighting was called for; they were the real soldiers of Confederacy, they were the true patriots of the South, they were their young nation's last, best hope.[7]

Alabama soldiers typified the warrior image. "The spirit of the troops at the front was high to the last," Walter L. Fleming says of the state's volunteers. They were, in other words, unabashed war Confederates. At the time of the 1863 election, Alabama's official contribution to the Confederate army amounted to approximately seventy-three thousand men (table 7). These men were distributed among fifty-five infantry regiments, fourteen cavalry regiments, eighteen artillery batteries, and a half dozen or more specialized battalions. In actuality, just under thirty thousand were on active duty, with about 6,700 of them serving in the Army of Northern Virginia, another 6,300 defending the Vicksburg–Port Hudson area, upwards of twelve thousand in the Army of Tennessee, some 2,500 guarding Mobile Bay, and at least two thousand (mostly cavalry) operating in the Tennessee River valley, as well as several hundred Alabamians serving as field-grade officers, staff personnel, surgeons, and chaplains. This disparity between strength on paper and strength in the field is a product of wartime wear and tear that was common to all Civil War units. In addition to an estimated twelve thousand or so Alabamians who had already died after two years of rebellion, thousands more had been discharged with wounds, perhaps another eight thousand or so had deserted, and an indeterminate number were simply absent for reasons ranging from self-extended furloughs to special assignments to just plain malingering. Replacements grew increasingly scarce even with conscription. Historian James M. McPherson notes that by summer 1863, the average strength of Confederate line units was around 40 percent of the original muster. Therefore, the twenty-nine thousand Alabamians who were still in the ranks constituted the state's warrior class. They were, as Lieutenant Samuel Sprott of the Fortieth Alabama Infantry proudly said, "the last to give up hope in the final success of the southern cause."[8]

The prevalent war Confederate mindset of Alabama soldiers cannot be overstated, and it is crucial to qualifying the results of the 1863 election. There is perhaps no better statement of the men's combat creed than that of Private Henry Wood of the Twelfth Alabama Infantry. An overseer from Coosa County, Wood penned a lengthy letter to his father in May 1862 in which the private forcefully explained his motivation: "I am in for the war; I shouldered my musket, and it must not be thrown down . . . until the nations of the earth, including the proud boasting North, shall confess that we are not rebels; but a nation of freemen, who know our rights, and knowing dare maintain them." Captured at Gettysburg, Wood subsequently died in a Union prison camp. His father published this letter in November 1864 as a reminder to all of his son's honorable sacrifice.[9]

Alabamians serving in units deployed all over the South echoed Wood's resolve in the early months of 1863. In February, the officers and men of the Twenty-Ninth Alabama Infantry (then stationed along the Florida border) unanimously adopted a resolution pledging to follow the patriotic example of the Revolutionary generation in never giving up the fight: "As long as the foe advances, or his foot pollutes our soil, we will be found ready to combat him." That same month, Henry Pond, a lieutenant in the Thirteenth Alabama Infantry wrote home from Virginia a letter that revealed a mixture of optimism and anxiety. "I have come to the conclusion that this war, the wicked war, will *Soon* Cease, for I *cannot* see how it can much longer exist," he informed his father. Rightly convinced that something decisive awaited his regiment for the summer, he concluded his correspondence, "I believe the glory will be ours, what do you say Pa?" Pond did win glory, though not victory. He was captured at Gettysburg on July 3, while participating in what became known as Pickett's Charge.[10]

April 1863 marked the second anniversary of the war's beginning. Several Alabama soldiers reflected on the moment both with pride in having held out for so long against the vaunted power of the North and with a renewed devotion to their young nation. "I believe our cause is just," Lieutenant Elias Davis of the Tenth Alabama Infantry explained to his wife back in Shelby County, "and believing it to be just, I am confident that God will not allow us to be starved into submission." He then glibly added, "I have no fear of Enemy shooting us into subjugation." A few weeks later, after Davis and his regiment fought in the great rebel victory at Chancellorsville, Virginia, he jubilantly wrote to his wife again: "Mr. Lincoln must raise new armies or cease

Table 7. Alabama Soldiers—August 1863 (by County)

County	Companies/Batteries[a]	Official[b]	Actual[c]	Voters[d]	WC[e]
Autauga	4.5 Infantry; 2.5 Cavalry	700	280	168	134
Baldwin	2 Infantry	200	80	48	38
Barbour	20.5 Infantry; 4 Cavalry; 1.5 Artillery	2,600	1,040	312	250
Bibb	9.5 Infantry	950	380	228	182
Blount	11 Infantry; 1 Cavalry	1,200	480	288	230
Butler	15 Infantry; 2 Cavalry; 0.2 Artillery	1,720	688	413	330
Calhoun	19 Infantry; 4 Cavalry; 0.2 Artillery	2,320	928	557	445
Chambers	10.5 Infantry; 3 Cavalry	1,350	540	324	259
Cherokee	14 Infantry; 3 Cavalry	1,700	680	408	326
Choctaw	7.5 Infantry; 1 Cavalry	850	340	204	163
Clarke	10 Infantry; 1 Cavalry	1,100	440	264	211
Coffee	8 Infantry; 1.5 Cavalry	950	380	228	182
Conecuh	8 Infantry	800	320	192	154
Coosa	15.5 Infantry; 1.5 Cavalry	1,700	680	408	326
Covington	5 Infantry	500	200	120	96
Dale	7.5 Infantry; 0.5 Cavalry	800	320	192	154
Dallas	9 Infantry; 2.5 Cavalry; 0.45 Artillery	1,195	478	287	229
DeKalb	6 Infantry; 5 Cavalry	1,100	440	264	211
Fayette	13.5 Infantry; 1 Cavalry	1,450	580	348	278
Franklin	8 Infantry; 4.5 Cavalry	1,250	500	300	240
Greene	9.5 Infantry; 2 Cavalry	1,150	460	276	221
Henry	10 Infantry; 1 Cavalry	1,100	440	264	211
Jackson	16.5 Infantry; 4 Cavalry	2,050	820	492	394
Jefferson	11 Infantry; 2 Cavalry	1,300	520	312	250
Lauderdale	10 Infantry; 3 Cavalry	1,300	520	312	250
Lawrence	8 Infantry; 7 Cavalry	1,500	600	360	288
Limestone	7.5 Infantry; 1 Cavalry	850	340	204	163
Lowndes	11 Infantry; 2 Cavalry; 0.2 Artillery	1,320	528	317	253
Macon	21.5 Infantry; 0.5 Cavalry; 0.3 Artillery	2,230	892	535	428
Madison	8 Infantry; 5 Cavalry; 1 Artillery	1,400	560	336	269
Marengo	8.5 Infantry; 1 Cavalry; 0.45 Artillery	995	398	239	191
Marion	6 Infantry; 2.5 Cavalry	850	340	204	163
Marshall	10.5 Infantry; 2 Cavalry	1,250	500	300	240
Mobile	42.5 Infantry; 1 Cavalry; 6 Artillery	4,950	1,980	1,188	950
Monroe	7.5 Infantry; 3 Cavalry	1,050	420	252	202
Montgomery	16.5 Infantry; 10 Cavalry; 2.5 Artillery	2,900	1,160	696	557
Morgan	3.5 Infantry; 6 Cavalry	950	380	228	182
Perry	10.5 Infantry; 0.5 Cavalry; 0.45 Artillery	1,145	458	275	220

Table 7. *Continued*

County	Companies/Batteries[a]	Official[b]	Actual[c]	Voters[d]	WC[e]
Pickens	14 Infantry; 2 Cavalry	1,600	640	384	307
Pike	23.5 Infantry; 3.5 Cavalry	2,700	1,080	648	518
Randolph	15 Infantry; 4 Cavalry	1,900	760	456	365
Russell	9.5 Infantry; 1.3 Artillery	1,080	432	259	207
Shelby	11.5 Infantry; 2 Cavalry; 0.25 Artillery	1,375	550	330	264
St. Clair	9 Infantry; 1 Cavalry	1,000	400	240	192
Sumter	7 Infantry; 1 Cavalry	800	320	192	154
Talladega	19.5 Infantry; 2 Cavalry; 0.2 Artillery	2,170	868	521	417
Tallapoosa	17 Infantry; 4 Cavalry; 0.3 Artillery	2,130	852	511	409
Tuscaloosa	13 Infantry; 2 Cavalry; 2.5 Artillery	1,750	700	420	336
Walker	13.5 Infantry; 1 Cavalry	1,450	580	348	278
Washington	3.5 Infantry	350	140	84	67
Wilcox	9.5 Infantry; 4 Cavalry	1,350	540	324	259
Winston	None	100	40	24	19
Misc.	6 Artillery	600	240	144	115
F & S[f]		400	400	400	320
Total		73,480	29,632	17,628	14,097

[a] Companies/Batteries are either infantry or cavalry companies and artillery batteries. The numbers in this column indicate the sum of the units of this type raised within a given county. For example, Tuscaloosa raised thirteen companies of infantry, two companies of cavalry, and two and a half batteries of artillery, for an official manpower total of 1,750 soldiers.
[b] Official refers to the number of men stipulated by the designated unit if it were at full strength (one hundred men for all unit types).
[c] Actual refers to the number of men actually present for combat (40 percent of the official figure by 1863), although batteries were usually kept near their full complement.
[d] Voters refers to the number of men who were twenty-one years of age or older, hence eligible to vote (60 percent of those actually present).
[e] WC indicates the number of men who identified with the War Confederate outlook (80 percent of those who could vote).
[f] F & S (Field and Staff) were the headquarters element within every regiment and typically comprised one colonel, one lieutenant colonel, one major, one adjutant, one surgeon, and one chaplain, for at least six additional personnel for each of the sixty-nine active duty infantry and cavalry regiments.

Sources: Willis Brewer, *Alabama: Her History, Resources, War Record, and Public Men from 1540 to 1872* (Montgomery, AL: Barrett and Brown, 1872), 589–705; Donald Bradford Dodd, "Unionism in Confederate Alabama" (PhD diss., University of Georgia, 1969), 151 (for Winston).

to fight us. . . . Let them tremble for their day of retribution is not far distant." In the western theater, Lieutenant Joshua Callaway of the Twenty-Eighth Alabama Infantry expressed similar certitude in a letter to his own wife. "I feel confident that the war is now in its 'last stage' . . . it will be the final, Death struggle of the expiring Despotism," he said of the North, whose soldiers he referred to as an "immense Conscript army." "If we can foil him at every point during the next six months," Callaway predicted, "the States will all secede from the old union, and one by one they will ask admittance into the Confederacy." Back home in Pike County, local lawyer John Hubbard shared Callaway's defiance. Addressing a company of men serving in the newly raised Fifty-Seventh Alabama Infantry, he warned the recruits that their state faced "total extermination" at the hands of invaders that were "more cruel than the hordes of Attila." He then reassured them that "war is liberty's trysting time, and in it she sows the seeds of national greatness—and from the blood of heroes springs the noblest spirit of Independence." Hubbard had been wounded a year earlier at Shiloh, and so his words carried the imprimatur of one of those very heroes. His speech was mass produced and distributed throughout the ranks.[11]

All this Confederate jingoism received a devastating jolt during the first week of July. On July 3, Lee's vaunted Army of Northern Virginia suffered a resounding defeat at Gettysburg, and on July 4, the Vicksburg garrison capitulated after enduring a seven-week-long siege. Historian Chandra Manning speaks of widespread demoralization in the days that followed, though she stresses that the sudden reversal of military fortune produced more anxiety in the ranks than it did defeatism. "It did not amount to a desire to return to the Union," she says of the twin defeats, "but it taxed the Confederate cause and the men who fought for it." Jason Phillips further downplays the situation, contending that rebel soldiers viewed the summertime losses mostly as an unwelcome prolongation of the struggle. For one Alabamian serving in Virginia, the setbacks only hardened his resolve to fight a protracted war. "I expect to see the black flag floating over our two armies," he predicted; "All these things have a tendency to make us more desperate, rather than despond and feel like giving up." This "Voice from the Army" captured the prevailing attitude of Alabama's front-line fighters.[12]

Gettysburg and Vicksburg are often coupled together in discussions of the impact of defeat on the Confederate soldiers' mindset, but as Phillips notes, "contemporaries treated the events quite differently." Examining the outcome of each battle individually reveals a more qualified reaction. At Gettysburg, the Army of Northern Virginia suffered an astounding twenty-four thousand casualties as Lee's second invasion of the North came to a decisive end. Among the losses were 2,200 Alabamians. Nonetheless, this army remained a formidable and highly motivated fighting organization. It is well understood by historians that morale in the Army of Northern Virginia was the highest anywhere in the Confederacy. Under its beloved commander, General Robert E. Lee, this army had compiled a most impressive military record. It scored victories at the Seven Days, at Second Manassas, at Fredericksburg, and at Chancellorsville. Even the strategic setback at Antietam in 1862 could be spun into a worthy tactical success. Gettysburg was that army's first real defeat, yet it only temporarily dampened the spirit of the rank and file, including those from the Alabama regiments. "You seem to be discouraged at the late reverses to our cause," Private James Branscomb of the Third Alabama Infantry chided his sister a month after the battle, "but wait a while and you will hear of another great victory from Genl Lee's army that will cheer every southern heart." Lieutenant Elias Davis of the Tenth Alabama shared Branscomb's optimism. "We can whip Federal Army of Potomac," he wrote to his wife in a letter that dismissed Gettysburg as an aberration. "Enemy will have it that our army is demoralized," he went on; "We will prove to the world to the contrary." Likewise, Lieutenant Ebenezer Coggin of the Forty-Seventh Alabama Infantry expressed unshakeable faith in the Army of Northern Virginia, though he did wonder whether its Federal adversaries would ever realize their military inferiority. "We will fight them any time and we generally git the Best of it according to our Number," he wrote to his wife after Gettysburg; "But they allways have as many more men as we Do." Nonetheless, Coggin was committed to a total victory no matter the cost in time or lives: "I think that we will fight the Enemy for the Next 10 years to come," he further elaborated, "the yanks may Kill all of us though they Cannot Never whip General Lee."[13]

For many of Lee's Alabama boys, the carnage at Gettysburg actually clarified why they were fighting in the first place. Three veterans, two from the Ninth Alabama Infantry and one from the Sixth Alabama Infantry, composed prose paeans that, taken together, serve as a rebel version of the Gettysburg Address. "Eighty Seven years ago today, our forefathers declared that henceforth and forever they were and of right ought to be free," penned Lieutenant Edmund Patterson in his journal the day after his capture on July 3, in a phrase strikingly similar to the opening line of Lincoln's address. "Today the South contends for the same principles which fired the hearts of our ancestors in the revolutionary struggle," Patterson continued, "and as sure as right and justice prevail, so surely will we finally triumph." Back in northern Virginia, Private William McClellan resumed Patterson's peroration with a patriotic affirmation of his own (one that he wrote in a letter to his sister): "We have fought too much to give up now, too many gallant Spirits have been Slain; too many voices would cry out from their graves for revenge to give up the Boon for which they died. No we must fight on, fight ever until the end of time." And on a nearby campground, Lieutenant Thomas Taylor expressed comparable resolve to his own sister. "We must fight if we expect to be free," he explained, "Let us be as determined to be Free as they are to subjugate us & all will be well." These are powerful statements. Had they not been proclaimed for the lost cause, they might enjoy the same veneration that Americans now bestow on similar words uttered in behalf of the Union. They are also statements from soldiers who epitomize the war Confederate mentality.[14]

Although the impact of Gettysburg seemed relatively insignificant to Alabama soldiers, the same cannot be said about Vicksburg. The capitulation of this citadel elicited genuine consternation among the men, particularly those in the western armies, about the fate of the Confederacy. In his definitive study of the siege, Michael B. Ballard reiterates the prevailing scholarly assessment of Union success at Vicksburg. In taking the city, the Federal army not only gained permanent control over the Mississippi River, it unhinged the entire Confederate defense in the West. Moreover, its victory set in motion a noticeable panic among southern soldiers and civilians alike. "In regard to our country's afflictions, I have never yet despaired," Captain George K. Miller, an Alabamian in the Eighth Confederate Cavalry, wrote to his wife prior to the surrender of Vicksburg. His tone changed afterward: "Upon hearing of the fall of our great Stronghold I felt myself as tho' I would never live to see peace." Private Grant Taylor of the Fortieth Alabama Infantry experienced a similarly unhappy volte-face. In the months before Vicksburg fell he expressed optimism. "This is the strongest natural position that I ever saw and then it is well fortified," he wrote in January 1863 to his wife in Pickens County, "I do not believe there is any chance for the Yanks to get it." But in the months after the battle, he described serious morale problems among his comrades: "They are generally low spirited and think our cause is gone. . . . They feel like they are sacrificing their lives and their all for nothing." Lieutenant Samuel Sprott, also from the Fortieth Alabama, was more blunt. "The fall of Vicksburg sounded the death knell of the Confederacy," he said, years after the war, "and from that time on it was a hopeless struggle." Sprott did, however, equate Vicksburg to the great Siege of Sevastopol during the Crimean War; he drew immense pride from having participated in it even as he acknowledged its military import. It must be noted that despite their misgivings, all three of these men remained on active duty until the war's end.[15]

Many Confederate soldiers, however, did not stay on to the end. The loss of Vicksburg (and to a lesser extent the defeat at Gettysburg) inaugurated a wave of desertion, one that several historians emphasize as a sign of diminishing fervor for the rebellion. "Men were leaving through every door possible," Mark A. Weitz contends in his comprehensive study of the topic; "desertion was killing the Confederate army." Such comments, however, are overstated. The only specific numbers that anyone cites for Alabama deserters in 1863 are between six thousand and ten thousand—admittedly a large figure, but hardly the epidemic that Weitz describes. Besides, desertion rates within the Confederacy at this time were comparable to those in the Union army, yet few have used this fact to argue that Federal troops were ready to call it quits. Desertion did rise in the wake of Vicksburg, but the phenomenon did not significantly undermine Confederate combat ability until the latter half of 1864, when virtually all southerners realized that military defeat was a certainty. (An estimated nineteen thousand Alabamians deserted over the course of the entire war.) The truth is that most soldiers, especially those with war Confederate convictions, generally despised desertion, seeing it as both dishonorable and criminal. "I want to come home," Private John W. Cotton of the Tenth Confederate Cavalry confessed to his wife in May 1863, "but I shant run away." A yeoman farmer from Coosa County, Cotton exemplified the common southerner's sense of duty: "I don't want it throwed up to my children after I am dead and gone that I was a deserter from the confederate army . . . that will leave a stain on my posterity." Private Hiram T. Holt of the Thirty-Eighth Alabama Infantry considered desertion to be the most heinous act of wartime cowardice. On learning that two of his comrades had absconded back to Choctaw County, he fumed to his wife, "let the people shoot them just where they find them."[16]

Part of the misperception about rebel desertion in summer 1863 stems from a misunderstanding of what happened to the Vicksburg parolees. After capturing the city, Union general Ulysses S. Grant opted not to imprison the rebel garrison of nearly thirty thousand men (including over three thousand Alabamians) until the usual exchange could be arranged. Instead, he paroled them on the condition that they not take up arms again. The Davis administration, however, accused the North of subverting the long-standing prisoner exchange policy. Accordingly, it unilaterally declared that the former Vicksburg defenders had been exchanged and placed them on furloughs of up to thirty days with orders to then return to duty (Alabamians were told to rejoin their regiments in Demopolis). Not surprisingly, these conflicting directives produced confusion within the ranks. Major Stephens Croom, a staff officer from Greene County, observed what he considered to be a shocking breakdown in discipline. "The men got a notion into their heads that they were entirely free & would not submit to any military control whatever, but straggled all over the country going to their homes." And so hundreds of Alabamians trekked back to their communities; however, this should not be construed as deserting. To be sure, a considerable number did desert, but most eventually returned. Some, like Private James D. Harwell of the Twentieth Alabama, trusted the validity of their "exchange" and willingly reported right away; others needed some coaxing to reassure them that their own government's exchange policy superseded the enemy's parole policy. "But at last orders were peremptorily issued demanding all to assemble at Demopolis," Captain George E. Brewer of the Forty-Sixth Alabama later recalled. In his recent history of the Thirtieth Alabama Infantry, Larry D. Stephens is hesitant to condemn those who stayed at home. "These men had been to hell and back," he explains. "They were far from cowards." Fair enough, but his characterization of those who returned is more telling: "These were the *real heroes* of the 30th Alabama—the men who would keep fighting." During autumn 1863, Confederate authorities reconstituted a great portion of the old Vicksburg garrison, including all eight of the infantry regiments from Alabama that had helped defend the city. The editors of the *Eutaw Whig* declared this development to be a sign that the now-exchanged parolees "burn with anxiety to repay the Yankees the debt they owe for the hardships they underwent at Vicksburg." The newspaper likely exaggerated, but had these men truly turned against the war, then it is most unlikely that so many would have gone back to camp, whether of their own volition or not.[17]

Caught in the middle of the Gettysburg and Vicksburg fiascos was the Army of Tennessee, which was stationed in southeastern Tennessee at the time. The reaction of its soldiery to these battles is revealing. To these soldiers, the disaster at Vicksburg was worrisome, but it also appears to have intensified their patriotic fervor. This army never won the laurels of its storied counterpart in Virginia, but it had handled itself with courage and ability in such battles as Perryville and Murfreesboro, developing what historian Larry J. Daniel calls an "indomitable spirit." With the fall of Vicksburg, the men in the ranks understood that they were, for all practical purposes, the last real defenders of the Confederate heartland. "Cheer up," Colonel John Sanford of the Sixtieth Alabama Infantry consoled his mother in mid-July, "The enemy cannot subdue us. Our independence will be established and our liberties secured." In correspondence less blasé, Sergeant Edward N. Brown of the Forty-Fifth Alabama Infantry regarded Vicksburg as merely part of the conflict's inevitable vicissitudes. "War has become a business with us & we have learned to bear misfortunes as if they must come as a matter of course," he reassured his wife back in Barbour County. "The tide will turn again in our favor. . . . Battles are only incidents to the great end to be obtained. . . . Fight on, fight ever is my motto." Captain Stouten Dent echoed Brown's stoic optimism in a letter to his family, also from Barbour County. "I expect you all have the blues over the military news," he wrote in mid-July, adding, however, "I am getting accustomed to it—and do not feel dispirited either." Dent then went on to qualify the bad news: "Fifteen months ago affairs were as gloomy as they are now and we redeemed them. We may do it again. Let us hope for the best."[18]

Among the most devoted soldiers in the Army of Tennessee was Joshua K. Callaway, a schoolteacher from Dallas County serving as a lieutenant in Company K, Twenty-Eighth Alabama Infantry. The loss of Vicksburg admittedly left him feeling "sad and depressed," but he rebounded quickly. In the immediate wake of that defeat, Callaway authored a series of letters over the course of a fortnight that not only conveyed his own rejuvenated patriotism, but cogently articulated the front-line resolve of most Confederate soldiers. "We are not whipped by any means," he bluntly exclaimed to his wife on July 11, adding that he was prepared to fight the war "for the next 50 years." "There is no telling where our reverses are going to end," he related on July 16; "But our trust is in God and our cause is just." (This last statement became a refrain in many of the lieutenant's subsequent letters.) "The Yankees have largely the advantage of us," he elaborated on July 19; "Nevertheless I am not out of heart." Finally, on July 23, Callaway expressed a sentiment that succinctly epitomized the war Confederate outlook: "I have never thought for a moment that we would finally fail, but I am almost sick at the thought of the blood, treasure and long war it is going to take before we establish our independence." Tragically, the end for the twenty-eight-year-old lieutenant came sooner than he could have known. On November 25, 1863, Joshua Callaway suffered a mortal bullet wound to his stomach while serving as his company's acting commander during the Battle of Missionary Ridge.[19]

Obviously, soldiers recognized both Gettysburg and Vicksburg as military failures, but they were hardly a broken force. "Gloom and despair could trouble diehards for a while," Jason Phillips aptly explains, "but they often restored their faith during the worst circumstances." Anne Sarah Rubin concurs, stating that "with the passage of time, soldiers' spirits rebounded from the defeats of early summer." So it was that thousands of officers and men rallied with remarkable speed. Those in the Army of Northern Virginia were just as upbeat after these defeats as they were before; those in the Army of Tennessee were a bit less cocky, but no less committed; and the Vicksburg parolees, though momentarily downcast immediately after their surrender, still willingly returned to the ranks once more. "Fellow soldiers never question our ultimate success," Brigadier General Henry Clayton exhorted his Alabama regiments at the end of that rough summer, "Our cause is righteous, being the defense of our homes, and our families." Taking such words to heart,

Alabamians stood by their country's flag in sufficient numbers to maintain a viable battlefield presence for another year and half.[20]

Given their manifest commitment to southern independence, it is a terrible irony that Alabama's soldiers were unable to participate in the election of 1863. According to Article III, Section 5, of the 1861 state constitution, voters had to be twenty-one years of age *and* maintain residence in their precinct for "the last three months" prior to an election. Obviously, soldiers at the front did not qualify under the letter of the law. Private William McClellan of the Ninth Alabama Infantry joked that if residency was the principal issue, then he should have been allowed to vote in Virginia's state elections, having been stationed there for nearly two years. All kidding aside, toward the end of 1862, war Confederates began to realize that this technicality might not only bode ill for their political prospects in 1863 but also represent a slap in the face to the valor of the fighting man. Twice that autumn (October 29 and November 12), Levi W. Lawler, a prowar legislator from Talladega County, introduced a bill in the House to "prevent the disfranchisement of soldiers in the army from Alabama." In essence, Lawler was resurrecting and expanding a recently expired law that had authorized soldiers in the field to vote in the national elections of 1861. Both times, however, the Judiciary Committee, though sympathetic to the soldiers' plight, reported adversely on Lawler's bill, arguing that the 1861 act was a special exception, whereas any further changes to voter qualifications would require a constitutional amendment; and that was a change that the committee deemed too impractical during the stress of war. The Alabama Senate concurred. Naturally, the soldiers were upset. In response, the *Montgomery Advertiser* offered a legal justification for the assembly's action before it condescendingly dismissed further objection. "We are sure," the editors lectured, "it is a matter about which the great body of the soldiery feel comparatively indifferent as long as there is a foe in front of them to engage their attention." John Hubbard, a veteran and editor of the prowar *Southern Advertiser*, was more understanding. "Shall the people at home bargain away our brave heroes in the field?" he asked immediately after the election, when it became apparent that peace Confederates had won many races. "Surely the men who endure all should have some right to end the contest." It was not to be.[21]

Alabama's soldiers were displeased by their government's failure to reform the voting requirements, but they obeyed the law all the same. Consequently, the election returns would not reflect the political outlook of the state's most devoted citizens. Using twenty-nine thousand as a working figure for the number of Alabamians who were outside of their home precincts on the day of the election, and reducing the tally by approximately twelve thousand to account for those under twenty-one years of age, it is fair to say that about seventeen thousand potential votes were never recorded. Officially, around thirty-nine thousand Alabamians voted in the election. Had the front-line soldiers also voted, then their portion of the returns would have composed an impressive 30 percent. This possibility is especially significant when compared to the much discussed Union soldier vote for Abraham Lincoln in 1864. In that election, absentee ballots from the field amounted to only 4 percent of the total cast, yet because most of these ballots went for the incumbent, they are rightly seen as a powerful testament of bluecoat commitment to total victory. In the case of Alabama, however, the state readily gave its soldiers bullets with which to kill the enemy, but deprived them of ballots with which to ensure the election of leaders who would honor their service. Captain Henry Semple, an artillery officer in the Army of Tennessee, considered the soldiers' impotence in political matters to be a great misfortune. "I think if the peace question could be submitted to our own troops & the troops of the enemy we could speedily come to an understanding," he wrote to his wife back in Montgomery, "but the men who fight the battles have little to do with the arrangement of difficulties beyond the fighting out of them." In one of his Civil War essays, David Herbert Donald quipped that the Confederacy "Died of Democracy" because the government ostensibly permitted the rank and file too much freedom, individualism, and insubordination. As a consequence, the rebel armies never matured into brutally efficient killing machines like their Union counterparts. Donald's argument is provocative but unconvincing, for the suffrage is a fundamental right of any democracy, yet Alabama quashed the political liberty of its warrior class. Seen in this context, Donald's epitaph would be more apt if it read "Death by Democracy Denied."[22]

Their de facto disfranchisement notwithstanding, Alabama soldiers still paid attention to the August elections. The three gubernatorial candidates attracted a fair amount of interest. Private James B. Daniel of the Forty-Seventh Alabama Infantry evidently disliked the incumbent John Gill Shorter, particularly given the administration's policies on conscription and the militia. "I Surpose the governor is a going to take all hands and the cook," he grumbled to his wife in July. Neither endorsing nor condemning any of the candidates, Daniel glumly predicted that "we may fight a long time yet," no matter the election's outcome. Lieutenant James B. Mitchell of the Thirty-Fourth Alabama Infantry seemed inclined to support the incumbent, but he solicited his father's opinion on the matter: "Do you thinke Gov. Shorter will be reelected? Who Will?" An anonymous Alabamian in the Army of Tennessee, however, expressed no indecision. In a letter to the *Montgomery Advertiser*, this soldier, who went by the moniker "A Voice from the Army," urged his readers to vote for Shorter. Listing the governor's many accomplishments on behalf of the war effort, he asked whether anyone could have done better under the circumstances. "The man don't live who can preserve his self-respect and say Gov. Shorter is not *capable* or that he is not *honest*." Matthew Sanders, an artillery lieutenant from Greene County, agreed, praising the governor for his "great energy and zealous vigilance." Even a soldier from beyond Alabama found Shorter's leadership impressive. While visiting Montgomery in October 1862, Sergeant Joe T. Scott of the Twentieth Georgia Infantry spoke highly of the governor's efforts at prosecuting the war, particularly the relief programs for war-torn families. "A truer, nobler Southern patriot never breathed," Scott said of Governor Shorter.[23]

Thomas Hill Watts had his fans among the rank and file, too. On July 18, the men of the Twenty-Fifth Alabama Infantry—a regiment drawn from the state's eastern and southeastern counties—signed a petition titled, "Soldiers for Judge Watts." With a touch of resentment, the petitioners acknowledged the legal ban on their right to participate in the election, but they insisted that their preference for governor be made known to the electorate, "if for no other reason [than] from a sense of justice to the absent and disfranchised soldier." Describing their man as "indomitable" and "indispensable," the soldiers "earnestly" recommended that the voters "give to Hon. Thomas H. Watts, their warm and unqualified support." The extent to which this petition was circulated through the newspapers is unknown.[24]

Prior to their surrender, Alabamians in the Vicksburg garrison exerted some genuine influence over the gubernatorial contest. With all due respect to Governor Shorter, the men of the Twentieth Alabama Infantry thought that their state needed a war veteran at the helm. To this end, they nominated their commander, Colonel Isham W. Garrott. As a former states' rights Democrat and secession commissioner, as well as a proven combat leader, Garrott was unimpeachable in his war Confederate credentials. He declined to run, however, preferring, as he said, "to remain at my post in defense of the great cause for which we are struggling." On June 17, a Union sniper killed Garrott as the colonel inspected his regiment's entrenchments outside Vicksburg. Determined to put one of Vicksburg's defenders in the statehouse, the men of the Thirty-Seventh Alabama Infantry then nominated for governor their own colonel, James F. Dowdell. Unlike Garrott, Dowdell humbly agreed to run even though both he and his men were then besieged inside the port city.[25]

At the end of May 1863, soldiers in the Fifteenth Alabama Infantry conducted a straw poll for governor, even as they prepared to embark on the Gettysburg Campaign. The outcome saw votes evenly distributed between Shorter and Watts. Those who liked Shorter stressed his "purity of character."

Those who liked Watts emphasized his "capacity" for the job. Apparently, as far as the extant sources indicate, there was no overwhelming favorite for governor among the ranks. Significantly, while soldiers certainly preferred a particular candidate, there was very little disparagement of the other contenders. This lack of vitriol is probably because all three candidates were solid war Confederates. In the end it really did not matter to the soldiers who became governor, provided he was committed to military success. Watts's eventual victory elicited no dissatisfaction from the ranks. The same cannot be said of the other electoral outcomes.[26]

Soldier views on the three most hotly contested congressional races reveal more emphatically the front line's preference for war Confederates. Popular among the ranks was Congressman Jabez Curry, a hard-liner from the state's Fourth District. On July 13, Curry toured the campgrounds of the Army of Tennessee, then stationed near Chattanooga. As part of his visit, the incumbent delivered a political speech to the five regiments in General Zachariah Deas's all-Alabama brigade. Listening attentively was Calvin J. C. Munroe, a private in the Twenty-Fifth Alabama Infantry and a fellow resident from Curry's home county of Talladega. A few days later, Munroe related to his sister how the congressman's words noticeably lifted the men's spirits at a time when "our fate as a nation looks very gloomy." While neglecting to mention any of the details, Munroe exclaimed that the speech "was the best thing I have ever heard he made a great many of his enemys open their eyes." Still, Munroe was aware of the Peace Society's influence back home: "for all that I am afraid he will get beat." And Curry did, indeed, lose to the peace Confederate Marcus Cruikshank, an outcome that infuriated Captain Joseph R. Cowan of the Twenty-Second Alabama Infantry. Cowan, too, presumably heard the speech and angrily queried the citizens back home, "Why was Curry beaten for Congress?" Appalled by what he described as "the ideas and hints of reconstruction," Cowan castigated the people for electing a defeatist to represent Alabama's Fourth District. "The Rubicon is crossed, and it is too late to turn back," he growled, "*Subjugation means extermination.*"[27]

Alabama soldiers from Jackson County (part of the Second District) displayed their war Confederate sympathies through deeds rather than words. On the day of the election, twenty-seven cavalry troopers under Captain Francisco Rice marched to the polling place in Princeton, the county seat. Rice, who was also a sitting member of the state Senate, decided that his men would vote for their representative, the law be damned. Evidently, the precinct commissioner acceded, though he marked their ballots "illegal" and refused to include them in the official tally. Nonetheless, he forwarded these soldiers' votes to the secretary of state, and the results are telling. The incumbent John Ralls and war hero Colonel James Sheffield, both war Confederate candidates, received respectively ten and sixteen votes, while the man who actually won the race, peace Confederate Williamson Cobb, received a mere two soldier votes. However small this sample may be, it is a revealing glimpse into the political views of the fighting man. Incidentally, Captain Rice continued to serve in the state assembly as an avowed war Confederate.[28]

Soldiers from the Eighth District, comprising the southeastern counties of the state, also evinced a desire for prowar leadership. This wiregrass region is often seen as a stronghold of unionism, but according to historian Tommy Brown, its residents proved as fervent for the cause as did any other in the state. In June, over one hundred wiregrass men from the Sixth Alabama Infantry (stationed in Virginia) signed a petition urging their neighbors back in Henry County to vote for James L. Pugh, a stalwart war Confederate. Describing Pugh as the "right man in the right place," the petitioners pledged their "zealous and cordial support" for his reelection. Pugh reciprocated the regiment's good will. "To these men the government owes its existence," he explained in a public letter, "to them the people at home are indebted for every thing sacred and valuable, and if hard policy and cold constitutional provisions could be ignored, nothing would be accepted with more pleasure than the ballot of the soldier." The congressman did sweat out a plurality win, but he would certainly have breathed easier had the moral support of his uniformed constituents been translated into real votes. Evidently, that is what the men of the Fifty-Seventh Alabama Infantry had hoped to do. Stationed in Pollard, a town not far from the unit's muster counties in the Eighth District, these particular soldiers queried the governor about whether they could "vote legally." The reply is no longer extant, but it probably instructed the regiment to comply with the law. One of the few dissenting voices from the front line came from Captain Sherman K. Fielder of the Eighteenth Alabama Infantry. Fielder leaned toward the peace Confederate candidacy of McCaleb Wiley, but he did so primarily because both he and Wiley lived in Pike County, whereas Pugh came from Barbour County. "Rotation is fair," Fielder explained in a newspaper letter, "and Pike ought to have one representative in Congress, while Barbour furnishes so many."[29]

Soldier commentary on the legislative races further reflects the fighting man's contempt for antiwar politics. Captain Joab Goodson of the Forty-Fourth Alabama Infantry was especially appalled by developments in his native Bibb County, where James W. Davis, a peace Confederate, won the race for the House seat. "Is Bibb County for the Union, with the Yankees? God forbid," queried the captain in a postelection letter to his niece, "what are we coming to, whither are we drifting? We are fast losing confidence in the patriotism of a great many of the people at home." Colonel Bolling Hall Jr. of the Fifty-Ninth Alabama Infantry was equally disturbed. "The elections at home have had a bad effect among the men," he wrote to his father back in Autauga County, "they think the Unionists & reconstructionists in majority at home & will protect them if they desert." Fearing that Lewis E. Parsons, one of the leading peace Confederates, would go on to become a senator, Hall recommended that such men "come out in strong Southern letters and correct the impressions (if they are really false) which have obtained in the army" that they no longer supported the war. Private William McClellan of the Ninth Alabama Infantry also lamented the prospect of peace Confederates winning so many seats. He dubbed such men "skallawags"; however, he made an exception in the case of his older brother, John B. McClellan. John was a convert to the peace Confederate platform, but he was also a war hero. (As a company commander in the Fiftieth Alabama Infantry, he lost his right arm to enemy fire at the Battle of Murfreesboro.) Even though William disagreed with his big brother's political stance, he believed that his sibling had earned the right to protest the war, unlike so many others who criticized the struggle yet refused to don the uniform.[30]

Although soldiers in general could not vote, quite a few veterans ran for the state legislature. Captain Thomas Clark of the Twentieth Alabama Infantry, for instance, graciously accepted a call to stand for election in Greene County as "the Soldier and the Soldier's Friend." His only caveat was that he be allowed to "remain in the army" whenever the assembly was not in session. Many other prowar officers, including Colonel William Oates of the Fifteenth Alabama Infantry and Captain George Brewer of the Forty-Sixth Alabama Infantry, considered running but ultimately preferred staying in the army. Looking back on the election, Brewer insinuated that he would have won the Senate race in his home county of Coosa. He had held the seat until the call to arms took him away, having defeated in 1859 the man—peace Confederate William Garrett—who won in 1863. In all, of the 230 candidates who ran for the 116 open assembly seats in 1863, about seventy had genuine military credentials, meaning a regular service record in the Confederate army (not some nebulous duty in the state militia or home guard).[31]

Wearing the uniform, however, does not seem to have influenced the balloting. Only twenty-two veterans prevailed at the polls: six won Senate seats, and sixteen won House seats. (Captain Clark was among the losers.) This paltry outcome should come as no surprise given that a great many of their likely supporters were in the ranks, hence disfranchised. Of the soldier politicians who did win, fifteen displayed a pronounced war Confederate mindset. Notable among this group was Lieutenant Colonel Mitchell T. Porter of Jefferson County, who commanded the Twentieth Alabama Infantry at Vicksburg; Captain John Y. Kilpatrick of Clarke County, who made a point of wearing his full-dress cavalry uniform throughout the ensuing legislative session; and Captain Nathaniel H. R. Dawson of Dallas County, a signatory of the Ordinance of Secession and a veteran of First Manassas, where he commanded a company in the Fourth Alabama Infantry. Only five soldier politicians openly caucused with the peace Confederates, including Captain Augustus A. West of Randolph County, who served in the Thirty-First Alabama Infantry and was a known member of the Peace Society, and Captain John B. McClellan. The political affiliation of two veterans is unclear. This 3–1 prowar ratio among veterans mirrors the martial patriotism of Alabama's active-duty soldiery. Unfortunately, the dearth of such veterans in the assembly also reflects the inadequate representation of the fighting man, particularly for a state engaged in an all-out war. Regardless of whether they were for war or peace, veterans accounted for barely 17 percent of Alabama's legislators. Only they could truly empathize with the plight of those at the front, let alone the cause for which so many had and would make the ultimate sacrifice.[32]

While not all soldiers weighed in with a political opinion, those who did were clearly unhappy with the results of the election. Historian Joseph Allen Frank notes that during the Civil War, "the army needed society's reaffirmation of its commitment to the cause." Anything less than unconditional support on the home front bordered on treason. This claim holds true for Alabama. Its soldiers had suspected a decline of will among civilians prior to the election, but such concerns exploded into outrage in its aftermath. In a letter published in the *Montgomery Advertiser*, Captain Thomas R. Lightfoot of the Sixth Alabama Infantry denounced as "the veriest cowards" those who promoted peace without victory. "While the true men of the South are fighting its battles," the captain further ranted, "these miscreants croak of submission—of reconstruction!" Lieutenant L. C. Apperson of the Twenty-Second Alabama Infantry similarly recoiled at the prospect of reconstruction. "Tell all you hear talking about succumbing to the Yankee baboon that the soldiers have no such idea," he lectured his sister in a letter published in the *Southern Advertiser*, "we are not whipped and don't intend to be." Other soldiers shared this sense of betrayal. In the same newspaper issue, Private William M. Bledsoe of the Sixtieth Alabama Infantry posed a rhetorical question to incoming peace Confederates: "When this war has ceased and the brave soldiers have returned home how will you feel when called upon for your experience in this war by those brave soldiers, you will feel ashamed to face them . . . there is no liberty without victory in this noble cause."[33]

Later in the year, soldiers began blaming the home front more broadly, lumping conscript evaders and profiteers into the peace Confederate camp. "I find the majority of the people cold, spineless, apathetic," an angry Captain George Miller wrote to his wife toward the end of September, "a set of demoralized extortioners, ready and willing to drink the very life blood of the widow and rush on." Lieutenant Thomas S. Taylor of the Sixth Alabama Infantry similarly fumed to his own wife: "If we are not successful in gaining our independence the fault will be with the people who are out of the Army & not the soldiers." Sergeant Edward N. Brown of the Forty-Fifth Alabama echoed Taylor's rage. "The Yankees never could conquer us if we were true to our country, true to the last man & the last loaf of bread," he wrote to his wife, "thousands who ought to be in the army are at home speculating." Private William A. Stephens of the Forty-Sixth Alabama Infantry glumly commented to his wife that he thought "nearley all the leden men is more for money than for the good of thiser contery." The visceral tone of these letters reveals the fighting man's irate frustration with home-front politics and his own powerlessness to do anything about it. Chandra Manning is close to the mark when she states that most of the South's wartime elections "showed that soldiers . . . did not like the Confederacy they had, but neither did they share a coherent vision of the Confederacy that they wanted in its place."[34]

Folks back home attempted to reassure the soldiers that their worries were misplaced. On August 29, judge William Jones of Greene County visited the campgrounds of the Fifth Alabama Infantry, then recuperating from the Gettysburg Campaign, and spoke to many of the men whom he had watched march off to war two years earlier. Hearing their complaints about political defeatism, he delivered "a short address" in which he emphatically denied that Alabamians favored reconstruction and then insisted that "never before were the people more united & more determined to prosecute the war." Private Sam Pickens, for one, appreciated the judge's speech and recorded the moment in his diary. State newspapers also tried to restore harmony between soldier and civilian. For instance, the *Democratic Watchtower* called for a celebration in honor of the Thirtieth and Thirty-First Alabama Infantry Regiments, whose rank and file came from Talladega and the surrounding counties. The units had just reconstituted after their surrender at Vicksburg and were soon to depart for Demopolis. "Let us show by our actions where our sympathies are," the editors exclaimed, "that we appreciate and have treasured their daring deeds in our hearts." Evidently, the locals turned out, and the planter class pledged several thousand bushels of corn and wheat, along with bags of salt and stacks of blankets, not just for the men, but for their families. "They are our boys and we are proud of them," said the newsmen.[35]

The soldiers certainly welcomed gestures of goodwill and words of praise, but nothing could quite atone for their disfranchisement. The *Montgomery Advertiser* agreed. "There are too many weak, vacillating and vain men aspiring to civil positions now to be entrusted with the ordinary functions of legislation," it remarked more than a month after the election; "that the spirit and vigor of our soldiery needs to be infused into the old leaven is too manifest to be denied." The logical deduction was obvious: if Alabama's soldiers were war Confederates (and most of them were), then their absence from the polls enabled too many peace Confederates to gain office, which in turn jeopardized the South's chance for military victory.[36]

A hypothetical election in which soldiers did vote is worth serious contemplation. Approximately seventeen thousand eligible voters were in the ranks on the day of the election. In light of these Alabama soldiers' compelling prowar testaments, it is fair to assume that 80 percent of them would have voted for war Confederate candidates. This percentage is no arbitrary figure; rather it is based on voter analysis coming out of the North Carolina gubernatorial election of August 1864. In a careful study of this event, Marc W. Kruman demonstrates that not only did Tar Heel soldiers vote, but that they cast a whopping 88 percent of their ballots for the prowar incumbent, Zebulon Vance, who went on to crush his antiwar opponent, William Holden, a man associated with the Heroes of America, North Carolina's version of the Peace Society. If so many North Carolina veterans were voting for war Confederates at a time when it was plain to any rational observer that the cause was doomed, then it is no stretch to hypothesize that a large majority of Alabama soldiers would have done the same in their own election a year earlier. That a minority would have voted for peace Confederates is undeniable. In fact, some from this group did just that in violation of the law. According to Major W. T. Walthall, the conscript officer for Talladega County, an unspecified number of "paroled prisoners" voted illegally, evidently at the behest of the Peace Society, thereby contributing to the defeat of war Confederate Jabez Curry. Illicit soldier voting seems to have been an aberration, however, perhaps even an exaggeration, for there is no record of parolees voting in other counties. The truth is that most Alabama soldiers—80 percent—were advocates of total victory. Thus, of the seventeen thousand potential soldier votes in August 1863, about fourteen thousand would have gone to Alabama's war Confederates (table 7).[37]

The inclusion of soldier votes would have had little impact on the gubernatorial race, where all candidates were war Confederates, but they would have made a major difference when woven into the most closely contested congressional races. In the Second Congressional District, nominal peace Confederate William Russell Smith defeated war Confederate William H. Fowler

1,756–1,108. Under the 80 percent formula, however, Fowler would have reversed this outcome decisively, beating Smith 2,662–2,146. In the Third Congressional District, the unionist Williamson Cobb won a majority over his two war Confederate opponents, but under the 80 percent formula, his margin would have been reduced to a plurality. In the Fourth Congressional District, the one most often cited as proving Alabama's loss of will, war Confederate Jabez Curry would not have lost by nearly one thousand votes to the defeatist Marcus Cruikshank, but—thanks to soldier ballots—won by nearly two hundred: 3,789–3,610. And if Major Walthall is right in saying that antiwar parolees voted illegally, then Cruikshank's tally already included his 20 percent of the potential soldier vote. Thus, Curry would actually have won by a wider margin. These three counterfactual results constitute a powerful rebuttal to the standing belief that the hill counties of Alabama were anti-Confederate. For the other races, Francis Lyon's landslide over Jack F. Cocke would have become an utter obliteration of the peace Confederate candidate; William Chilton, David Clopton, and James Dickinson would have won by more comfortable margins; and James Pugh's plurality would have become a majority. So, under a hypothetical election with soldiers voting, Alabama's delegation to the Confederate Congress would have comprised eight war Confederates. Moreover, had an official war party formed, one that both conducted a proper canvass and persuaded either James Sheffield or John Ralls to step aside in the interests of unity against Williamson Cobb, then it is plausible that a full slate of nine war Confederates would have prevailed at the polls.

The results are similarly striking when the 80 percent formula is applied to the legislative races. In the actual election, fourteen veterans lost in races that were swept by known peace Confederates. The inclusion of soldier votes, however, would have dramatically altered the outcome in at least one race for the Senate and seven for the House. The senatorial contest pitted Curtis G. Beeson of St. Clair County against William N. Crump of Blount County. Beeson was a member of the Peace Society; Crump was a lieutenant colonel in the Forty-Ninth Alabama Infantry who exhibited the war Confederate outlook. In the actual election, Beeson won 665–475, racking up a crushing margin in his home county, one reputedly crawling with deserters and draft dodgers. Had the eligible 528 active-duty soldiers from these two counties been permitted to vote, however, Crump would have turned his shortfall into a clean majority: 897–771. In the House, Captain John A. Steele of the Fourth Alabama Cavalry would have defeated Anderson Orr in Franklin County; Captain Frances A. Musgrove of the Twenty-Eighth Alabama Infantry, who was wounded in action at Mufreesboro, would have defeated John Manasco in Walker County; Captain Thomas A. Davis of the Sixth Alabama Infantry would have defeated

Leonidas Howard in Autauga County; Private Arnold Shamblin and Chaplain Samuel L. Russell (both of the Nineteenth Alabama Infantry) would have outpolled George W. Howell and William A. Vincent in Cherokee County, thereby splitting that county's four-man delegation; and Private James M. K. Little of the Fortieth Alabama Infantry would have defeated the avowed unionist Alfred Holley in Covington County. It is more than coincidence that in all eight of these potential outcomes, the man with military experience would have prevailed over the man who did not serve. Thus, the 80 percent formula produces a legislative realignment that is markedly in favor of the war Confederates. Such a development would have had huge implications for the later election for the Confederate Senate. If eight peace Confederates had been replaced with eight war Confederates, then Jabez Curry would have won the Senate seat—unless of course he already retained his congressional seat, in which case Clement Clay would have gotten reelected. Either way, the peace Confederates would have suffered a terrible blow.

This carefully constructed hypothetical exercise is useful in reevaluating the significance of the election of 1863, but of course it can never substitute for the actual outcome. Against the wishes of Alabama's fighting men, peace Confederates gained real political influence. Months before this development, Private Thomas Caffey of the Third Alabama Infantry had already come to believe that only patriotic volunteer citizen-soldiers could win the day for the South. "The country is indebted to the original regiments for its salvation," he wrote to his sister in February 1863, "and though our ranks have been badly thinned by disease and losses in battles, the Confederate States will have to still rely on those gallant veterans." The August election only confirmed this opinion; and so Alabama soldiers doubled down on winning the war with more bullets. At Chickamauga, in northern Georgia, the gamble seemed to pay off. Over the course of September 18 to 20, Alabamians in the Army of Tennessee helped smash the Federal Army of the Cumberland in what became the Confederacy's greatest military success outside of Virginia. Coming just seven weeks after the disappointing state elections, Chickamauga was precisely the turn of events that so many Alabamians had been yearning for after a disastrous summer of defeats. A relieved Captain Daniel Coleman of the Thirty-Third Alabama Infantry penned in his diary the night after the battle, "we gained, through the blessings of our Father, a great victory over our enemies." Captain George Miller was more ecstatic. "The great battle that has just been so gallantly fought and won by our Southern chivalry," he wrote to his wife at the end of September, "seems to have lifted a terrible weight from the public mind, and the whole country seems to breathe free." To his own wife, Private John Cotton confided, "I think that it will bring about peace."[38]

Moved by their countrymen's persistent devotion in the field, poets from Alabama paid special homage to the fighting man. The *Mobile Register* published the verse of an anonymous veteran. One particular stanza captured the front line's dedication to the struggle:

> Two years have I fought for freedom
> Two more will I stay in the field
> Nor ne'er will retire from the contest
> While a weapon I can wield
> No, I ne'er will see my Mary
> Whilst a foeman threatens her door
> In the ranks I can best protect her
> Till the strife for victory's o'er.

Complementing this sentiment, Alexander B. Meek, whom Benjamin Buford Williams calls "the foremost literary figure in Alabama in the pre–Civil War period," composed a tribute to the whole rebel army shortly after Chickamauga, one titled "Martyrs of the South." Among the verses is a listing of thirteen Alabama infantry officers who had all been killed in action. "They well performed their hero parts, And passed from earth away," Meek wrote, "They lie asleep on honor's bed—Young Freedom's martyr band—For all that's dear to man they bled—For God and native land!"[39]

Confederate euphoria did not last long. The Army of Tennessee went on to besiege its vanquished foe at Chattanooga, but Union reinforcements under Ulysses S. Grant soon arrived, and between November 23 and 25, they sent the rebels packing in a series of clashes that utterly negated the practical results of Chickamauga. Psychologically, however, victory at Chickamauga proved that the rebel army could rebound, and there was no reason why it could not do so again. In a series of December letters to his home in Pickens County, Colonel Newton N. Davis of the Twenty-Fourth Alabama Infantry consoled his wife (and perhaps himself, as well). "We should never be discouraged by defeat. . . . We should never despair. . . . This is certainly a dark hour for our Confederacy, but still I believe there is a bright future in store for us yet." Similarly, defeat at Chattanooga actually seemed to intensify the defiance of some Alabama soldiers. For instance, Lieutenant Colonel John W. Inzer of the Fifty Eighth Alabama Infantry had been a cooperationist in 1861 and a dutiful officer thereafter. Following his capture at Missionary Ridge, however, he transformed into the most fanatical of rebels. "I live to hate the U.S. flag," Inzer ranted in one entry of his prison diary. "I am for continuing this war until the last man of the South shall have been killed," he fumed in another.

"I am willing to spend my days in killing yankee vandals," he went on in still another. Now here was a man who exemplified Grady McWhiney's recklessly aggressive Celtic southerner—a soldier unafraid to "attack and die." More measured, but no less resolved, is the sentiment of Lieutenant Elias Davis of the Tenth Alabama Infantry, who in a December letter to his mother articulated the stolid diehard mindset that had become the Confederate army. "We have suffered much during this war, but I am willing to fight forever," the lieutenant professed; "I conscientiously believe that our cause is just and consequently can't believe that we will not be successful." For these Alabama veterans, Confederate defeat was unthinkable.[40]

In supporting its thesis, this study includes dozens of prowar views from soldiers all over Alabama and from Alabamians serving in all of the Confederacy's principal armies. The perspectives of some are discussed more extensively than others, but every voice cited comes from a man who absolutely wanted to win the war. Several of these men subsequently died in service; the remainder all persevered to the end. "But then," thundered army chaplain J. J. D. Renfroe of the Tenth Alabama Infantry, "this is the price of liberty!" In a widely published Fast Day sermon, initially delivered on August 21 to the veterans of Wilcox's Brigade (whose five Alabama regiments endured heavy losses at Gettysburg), Renfroe exhorted his fellow Alabamians to stay the course: "We have to fight on! We cannot make peace. We cannot even propose peace." That neither he nor any of his comrades were allowed to vote in an election that centered on that very issue is a travesty of political injustice. That most of them nonetheless complied with Renfroe's plea and continued to rally around their nascent country's flag is telling proof of the soldiers' nationalism. The historian Peter S. Carmichael contends that this fanatical devotion of rebels to their cause was a product of an "absolutist" frame of mind where the war was a simple case of right versus wrong. The Confederacy was right to defend its bid for independence, whereas the North was wrong to punish the South over an abstraction like the Union. Alabama's fighting men certainly exemplified this absolutist outlook in 1863; their war Confederate mien is undeniable.[41]

In and of itself, the absence of Alabama soldiers from the polls is not the difference between Confederate victory and defeat in the Civil War. It is, however, an essential factor in determining whether the August election marks a shift in the state's commitment to the rebel cause. Coming at the war's midpoint, it was a crucial test of Confederate nationalism for white Alabamians, yet the constituency that was possessed of the greatest political clarity was absent from the process. If the soldiers had been involved, then war Confederates would have dominated state politics. As it turned out, the state's polity did lean prowar after the election anyway, although the presence of many peace Confederates plagued efforts to implement harsher policies. That the peace Confederates enjoyed any success at all is because soldiers could not weigh in directly on the political issues. And the peace Confederates understood this situation, so much so that, according to Walter L. Fleming, they exhibited a tacit "fear of the soldier class," one that compelled them to pursue policies of reconstruction with hesitation lest the southern war effort degenerate into a bloodbath of political proscription. Perhaps this conjecture is taking the fighting man's enmity too far, but historian Joseph Allen Frank calculates that nearly two-thirds of active-duty Confederate soldiers regarded antiwar politicians across the South with profound antipathy. Henry Coyne, the fiery editor of the *Montgomery Mail*, went so far as to call on soldiers to stand ready as executioners should the peace Confederates gain too much power: "the first man . . . who publicly proposes a reconstruction of the Union should suffer death." Talk of military usurpation, with perhaps Robert E. Lee taking over, was not uncommon after 1863. Lee, of course, was no Napoleon, at least not in political ambition, but given the revolutionary dimensions of the rebellion, a war Confederate version of France's infamous Reign of Terror is not so outlandish. If stringing up the likes of Marcus Cruikshank or Lewis E. Parsons could have altered the fate of the Confederacy, then there can be little doubt that thousands of truculent Alabama soldiers would have happily furnished the rope. The peace Confederates were, after all, the metaphorical yellow jackets stinging the soldier from the rear, the harmful insects that one hapless Alabama private on Culp's Hill tried in vain to stomp out.[42]

Conclusion

IN THE LATTER HALF OF 1864, Union forces militarily broke the Confederacy. Admiral David Farragut shut down Mobile as a port of call for blockade runners; General Ulysses S. Grant intensified his siege of Lee's army around Petersburg; General William Tecumseh Sherman captured Atlanta and shortly thereafter commenced his destructive March to the Sea; and General George Henry Thomas repulsed a desperate Confederate foray into Middle Tennessee. In the midst of these bleak developments, the Alabama state legislature met twice, once in late September (a called session) and again in early November (the regular session). The proceedings at both addressed the militia system; Governor Watts wanted greater authority over the county reserves. The dominant issue, however, was the course of the war; everyone knew that the game was up, especially after Lincoln won reelection in November, but not everyone was ready to call it quits. Peace Confederates in the assembly exploited the mood and pushed for reconstruction; they were asserting themselves at last. War Confederates betrayed signs of weariness, but they stymied their opponents all the same; there would be no political capitulation.

During the called session (September 26–October 7), the two legislative chambers operated as if they had no connection to each other. The prowar Senate stayed on task and revised the militia law according to the governor's wishes. Turner Reavis of Sumter County proposed a bill "of a certain sweeping character," to wit: the county reserves were eliminated, and the executive branch was granted discretionary powers over every able-bodied man between sixteen and fifty-five years of age. Floor debate was brief, and on October 1, the bill passed. In the Alabama House, however, peace Confederates attempted to steer the proceedings toward reconstruction. On September 27, James J. McLemore of Chambers County proposed a resolution calling for Alabama's participation in a southern-wide peace conference with northern Democrats. When he hinted that a separate peace might also be desirable, war Confederates reacted "as if a real bomb shell had exploded in the hall." Augustus Benners rebuked McLemore and moved to table the whole idea of reconstruction, but parliamentary protocol faltered in the bedlam. Lewis E. Parsons then took the floor and exhibited the defiant leadership that peace Confederates had long expected of him. At first, Parsons sought common ground by denouncing the Lincoln administration and praying for a George B. McClellan victory in the upcoming presidential election. But when he suggested "open negotiations for peace" in accordance with the Democratic platform that called for "the restoration of the Union," the catcalls resumed. John Y. Kilpatrick, in particular, tried to get Walter H. Crenshaw to silence Parsons, but the Speaker seemed resigned to letting the peace Confederates finally have their say. Urged on by John Manasco of Walker County, Parsons finished his presentation, but the war Confederates were furious. William B. Modawell of Marengo County wanted blood and called for the expulsion of the most obvious anti-Confederate in the chamber, the unionist Alfred Holley of Covington County. No roll call vote was recorded, but the measure was "adopted unanimously." Evidently, the peace Confederates made no effort to protect their colleague—inexcusable conduct if true. Instead, they retaliated on October 3, by throwing their votes against the Senate's militia bill, preventing its passage. They did so again on October 6, when Levi W. Lawler of Talladega attempted without success to revive the issue.[1]

The stormy called session accomplished virtually nothing other than to intensify the rancor between the rival factions. It did, however, reveal that Alabama remained a prowar polity, though with significant qualifications. The legislature's refusal to grant the governor carte blanche over the militia showed that even a total war had its limits. The peace Confederates did not have the numbers to stop the militia bill on their own. When the House tabled the Senate version (52–16) and Lawler's version (59–20), it did so with many war Confederates voting in the majority. Going into the called session, several newspapers that were usually prowar had questioned the wisdom of dispatching "old men and boys, the blind, lame and halt . . . to little purpose." Citing widespread lawlessness and derelict farm fields, John Hubbard of the *Southern Advertiser* beseeched the legislature to leave the county reserves alone: "Men are as necessary at home as in the army." Prominent war Confederates such as Augustus Benners, Tristam B. Bethea, Walter H. Crenshaw, Nathaniel H. R. Dawson, and William B. Modawell apparently agreed; they all voted against the militia bill. Their commitment to the war, however, remained undiminished, as demonstrated by their strident opposition to any overture about reconstruction.[2]

At the regular session (November 19–December 13), the militia system and reconstruction once again consumed the legislators' energies, albeit for the last time. As before, the Senate dutifully passed a strong militia bill, a virtual facsimile of its September version save that the governor could only deploy the force for forty days. How individual senators actually voted is unknown, but at least one war Confederate, Theophilus Toulmin of Mobile, thought that fielding the militia had become "inexpedient" with imminent defeat looming. Nevertheless, the forty-day caveat was designed to make the bill more appealing to the House. That chamber, however, did not commence serious discussion of the topic until the final days of the session. The floor debate lacked any sense of urgency, and when the Senate version finally came to a vote the members responded 54–15 against making any further revision to the existing law.[3]

A majority of war Confederates may have agreed with their political adversaries that a revised militia system was unnecessary, but they continued to reject all talk about a negotiated peace. In fact, Lincoln's presidential victory seemed to render the notion of reconstruction even more hateful. On the first day of the session, in a power-play reversal of what had happened back in September, John Y. Kilpatrick entered a House resolution that was explicitly "against Reconstruction." The peace Confederates feigned disinterest, it having become obvious that the North would settle for nothing less than the South's unconditional surrender. Alabama's war Confederates, however, were hell bent on pillorying men whom they considered to be traitors. In the Senate, Lewis L. Cato of Barbour County expanded Kilpatrick's draft resolution into a nationalistic litmus test: "This state hereby affirms and reiterates her unalterable determination to maintain her stand for the independence of the Confederate States." Averring that the Lincoln administration's goal was "to subjugate us or destroy us," the resolution importuned the citizenry to pledge "unreservedly" their lives, property, and honor to the southern cause. Peace Confederates tried in vain to postpone a final vote, but war Confederates pressed their majority. The resolution passed "unanimously" in the Senate (though no roll call tally was recorded) and barely in the House, 32–28. Some forty House members were either absent or abstained, but the breakdown of those who did vote could not have been starker. All twenty-eight nay votes (including Parsons) came from legislators who had voted for the antiwar John Jacob Seibels in the senatorial election the year before. The thirty-two yea votes came almost entirely from men who had voted for either Jabez Curry or Clement Clay. Peace Confederate opposition in the House notwithstanding, the Joint Resolution against Reconstruction (approved December 13) was a fitting coda for a war state all over.[4]

Histories of the Confederacy invariably present a variety of explanations for why the rebellion failed. The debate typically falls somewhere along a continuum of internal versus external factors. The internal school of thought asserts, among other reasons, that southern nationalism was too weak to sustain popular support for an unwelcome war, or that the Confederate government was too fractious to cope with the rigors of a protracted war, or that the region's agrarian economy was woefully inadequate for the demands of a modern war. The external school of thought posits that southerners were perfectly willing to resist, but that their military lacked the capacity to withstand indefinitely the unremitting pressure of a Union war machine that benefited from industrial abundance coupled with implacable generalship (at least after the first half of the war). This study complements the external theory. It was the Yankees who beat the South; southerners did not beat themselves. Confederate Alabama did its part for the cause in herculean proportions. Its polity displayed pronounced nationalism, collaborated in a mammoth war effort, and channeled more than the state's fair share of the public weal into the country's bid for independence. Only with the gradual demise of Confederate arms did internal fissures within Alabama—namely the peace movement—become something more than an irritation.[5]

Nevertheless, there is a tragic dimension to Alabama's wartime polity. Both the war Confederates and the peace Confederates pursued will-o'-the-wisps of their own design. War Confederates displayed an admirable zeal in pursuing the lofty goal of nationhood, and their actions reflected a rational calculus. Maximizing manpower through conscription and militia laws was a hard policy, but it made sense under the circumstances. The same can be said for impressment and taxation. That war Confederates could have implemented total war more efficiently is beyond dispute, but it was not the work of fools, at least not until late 1864, when prowar optimism became increasingly divorced from reality. Thereafter, mere victory, whatever that precisely meant, became the war Confederates' monomaniacal focus. Peace Confederates engaged in similar acts of delusion. Convinced by 1863 that the war was hopeless, they encouraged internal opposition through the Peace Society and sought external salvation through reconstruction. Unfortunately, both actions crossed the threshold of treachery. Peace Confederates always insisted that war termination could be done responsibly, with honor intact, but they never figured out how to actually pull off that feat. Peace talks with the enemy could only work from a position of strength, yet any military success invariably played into the hands of war Confederates as proof that the cause was still alive. In the end, the peace Confederates failed because their agenda ran against the will of the people—or more precisely the majoritarian will of those who participated in the state elections—and consequently they never came close to displacing the war Confederate hold over the polity. Their agenda also failed because the North refused to negotiate; the Lincoln administration was waging a total war of its own in pursuit of a total victory—unconditional reunification with wholesale emancipation. Therefore, reconstruction on southern terms was a naive and futile quest.

Some thirty years before the Civil War, a Prussian officer named Carl von Clausewitz authored *On War*, an intrepid study of military theory. A passage from that work, in a chapter titled "The People in Arms," presciently captures the plight of Alabama (and the Confederacy more broadly) in 1863: "A government must never assume that its country's fate, its whole existence, hangs on the outcome of a single battle, no matter how decisive. Even after a defeat, there is always the possibility that a turn of fortune can be brought about by developing new sources of internal strength or through the natural decimation all offensives suffer in the long run or by means of help from abroad. There will always be time enough to die; like a drowning man who will clutch instinctively at a straw, it is the natural law of the moral world that a nation that finds itself on the brink of an abyss will try to save itself by any means."[6]

Rather than losing a single, decisive battle, the Confederacy suffered two defeats: Gettysburg and Vicksburg. Still, the South persevered, with Alabama lawmakers doing their part to find "new sources of internal strength." In practical terms, this search meant more impressments, more taxation, and more conscription (to include a backdoor draft via the militia). Alabama's soldiers also pitched in, bringing about the "natural decimation" of Union offensives through a counterattack of their own at Chickamauga later in the year. And only a desperate master class—"like a drowning man"—would contemplate the paradox of arming its own chattel as a means of saving itself from the "abyss" of Yankee emancipation. But it was more than instinct that had Alabamians clutching "at a straw." Growing apprehensions aside, total war was a deliberate choice made at the polls by an electorate that wanted war Confederates at the helm, ideally to attain the elusive independence, but at the very least to stave off for as long as possible the disgrace of submitting to a hated foe. "All have in some form participated in the war," Governor Thomas Hill Watts soberly noted in March 1865. "We have all taken part in electing to the presidency, to the governorship, to Congress and our state legislature those who have sworn to support the Constitution and the cause of the Confederate States."[7]

Implicit in the governor's gesture to "all" is the white male electorate, but Watts's conclusion about Alabama's entire polity after 1863 is correct in its essentials. It hardly mattered that only a plurality of citizens had voted. The outcome produced a body of officeholders that would carry on the struggle. Frankly, what else could that government really do? Alabama was a war state all over because the war was all over the state, be it interminably harsh policies, ongoing social disruption, mounting casualty reports, or increasing Yankee incursions. War Confederates naturally doubled down on trying to win the contest at any cost and proved steadfast in their support, but even the peace Confederates frequently acceded to extreme measures. They were certainly less strident in their patriotism, but most peace Confederates (sans the unionist minority in their ranks) wanted a southern nation triumphant; most of them hated the Lincoln administration; most of them abhorred the idea of a liberated black race; and all of them marveled at the sacrifice of the fighting men, many of whom were brothers or sons. War Confederates often questioned the loyalty of their peace Confederate rivals, but this disdain never materialized into outright retribution, in large part because antiwar rhetoric seldom amounted to anything more than words, vacillating ones at that. State senator Ezekiel A. Powell, a nominal peace Confederate from Tuscaloosa, commented years after the war that, for all the histrionics over the peace resolutions, "there was no faltering in the support given the Confederacy." Speaker Walter H. Crenshaw perceived a subconscious solidarity between the two camps. In his closing address to the Alabama House in December 1864, he observed how the "ebullience of ill feeling" during debates readily gave way to "pleasant intercourse" at the conclusion of business each day. The Speaker was especially touched by the consistent bipartisan sympathy and support for the soldiers and their families. To him, politics had devolved into a means of honoring the state's warrior class: "let us not dampen their ardor by exhibiting discontent at the further prosecution of the War for Independence." Setting aside some very real pessimism about an ultimate victory, we can see Alabama for what it was: a remarkably durable polity that practiced total war until the final surrender of its armies.[8]

Total war was also and absolutely the will of the state's soldiery. "Alabamians may be destroyed, but never conquered," a veteran of Lee's army said in November 1863. That same month, Henry St. Paul of Mobile published a fascinating piece of propaganda that elevated the Confederacy's fighting men above the planter class as the embodiment of southern values. Away with tired refrains that proclaimed "Cotton is King," St. Paul intoned, "Valor is King—the salvation of the South is within the South itself—it lies in those armies whose martial tread shakes the soil and strikes terror in the enemy's heart." These armies, St. Paul explained further, "[were] fighting neither for domestic institutions, or the Rights of the States, but for a free, distinct and independent place amongst the nations of the earth." For good reason does Frank E. Vandiver describe the rebel army as "a nationalizing agent." It was the lifeblood of the Confederacy, its battle flag the symbol. The men in the ranks believed in their young country and wanted to win; they expected the same from the men in the halls. Not even the prospect of a gory death on the battlefield deterred them. "The Southern soldier saw his own sacrifice of life in terms of a greater purpose," insists Wiley Sword, "as such, in a practical sense it was an investment in the future." An estimated thirty thousand Alabamians perished as a result of the war. This "casualty record," notes Don E. Fehrenbacher, "seems to be *prima facie* evidence of strong dedication to the idea of an independent southern nation." It does indeed.[9]

Alabama's polity was hardly alone in its commitment to the cause. The state elections of 1863 in Georgia provide a valuable point of comparison. For Georgia's electorate, much like the one in Alabama, the course of the war was the main issue in virtually every race. In the gubernatorial contest, Joseph Brown, the controversial incumbent, easily won reelection over the combined tallies of Joshua Hill, who promoted a reconstruction agenda, and Timothy Furlow, a prowar secessionist. Hill garnered just over 25 percent of the vote, Furlow just over 15 percent. Between the two losers, the peace Confederate outperformed the war Confederate. But as James Horace Bass explains in his analysis, Joseph Brown was essentially a war Confederate as well. The governor may have personally disliked President Davis, and he certainly offered greater resistance to total war policies than his peers elsewhere in the South, but Brown wanted the Confederacy to win, and the soldiers knew this. Georgia's congressional races also yielded telling results. In his careful study, Rod Andrew finds that they illustrate a broad-based nationalism. Most prowar incumbents lost, but none of the winners were advocates of peace. Instead, they were army veterans, new men whose legislative records evinced continued faith in the cause. Furthermore, the military credentials of these newcomers highlighted the impact of soldier voting. Unlike Alabama, Georgia made provisions for absentee balloting in the field; the soldiers cast their ballots for politicians who wanted to press on toward victory. For instance, of the nearly twenty-four thousand Georgia veterans who voted for governor, fewer than six thousand went for the antiwar candidate. "The whole idea of reconstruction appeared absurd," George C. Rable has said of Georgia's volunteers, "and in any event would simply become slavery by another name." A comparable mindset also applies to Alabama's soldiers, their practical disfranchisement notwithstanding. War Confederates in Alabama managed to retain power even without soldier votes, but with these votes the lawmakers would have smothered their peace opponents in many more races and perhaps established an outright mandate for total war.[10]

As the conflict dragged on, however, the notion of a total war seemed to offer reassuring rhetoric more than a valid prescription for victory. According to military historian Michael I. Handel's description of a "rational calculus of war," a sensible termination of a conflict occurs when one side realizes that it can no longer achieve its political objective—but such levelheaded thinking rarely occurs in an all-out struggle. "The passions involved, the desire to recoup investments made thus far, and the irresistible allure of wishful thinking all doom efforts to conduct the war rationally," notes Handel. "Even if the original calculations are rational, the war will become increasingly impervious to a rational approach as it progresses." Applying this concept to the Civil War, we see that most southern politicians trembled at the mounting cost of their rebellion but steadfastly pressed ahead all the same. They would either achieve an outright triumph or negotiate with the enemy only from a position of strength. Rebel arms were capable of neither after 1863, and so southerners proudly fought in vain as their homeland crumbled around them. This is the simplest, and somewhat pitiable, explanation for why Alabama remained a war state all over, why the southern polity at large rallied around the Confederacy even as defeat became both inevitable and obvious. Unable to attain, let alone sustain, decisive military success on the battlefield, Dixie succumbed to physical and economic exhaustion.[11]

By 1865, war Confederates had nothing left to fight with but defiant words. The Alabama legislature's closing, chest-thumping resolution reflected this pointless perseverance, as did its governor's final, delusional public addresses. State senator Augustus Benners was right when he ruminated, "the South cant stop & the North wont." The pedal point that undergirded this fatalistic adherence to the cause was the accusation posed by Private William M. Bledsoe, and shared by many other veterans like him, to the politicians back home: "When this war has ceased and the brave soldiers have returned home how will you feel when called upon for your experience in this war by those brave soldiers, you will feel ashamed to face them." The only acceptable and honorable response was to say that the polity had faithfully waged a total war, and done so, as Wilfred Buck Yearns poignantly remarks about the South's lawmakers, "with at least the satisfaction of never having begged for mercy."[12]

Their nation's defeat notwithstanding, Alabama's political leaders during the Civil War deserve credit for their conduct. Regardless of their attitude toward the conflict, virtually all of them were smart, capable men for whom there is no hint of scandal or corruption. Their records reflect the actions of normal individuals doing their conscientious best in trying times. A clear majority favored a fight to the finish, both before and after the 1863 elections. Going into that election, eight of Alabama's nine congressmen were stalwart war Confederates; coming out of it six remained true, though one of them—Thomas Jefferson Foster—lost heart near the end. Of the two war governors, John Gill Shorter stands out for his embrace of total war, but his successor, "Big Tom" Watts, proved just as devoted to the cause. In the general assembly, war Confederates maintained control in both chambers, solidly in the Senate, narrowly in the House. As a result, the position of the Confederate senator also remained in war Confederate hands, albeit of a variety more moderate than the hard-liners would have wished. This prowar political continuity may not have constituted a popular mandate, but it did reflect the overall attitude of those who actually voted. Moreover, it was the undeniable sentiment of a disfranchised soldiery. To be sure, an outspoken minority opposed any further radicalization of the war, but the verdict of the election of 1863 was plain enough. At every level of governance, at every point in the struggle, the polity of Confederate Alabama was a war state all over.

Notes

Introduction

1. *Clarke County Journal*, October 29, 1863.

2. Louise B. Hill, "State Socialism in the Confederate States of America," *Southern Sketches* 1st ser., no. 9 (1936): 3; John Brawner Robbins, "Confederate Nationalism: Politics and Government in the Confederate South, 1861–1865 (PhD diss., Rice University, 1964), 30–31; Frank E. Vandiver, "The Civil War as an Institutionalizing Force," in *Essays on the American Civil War*, ed. Frank E. Vandiver, Martin Hardwick Hall, and Homer L. Kerr (Austin: University of Texas Press, 1968), 79–82; Richard Bensel, "Southern Leviathan: The Development of Central State Authority in the Confederate States of America," *Studies in American Political Development* 2, no. 1 (1987): 134. For a fuller definition of total war, see Joseph Allen Frank, *With Ballot and Bayonet: The Political Socialization of American Civil War Soldiers* (Athens: University of Georgia Press, 1998), 146–48.

3. William L. Barney, *Flawed Victory: A New Perspective on the Civil War* (New York: Praeger, 1975), 96; Curtis Arthur Amlund, *Federalism in the Southern Confederacy* (Washington, DC: Public Affairs Press, 1966), 130; Michael Brem Bonner, *Confederate Political Economy: Creating and Managing a Southern Corporatist Nation* (Baton Rouge: Louisiana State University Press, 2016), 4–5, 13.

4. Malcolm C. McMillan, *The Alabama Confederate Reader* (Tuscaloosa: University of Alabama Press, 1963), 233; Bruce Levine, *The Fall of the House of Dixie: The Civil War and the Social Revolution That Transformed the South* (New York: Random House, 2013), 208; Armstead L. Robinson, *Bitter Fruits of Bondage: The Demise of Slavery and the Collapse of the Confederacy, 1861–1865* (Charlottesville: University of Virginia Press, 2005), 250; Anne Sarah Rubin, *A Shattered Nation: The Rise and Fall of the Confederacy, 1861–1868* (Chapel Hill: University of North Carolina Press, 2005), 79.

5. Christopher Lyle McIlwain, *Civil War Alabama* (Tuscaloosa: University of Alabama Press, 2016), 127, 132–33; George C. Rable, *The Confederate Republic: A Revolution against Politics* (Chapel Hill: University of North Carolina Press, 1994), 215, 221; Kenneth C. Martis, *The Historical Atlas of the Congresses of the Confederate States of America: 1861–1865* (New York: Simon and Schuster, 1994), 57. The total number of votes cast in the congressional races was 35,251; the number for the gubernatorial race was slightly higher at 38,907.

6. Joseph W. Danielson, *War's Desolating Scourge: The Union's Occupation of North Alabama* (Lawrence: University Press of Kansas, 2012), 125.

7. For good summaries of Alabama's home-front ordeal, see William Warren Rogers Sr., Robert David Ward, Leah Rawls Atkins, and Wayne Flynt, *Alabama: The History of a Deep South State* (Tuscaloosa: University of Alabama Press, 1994), 186–222;

and Ben H. Severance, *Portraits of Conflict: A Photographic History of Alabama in the Civil War* (Fayetteville: University of Arkansas Press, 2012), 233–73.

8. Georgia Lee Tatum, *Disloyalty in the Confederacy* (New York: AMS Press, 1934), 60; Bessie Martin, *A Rich Man's War, A Poor Man's Fight: Desertion of Alabama Troops from the Confederate Army* (1932; Tuscaloosa: University of Alabama Press, 2003), 109, 114–15; Rubin, *Shattered Nation*, 80; Barney, *Flawed Victory*, 112.

9. Martis, *Historical Atlas*, 67; Margaret M. Storey, *Loyalty and Loss: Alabama's Unionists in the Civil War and Reconstruction* (Baton Rouge: Louisiana State University Press, 2004), 16.

10. J. Mills Thornton III, *Politics and Power in a Slave Society: Alabama, 1800–1860* (Baton Rouge: Louisiana State University Press, 1978), 442. See also Thomas B. Alexander, "Persistent Whiggery in the Confederate South, 1860–1877," *Journal of Southern History* 27, no. 3 (1961): 305–29.

11. Jon L. Wakelyn, ed., *Southern Pamphlets on Secession, November 1860–April 1861* (Chapel Hill: University of North Carolina Press, 1996), 46. For in-depth discussions of Confederate nationalism, see Gary W. Gallagher, *The Confederate War: How Popular Will, Nationalism, and Military Strategy Could Not Stave Off Defeat* (Cambridge, MA: Harvard University Press, 1997); John McCardell, *The Idea of a Southern Nation: Southern Nationalists and Southern Nationalism, 1830–1860* (New York: W. W. Norton, 1979); Robert E. Bonner, *Mastering America: Southern Slaveholders and the Crisis of American Nationhood* (New York: Cambridge University Press, 2009); and Paul Quigley, *Shifting Grounds: Nationalism and the American South, 1848–1865* (New York: Oxford University Press, 2012).

12. Jabez L. M. Curry, *Civil History of the Government of the Confederate States* (Richmond, VA: B. F. Johnson, 1901), 160–61; Richard Bensel, "Rejoinder to 'Why No Parties? Investigating the Disappearance of Democratic-Whig Divisions in the Confederacy,'" *Studies in American Political Development* 13, no. 2 (1999): 275; Rable, *Confederate Republic*, 138, 157–59.

13. Levine, *Fall of the House of Dixie*, 214; *Southern Advertiser*, August 12, 1863; Walter L. Fleming, *Civil War and Reconstruction in Alabama* (New York: Columbia University Press, 1905), 132.

14. *Population of the United States in 1860: The Eighth Census* (Washington, DC: Government Printing Office, 1864), 8; Don E. Fehrenbacher, *Sectional Crisis and Southern Constitutionalism* (Baton Rouge: Louisiana State University Press, 1995), 87–88; Stephanie McCurry, *Confederate Reckoning: Power and Politics in the Civil War South* (Cambridge, MA: Harvard University Press, 2010), 80; Steven Hahn, *A Nation under Our Feet: Black Political Struggles in the Rural South from Slavery to the Great Migration* (Cambridge, MA: Belknap Press, 2003), 15, 19, 64–65, 82–88.

15. H. E. Sterkx, *Partners in Rebellion: Alabama Women in the Civil War* (Cranbury, NJ: Associated University Press, 1970); Laura F. Edwards, *Scarlett Doesn't Live Here Anymore: Southern Women in the Civil War Era* (Chicago: University of Illinois Press, 2000), 84; Victoria E. Ott, *Confederate Daughters: Coming of Age during the Civil War* (Carbondale: Southern Illinois University Press, 2008), 71; George C. Rable, *Civil*

Wars: Women and the Crisis of Southern Nationalism (Chicago: University of Illinois Press, 1989), 145.

16. For a fuller, technical definition of a polity, see Yale H. Ferguson and Richard W. Masbach, *Polities: Authority, Identities, and Change* (Columbia: University of South Carolina Press, 1996), 33–37.

17. Rable, *Confederate Republic*, 280.

Chapter 1

1. Kenneth C. Martis, *The Historical Atlas of the Congresses of the Confederate States of America, 1861–1865* (New York: Simon and Schuster, 1994), 32–33; David M. Potter, "Jefferson Davis and the Political Factors in Confederate Defeat," in *Why the North Won the Civil War*, ed. David Herbert Donald (Baton Rouge: Louisiana State University Press, 1960), 111; George C. Rable, *The Confederate Republic: A Revolution against Politics* (Chapel Hill: University of North Carolina Press, 1994), 221–35; Rod Andrew, "The Essential Nationalism of the People: Georgia's Confederate Congressional Election of 1863," in *Inside the Confederate Nation: Essays in Honor of Emory M. Thomas*, ed. Lesley J. Gordon and John C. Inscoe (Baton Rouge: Louisiana State University Press, 2005), 128–46.

2. Richard Bensel, "Southern Leviathan: The Development of Central State Authority in the Confederate States of America," *Studies in American Political Development* 2, no. 1 (1987): 76; E. Merton Coulter, *The Confederate States of America, 1861–1865* (Baton Rouge: Louisiana State University Press, 1950), 143; Wilfred Buck Yearns, *The Confederate Congress* (Athens: University of Georgia Press, 1960), viii; Frank E. Vandiver, *Rebel Brass: The Confederate Command System* (Baton Rouge: Louisiana State University Press, 1956), 75–76; James M. McPherson, *Ordeal by Fire: The Civil War and Reconstruction* (New York: McGraw-Hill, 1992), 360–61; Allan Nevins, *The War for the Union*, vol. 3, *The Organized War, 1863–1864* (New York: Konecky and Konecky, 1971), 45; Reid Mitchell, *The American Civil War, 1861–1865* (New York: Routledge, 2013), 43.

3. Thomas B. Alexander and Richard E. Beringer, *The Anatomy of the Confederate Congress: A Study of the Influences of Member Characteristics on Legislative Voting Behavior, 1861–1865* (Nashville: Vanderbilt University Press, 1972), 24–25; Jeffery A. Jenkins, "Examining Contemporary Congressional Theories Historically: Essays on the Congress of the Confederate States of America" (PhD diss., University of Illinois Urbana-Champaign, 1999), 15. For legal imprimatur, see Confederate Constitution, Article I, Section 8.1 (tax-in-kind), Section 8.12–14 (conscription), Section 9.3 (suspension of habeas corpus), and Section 9.16 (impressment).

4. Coulter, *Confederate States of America*, 145–46; Yearns, *Confederate Congress*, vii-viii; Vandiver, *Rebel Brass*, 77, Allan Nevins, *The War for the Union*, vol. 2, *War Becomes Revolution, 1862–1863* (New York: Konecky and Konecky, 1960), 89; Scott Nelson and Carol Sheriff, *A People at War: Civilians and Soldiers in America's Civil War, 1854–1877* (New York: Oxford University Press, 2008), 129. In his study of the US Congress during the Civil War, Allan G. Bogue finds that many northern legislators, especially

among the Republicans, could be petty and uncompromising toward Lincoln, even as they enacted laws that were necessary for the war effort. Bogue, *The Congressman's Civil War* (New York: Cambridge University Press, 1989).

5. Walter L. Fleming, *Civil War and Reconstruction in Alabama* (New York: Columbia University Press, 1905), 134; Frank L. Owsley, "Defeatism in the Confederacy," *North Carolina Historical Review* 3 (1926): 452; Bessie Martin, *A Rich Man's War, A Poor Man's Fight: Desertion of Alabama Troops from the Confederate Army* (1932; Tuscaloosa: University of Alabama Press, 2003), 109–11; Paul D. Escott, *The Confederacy: The Slaveholders' Failed Venture* (Santa Barbara, CA: Praeger, 2010), 94–95; John Brawner Robbins, "Confederate Nationalism: Politics and Government in the Confederate South, 1861–1865 (PhD diss., Rice University, 1964), 208–9; David Williams, *A People's History of the Civil War: Struggles for the Meaning of Freedom* (New York: New Press, 2005), 103.

6. Richard E. Beringer et al., *Why the South Lost the Civil War* (Athens: University of Georgia Press, 1986), 265, 292; Rable, *Confederate Republic*, 225–26, 234; Bruce Levine, *The Fall of the House of Dixie: The Civil War and the Social Revolution That Transformed the South* (New York: Random House, 2013), 206.

7. According to Emory M. Thomas, the concept of states' rights "was a political habit of mind so long and so articulately used to defend the Southern way of life that finally it became inseparable from that way of life." Thomas, *The Confederacy as a Revolutionary Experience* (Englewood Cliffs, NJ: Prentice-Hall, 1971), 7.

8. Ezra J. Warner and Wilfred Buck Yearns, *Biographical Register of the Confederate Congress* (Baton Rouge: Louisiana State University Press, 1975), 68; J. Mills Thornton III, *Politics and Power in a Slave Society: Alabama, 1800–1860* (Baton Rouge: Louisiana State University Press, 1978), 260, 335; Alexander and Beringer, *Anatomy of the Confederate Congress*, 363; *Representative Men of the South* (Philadelphia: Charles Robson, 1880), 287.

9. E. Grace Jemison, *Historic Tales of Talladega* (Montgomery, AL: Paragon Press, 1959), 257; Benjamin F. Riley, *Makers and Romance of Alabama History* (n.p.: n.p., 1915), 219; William Garrett, *Reminiscences of Public Men in Alabama, for Thirty Years* (Atlanta: Plantation, 1872), 647; *Representative Men of the South*, 287–88; Thornton, *Politics and Power*, 351.

10. Jabez Curry, *Progress of Anti-Slaveryism*, published speech (Washington, DC: Lemuel Towers, 1859), 1, 7–9; Hellen Jeanette Jackson, "The Work of the Alabama Delegation in the Confederate Congress," (master's thesis, Emory University, 1953), 3–6; Robert S. Tharin, *Arbitrary Arrests in the South; or Scenes from the Experience of an Alabama Unionist* (New York: John Bradburn, 1863), 62; Charles B. Dew, *Apostles of Disunion: Southern Secession Commissioners and the Causes of the Civil War* (Charlottesville: University Press of Virginia, 2001), 56–57.

11. Clarence Phillips Denman, *The Secession Movement in Alabama* (Freeport, NY: Books for Libraries Press, 1971), 155; Curtis Arthur Amlund, *Federalism in the Southern Confederacy* (Washington, DC: Public Affairs Press, 1966), 3–5, 11, 13, 17; Martis, *Historical Atlas*, 131.

12. Curry, *Progress of Anti-Slaveryism*, 13; "Proceedings of the Confederate Con-

gress," *Southern Historical Society Papers* (*SHSP*) 44 (1923): 101; 47 (1930): 183–84, 190; 49 (1943): 82; *Journal of the Congress of the Confederate States of America, 1861–1865* (*JCCSA*), 7 vols. (Washington, DC: Government Printing Office, 1904–5), 5:34, 228, 400, 516; 6:107, 382; Jackson, "Work of the Alabama Delegation," 85, 93, 100, 118, 161; Jessie Pearl Rice, *J. L. M. Curry: Southerner, Statesman and Educator* (New York: King's Crown Press, 1949), 41, 44; Edwin Anderson Alderman and Armistead Churchill Gordon, *J. L. M. Curry: A Biography* (New York: MacMillan, 1911), 163.

13. Alderman and Gordon, *J. L. M. Curry*, 10–11, 166; William C. Davis, *Look Away! A History of the Confederate States of America* (New York: Free Press, 2002), 101; Mary S. Estill, ed. "Franklin B. Sexton: Diary of a Confederate Congressman, 1862–1863," *Southwestern Historical Quarterly* 38, no. 4 (1935): 292; Clayton E. Jewett, ed., *Rise and Fall of the Confederacy: The Memoir of Senator Williamson S. Oldham, CSA* (Columbia: University of Missouri Press, 2006), 57; Willis Brewer, *Alabama: Her History, Resources, War Record, and Public Men; From 1540 to 1872* (Montgomery, AL: Barret and Brown, 1872), 542; Rice, *J. L. M. Curry*, 38; *The Papers of Jefferson Davis*, ed. Lynda Lasswell Crist, vol. 8, *1862* (Baton Rouge: Louisiana State University Press, 1995), 256–59, 314.

14. Rice, *J. L. M. Curry*, 39–40, 43; Rable, *Confederate Republic*, 112, 187; Rebecca Grant Sexton, ed., *A Southern Woman of Letters: The Correspondence of Augusta Jane Evans Wilson* (Columbia: University of South Carolina Press, 2002), 67.

15. Jackson, "Work of the Alabama Delegation," 43–44; Alexander and Beringer, *Anatomy of the Confederate Congress*, 381; Warner and Yearns, *Biographical Register*, 201; Thornton, *Politics and Power*, 427; Brewer, *Alabama*, 251–52.

16. Brewer, *Alabama*, 251; Martis, *Historical Atlas*, 131; Jack L. Dickinson, ed., *If I Should Fall in Battle: The Civil War Diary of James P. Stephens* (Huntington, WV: John Deaver Drinko Academy, 2003), 52; "Proceedings of the Confederate Congress," *SHSP* 44 (1923): 81–82; *JCCSA*, 5:228, 400, 518; 6:107, 234; Jackson, "Work of the Alabama Delegation," 118; Warner and Yearns, *Biographical Register*, 201; H. H. Cunningham, "Confederate General Hospitals: Establishment and Organization," *Journal of Southern History* 20, no. 3 (1954): 379–80; Estill, "Franklin B. Sexton," 39, no. 1 (1935): 39.

17. Garrett, *Reminiscences of Public Men*, 730; Jackson, "Work of the Alabama Delegation," 44–45; Alexander and Beringer, *Anatomy of the Confederate Congress*, 361; Warner and Yearns, *Biographical Register*, 54; *Representative Men of the South*, 476; Brewer, *Alabama*, 482.

18. Elizabeth H. Yamaguchi, "Macon County, Alabama: Its Land and Its People from Prehistory to 1870" (master's thesis, Auburn University, 1981), 110–11; Garrett, *Reminiscences of Public Men*, 730; Dew, *Apostles of Disunion*, 57–58; Edward S. Cooper, *Traitors: The Secession Period, November 1860–July 1861* (Madison, NJ: Fairleigh Dickinson University Press, 2008), 117; Warner and Yearns, *Biographical Register*, 54; *Representative Men of the South*, 475–76.

19. Jackson, "Work of the Alabama Delegation," 85, 93; *JCCSA*, 5:228, 400; Albert B. Moore, *Conscription and Conflict in the Confederacy* (New York: Hillary House, 1963), 13; *Montgomery Weekly Advertiser*, July 22, 1863; "Proceedings of the Confederate Congress," 46 (1928): 57.

20. Jackson, "Work of the Alabama Delegation," 124, 142–43, 161, 174; *JCCSA*, 5:508, 516–17; 6:107, 234, 382, 488; "Proceedings of the Confederate Congress," 47 (1930): 152; Warner and Yearns, *Biographical Register*, 54.

21. Jackson, "Work of the Alabama Delegation," 41–43; Warner and Yearns, *Biographical Register*, 198; Riley, *Makers and Romance*, 305–6; Anne Kendrick Walker, *Backtracking in Barbour County: A Narrative of the Last Alabama Frontier* (Richmond, VA: Dietz Press, 1941), 133, 164.

22. Alexander and Beringer, *Anatomy of the Confederate Congress*, 381; Mike Bunn, *Civil War Eufaula* (Charleston, SC: History Press, 2013), 36, 39, 75; Mary Jane Davidson, "James Lawrence Pugh: A Half Century in Politics" (master's thesis, Auburn University, 1971), 28, 31–32; Brewer, *Alabama*, 128–29; Malcolm C. McMillan, *The Alabama Confederate Reader* (Tuscaloosa: University of Alabama Press, 1963), 40–41.

23. Bunn, *Civil War Eufaula*, 51; Martis, *Historical Atlas*, 131; Warner and Yearns, *Biographical Register*, 199; Jackson, "Work of the Alabama Delegation," 85, 118, 160, 172; *JCCSA*, 5:68–70, 228, 400, 518; 6:107, 382, 474; *Southern Advertiser*, July 22, 1863; Estill, "Franklin B. Sexton," 39:34, 40; *Autauga Citizen*, August 27, 1863.

24. Jackson, "Work of the Alabama Delegation," 39–40; Warner and Yearns, *Biographical Register*, 69; Riley, *Makers and Romance*, 176–77; Garrett, *Reminiscences of Public Men*, 385–86; Brewer, *Alabama*, 411.

25. Riley, *Makers and Romance*, 178–79; Brewer, *Alabama*, 412; Garrett, *Reminiscences of Public Men*, 386; John Hope Franklin, "The Southern Expansionists of 1846," *Journal of Southern History* 25, no. 3 (1959): 331–32.

26. Thornton, *Politics and Power*, 254–56; Alexander and Beringer, *Anatomy of the Confederate Congress*, 363; James Benson Sellers, *Slavery in Alabama* (Tuscaloosa: University of Alabama Press, 1950), 238, 358; William Russell Smith, *The History and Debates of the Convention of the People of Alabama* (Montgomery, AL: White, Pfister, 1861), 94.

27. Robert Bradley, "Tattered Banners: Alabama's Civil War Flags," *Alabama Heritage* 96 (2010): 12; Smith, *History and Debates of the Convention*, 94, 325; Martis, *Historical Atlas*, 131. Dargan's rival Portis went on to command the Forty-Second Alabama Infantry Regiment.

28. Brewer, *Alabama*, 412; Warner and Yearns, *Biographical Register*, 70; *JCCSA*, 5:228, 400; Robbins, "Confederate Nationalism," 100; "Proceedings of the Confederate Congress," 45 (1925): 209–10; 46 (1928): 53; Estill, "Franklin B. Sexton," 38:277, 289; Riley, *Makers and Romance*, 179; Coulter, *Confederate States of America*, 143.

29. Jackson, "Work of the Alabama Delegation," 85, 93, 118, 142–43, 145, 160, 169; *JCCSA*, 5:518, 6:35, 107, 234, 382; Robbins, "Confederate Nationalism," 72; John Brawner Robbins, "The Confederacy and the Writ of Habeas Corpus," *Georgia Historical Quarterly* 55, no. 1 (1971): 88; Warner and Yearns, *Biographical Register*, 70; Estill, "Franklin B. Sexton," 38:298.

30. *The War of the Rebellion: A Compilation of the Official Records of the Union and Confederate Armies* (*Official Records*), 4th ser., vol. 2 (Washington, DC: Government Printing Office, 1900), 664–65; *Papers of Jefferson Davis*, 8:483; *The Papers of Jefferson*

Davis, ed. Lynda Lasswell Crist, vol. 9, *January–September 1863* (Baton Rouge: Louisiana State University Press, 1997), 335; Sellers, *Slavery in Alabama*, 387–88; Edward Younger, ed., *Inside the Confederate Government: The Diary of Robert Garlick Hill Kean* (New York: Oxford University Press, 1957), 67; John B. Jones, *A Rebel War Clerk's Diary at the Confederate States Capital* (Philadelphia: Lippincott, 1866), 1:391.

31. See Thomas B. Alexander, "Persistent Whiggery in the Confederate South, 1860–1877," *Journal of Southern History* 27, no. 3 (1961): 305–29; and a persuasive rebuttal by John Vollmer Mering, "Persistent Whiggery in the Confederate South: A Reconsideration," *South Atlantic Quarterly* 69, no. 1 (1970): 124–43.

32. Warner and Yearns, *Biographical Register*, 89; Brewer, *Alabama*, 304, 310; Alexander and Beringer, *Anatomy of the Confederate Congress*, 27, 367; Paul Horton, "Submitting to the Shadow of Slavery: The Secession Crisis and Civil War in Alabama's Lawrence County," *Civil War History* 44, no. 2 (1998): 116, 121; Spencer A. Waters and Betty R. Waters, *Lawrence County*, vol. 2, *Genealogical Records* (n.p.: B. R. Waters, 2009), 24; Martis, *Historical Atlas*, 131.

33. Jackson, "Work of the Alabama Delegation," 85, 93; *JCCSA*, 5:228, 400; Yearns, *Confederate Congress*, 69; "Proceedings of the Confederate Congress," 46 (1928): 136.

34. *Papers of Jefferson Davis*, 8:458, 467; 9:206; Beringer et al., *Why the South Lost*, 374; Jackson, "Work of the Alabama Delegation," 118, 161, 167, 172; *JCCSA*, 5:518; 6:107, 234, 382.

35. Warner and Yearns, *Biographical Register*, 47; Garrett, *Reminiscences of Public Men*, 116; Brewer, *Alabama*, 477; Riley, *Makers and Romance*, 81–83; Alexander and Beringer, *Anatomy of the Confederate Congress*, 361; Lewy Dorman, *Party Politics in Alabama from 1850 through 1860* (Montgomery: Alabama State Department of Archives and History, 1935), 152; Eric H. Walther, *William Lowndes Yancey and the Coming of the Civil War* (Chapel Hill: University of North Carolina Press, 2006), 149–50; Jackson, "Work of the Alabama Delegation," 9–11.

36. Martis, *Historical Atlas*, 100, 131; William Warren Rogers Jr., *Confederate Home Front: Montgomery during the Civil War* (Tuscaloosa: University of Alabama Press, 1999), 44; Brewer, *Alabama*, 477–78; Jackson, "Work of the Alabama Delegation," 79, 85, 118, 160, 172; *JCCSA*, 5:228, 400, 516–18, 6:107, 234, 382; "Proceedings of the Confederate Congress," 45 (1925): 30–31, 34; 47 (1930): 33, 86; 48 (1941): 8–9, 191–92; Alexander and Beringer, *Anatomy of the Confederate Congress*, 170; Warner and Yearns, *Biographical Register*, 48. Curiously, in May 1863, Chilton abstained on resolutions calling for the execution of Union officers who commanded black soldiers; *JCCSA*, 6:487–88.

37. Winston Smith, *The People's City: The Glory and Grief of an Alabama Town, 1850–1874* (Demopolis, AL: Marengo County Historical Society, 2003), 28–30; Grady McWhiney, "Were the Whigs a Class Party in Alabama?" *Journal of Southern History* 23, no. 4 (1957): 515; E. Bryding Adams, "William Frye, Artist," *Alabama Heritage* 32 (1994): 34; Alexander and Beringer, *Anatomy of the Confederate Congress*, 375; Brewer, *Alabama*, 375–76; Warner and Yearns, *Biographical Register*, 154; Garrett, *Reminiscences of Public Men*, 587–90; Thornton, *Politics and Power*, 112.

38. Dorman, *Party Politics in Alabama*, 155–56; Smith, *The People's City*, 30; Lonnie Burnett, "Precipitating a Revolution: Alabama's Democracy in the Election of 1860," in *The Yellowhammer War: The Civil War and Reconstruction in Alabama*, ed. Kenneth W. Noe (Tuscaloosa: University of Alabama Press, 2013), 23; Martis, *Historical Atlas*, 131. Lyon's opponent Herndon went on to command the Thirty-Sixth Alabama Infantry Regiment.

39. Warner and Yearns, *Biographical Register*, 155; Jackson, "Work of the Alabama Delegation," 85, 93, 118, 160, 167; *JCCSA*, 5:228, 400, 6:107, 234, 382; Yearns, *Confederate Congress*, 154; *Papers of Jefferson Davis*, 8:403; 9:340; Smith, *The People's City*, 30.

40. Douglas B. Ball, *Financial Failure and Confederate Defeat* (Chicago: University of Illinois Press, 1991), 32, 185–86; Richard C. Todd, *Confederate Finance* (Athens: University of Georgia Press, 1954), 119, 133–35; Jackson, "Work of the Alabama Delegation," 149–60; John Christopher Schwab, *The Confederate States of America, 1861–1865: A Financial and Industrial History of the South during the Civil War* (New York: Charles Scribner's Sons, 1904), 3, 99, 166–67; Allan Nevins, *The War for the Union*, vol. 4, *The Organized War to Victory, 1864–1865* (New York: Konecky and Konecky, 1971), 231–32; Robbins, "Confederate Nationalism," 145.

41. Bell I. Wiley, ed., *Letters of Warren Akin, Confederate Congressman* (Athens: University of Georgia Press, 1959), 105; Jewett, *Rise and Fall of the Confederacy*, 70; Jackson, "Work of the Alabama Delegation," 160–61; Schwab, *Confederate States of America*, 291–93; Estill, "Franklin B. Sexton," 39:57–58; "Proceedings of the Confederate Congress," 49 (1943): 10.

42. Warner and Yearns, *Biographical Register*, 227–28; Jackson, "Work of the Alabama Delegation," 48; Garrett, *Reminiscences of Public Men*, 558–59; Brewer, *Alabama*, 561–62; Benjamin Buford Williams, *A Literary History of Alabama: The Nineteenth Century* (Madison, NJ: Fairleigh Dickinson University Press, 1979), 28–31; Anne Easby-Smith, *William Russell Smith of Alabama: His Life and Works* (Philadelphia: Dolphin Press, 1931), 32–33.

43. Easby-Smith, *William Russell Smith*, 41–43, 59, 76–78, 83; Garrett, *Reminiscences of Public Men*, 562; Dorman, *Party Politics in Alabama*, 140; *The Heritage of Tuscaloosa County, Alabama*, Heritage of Alabama 63 (Clanton, AL: Heritage, 1999), 377. During these years, Smith experienced an erratic domestic life, losing his first wife in 1844 and his second in 1853, both to illnesses, before finding durable happiness in 1854 with Wilhelmine Easby, his third (and final) spouse. See Johanna Nicol Shields, "A Social History of Antebellum Alabama Writers," *Alabama Review* 42, no. 3 (1989): 183–84.

44. Smith, *History and Debates of the Convention*, 26, 67–68, 98, 118, 121; Easby-Smith, *William Russell Smith*, 94–124.

45. Brewer, *Alabama*, 561, 631; Easby-Smith, *William Russell Smith*, 140–41; Martis, *Historical Atlas*, 131. The official returns for Alabama's Second District in 1861 were Smith, 1,699; Browne, 1,458; P. Musgrove, 1,274; and William Earnest, 451.

46. Jackson, "Work of the Alabama Delegation," 85, 93, 97–98, 118, 142–43, 160–

61; *JCCSA*, 5:68–70, 228, 400, 518; 6:107, 234, 382; "Proceedings of the Confederate Congress," 46 (1928): 83; William M. Robinson, *Justice in Grey: A History of the Judicial System in the Confederate States of America* (Cambridge, MA: Harvard University Press, 1941), 417; Easby-Smith, *William Russell Smith*, 146.

47. Easby-Smith, *William Russell Smith*, 142–43, 145–46, 149–50; Jon L. Wakelyn, *Confederates against the Confederacy: Essays on Leadership and Loyalty* (Westport, CT: Praeger, 2002), 24.

48. Easby-Smith, *William Russell Smith*, 148; Coleman Hutchison, *Apples and Ashes: Literature, Nationalism, and the Confederate States of America* (Athens: University of Georgia Press, 2012), 111–12; Williams, *Literary History of Alabama*, 36.

49. William R. Smith, *The Royal Ape: A Dramatic Poem* (Richmond, VA: West and Johnson, 1863), 25, 31, 35–41, 43.

50. Smith, 12, 46–47.

51. Smith, 65, 74–75, 84–85.

52. Easby-Smith, *William Russell Smith*, 150; Smith, *The Royal Ape*, 37, 73, 80. Smith's work created a mild stir back in Alabama when two newspaper editors debated the sexual mores of the play, one considering them indecent, the other as vital to the story line. The play's negative portrayal of Lincoln also appears to have made the author persona non grata in the eyes of the North. See Rhoda Coleman Ellison, *Early Alabama Publications: A Study in Literary Interests* (Tuscaloosa: University of Alabama Press, 1947), 130–31; Christopher Lyle McIlwain, *1865 Alabama: From Civil War to Uncivil Peace* (Tuscaloosa: University of Alabama Press, 2017), 221.

53. Jackson, "Work of the Alabama Delegation," 173, 192–93; *JCCSA*, 5:34, 60, 68–70, 228, 400, 516–18; 6:107, 234, 382, 764. In his quantitative analysis of the Confederate Congress, Kenneth Martis gives the Alabama delegation a score of 4.77 on a scale of 0–9 for its support of the war effort, which is slightly higher than the overall southern average, which he fixes at 4.62 (*Historical Atlas*, 104).

54. Yearns, *Confederate Congress*, 218–19; Jenkins, "Examining Contemporary Congressional Theories," 22, 34; Jackson, "Work of the Alabama Delegation," 142–43, 156–57; "Proceedings of the Confederate Congress," 45 (1925): 217; 47 (1930): 45, 86–87; 49 (1943): 30; Don E. Fehrenbacher, *Sectional Crisis and Southern Constitutionalism* (Baton Rouge: Louisiana State University Press, 1995), 156; Robinson, *Justice in Grey*, 434, 449.

55. Alexander and Beringer, *Anatomy of the Confederate Congress*, 216, 296, 336–37; Martis, *Historical Atlas*, 100; Richard E. Beringer, "The Unconscious 'Spirit of Party' in the Confederate Congress," *Civil War History* 18, no. 4 (1972): 330–31.

56. Jenkins, "Examining Contemporary Congressional Theories," 62.

57. William J. Cooper, *Jefferson Davis and the Civil War Era* (Baton Rouge: Louisiana State University Press, 2008), 39–40; Emory M. Thomas, *The Confederacy as a Revolutionary Experience* (Englewood Cliffs, NJ: Prentice-Hall, 1971), 60; Rable, *Confederate Republic*, 126, 173, 210; Alderman and Gordon, *J. L. M. Curry*, 164; Davis, *Look Away!*, 74; Rice, *J. L. M. Curry*, 42; Escott, *Confederacy*, 29, 96; Paul D. Escott, *Military*

Necessity: Civil-Military Relations in the Confederacy (Westport, CT: Praeger, 2006), 19, 145, 151; "Proceedings of the Confederate Congress," 45 (1925): 76; Wakelyn, *Confederates against the Confederacy*, 24.

58. *Papers of Jefferson Davis*, 8:392; Walther, *William Lowndes Yancey*, 364–65; Stuart Flynn and T. J. Beitelman, "Demopolis: City of the People," *Alabama Heritage* 59 (2001): 18; Bensel, "Southern Leviathan," 128.

59. Yearns, *Confederate Congress*, 55; Rable, *Confederate Republic*, 138, 157–59.

60. Georgia Lee Tatum, *Disloyalty in the Confederacy* (New York: AMS Press, 1934), 26–31, 58–62; Malcolm C. McMillan, *The Disintegration of a Confederate State: Three Governors and Alabama's Wartime Home Front, 1861–1865* (Macon, GA: Mercer University Press, 1986), 41–42; Yearns, *Confederate Congress*, 56; Jemison, *Historic Tales of Talladega*, 109, 137; Reuben A. Mitchell to Lewis E. Parsons, August 5, 1863, folder 1, box 1, Parsons Papers, LPR248, Alabama Department of Archives and History (ADAH); *Alabama Reporter*, June 5, 1862; *Jacksonville Republican*, July 11, 1863.

61. Jemison, *Historic Tales*, 116; Rice, *J. L. M. Curry*, 43, 192; Alderman and Gordon, *J. L. M. Curry*, 168–70; Martin, *Rich Man's War*, 111; Kenneth Michael Murry, "Gubernatorial Politics and the Confederacy" (PhD diss., Columbia University, 1977), 394–96; Jack A. Bunch, *Roster of the Courts-Martial in the Confederate States of America* (Shippensburg, PA: White Mane, 2001), 267; *Jacksonville Republican*, May 30, July 11, and July 18, 1863; *Democratic Watchtower*, July 22, 1863.

62. Martis, *Historical Atlas*, 135; Election Files of the Alabama Secretary of State, folder 12, SG002475, ADAH; *Papers of Jefferson Davis*, 9:333; *Montgomery Weekly Advertiser*, August 12, 1863; Sexton, *Southern Woman of Letters*, 77; *Mobile Weekly Advertiser and Register*, August 1, 1863; McMillan, *Alabama Confederate Reader*, 236–38; Robbins, "Confederate Nationalism," 209–10; Rice, *J. L. M. Curry*, 44; *Montgomery Weekly Mail*, September 23, 1863.

63. Garrett, *Reminiscences of Public Men*, 395–97; McMillan, *Alabama Confederate Reader*, 38; Thornton, *Politics and Power*, 6, 333–34; Dorman, *Party Politics in Alabama*, 24, 37, 59, 91; Brewer, *Alabama*, 287; Leah Atkins, "Williamson R. W. Cobb and the Graduation Act of 1854," *Alabama Review* 28, no. 1 (1975): 17.

64. Atkins, "Williamson R. W. Cobb," 25, 28, 30; Brewer, *Alabama*, 252; Dorman, *Party Politics in Alabama*, 166; McMillan, *Alabama Confederate Reader*, 38, 43; Martis, *Historical Atlas*, 131.

65. Tatum, *Disloyalty in the Confederacy*, 61; *Jacksonville Republican*, July 18, 1863.

66. Brewer, *Alabama*, 384, 660–61; Smith, *History and Debates of the Convention*, 358; J. Gary Laine and Morris M. Penny, *Law's Alabama Brigade in the War between the Union and the Confederacy* (Shippensburg, PA: White Mane, 1996), 2, 29, 82, 90–96; Katherine McKinstry Duncan and Larry Joe Smith, *The History of Marshall County, Alabama*, vol. 1, *Prehistory to 1939* (Albertville, AL: Thompson, 1969), 50–51, 61, 64; *Official Records*, 1st ser., vol. 27, pt. 2 (1889): 395–96.

67. Martis, *Historical Atlas*, 67, 135; Election Files, folder 12, SG002475, ADAH; Sarah Rousseau Espy, diary, July 9, July 17, and August 3, 1863, SPR2, ADAH. Martis incorrectly ascribes to Cobb a Whig appellation.

68. *South Western Baptist*, July 23, 1863; "Our Harman Heritage Research Center," J & W Enterprises, accessed August 25, 2019, http://www.harmanheritage.net/genealogy/; "Alabama Civil War Service Database," ADAH, updated May 23, 2017, http://www.archives.alabama.gov/civilwar/search.cfm; Martis, *Historical Atlas*, 135; Election Files, folder 12, SG002475, ADAH.

69. Brewer, *Alabama*, 505–6; *The Heritage of Pike County, Alabama*, Heritage of Alabama 55 (Clanton, AL: Heritage, 2001), 685–86; Garrett, *Reminiscences of Public Men*, 351–52; Margaret Pace Farmer, *One Hundred Fifty Years in Pike County, Alabama, 1821–1971* (Anniston, AL: Higginbotham, 1973), 139, 143–45.

70. Martis, *Historical Atlas*, 135; Election Files, folder 12, SG002475, ADAH. Pugh may have been a jingo for the Confederacy, but he was not a blind fanatic. In a preelection letter to General Henry Clayton, a fellow member of the Eufaula Regency, Pugh revealed some anxiety about the rebellion: "The future is wrapt in darkness—some lights breaking out occasionally but they are very faint." J. L. Pugh to H. D. Clayton, February 18, 1863, Henry D. Clayton Papers, folder 6, box 312, W. S. Hoole Special Collections Library, University of Alabama.

71. *Mobile Advertiser and Register*, April 18, 1863; Warner and Yearns, *Biographical Register*, 78; Alexander and Beringer, *Anatomy of the Confederate Congress*, 365; Timothy H. Ball, *A Glance into the Great South-East, or Clarke County, Alabama, and Its Surroundings, from 1540 to 1877* (Tuscaloosa, AL: Willco, 1962), 234, 274, 547–49; *The Heritage of Clarke County, Alabama*, Heritage of Alabama 13 (Clanton, AL: Heritage, 2001), 151; Brewer, *Alabama*, 179; Glen Dedmondt, *The Flags of Civil War Alabama* (Gretna, LA: Pelican, 2001), 76; *Clarke County Journal*, April 16, May 7, and July 30, 1863.

72. Brewer, *Alabama*, 397–98, 425–26; Warner and Yearns, *Biographical Register*, 223–24; Garrett, *Reminiscences of Public Men*, 184; Denman, *Secession Movement in Alabama*, 102–3; *Mobile Advertiser and Register*, April 21, 1863; *Clarke County Journal*, July 9, 1863; Riley, *Makers and Romance*, 152–53; *Representative Men of the South*, 190–91, 540–52; Henry M. McKiven, "Secession, War, and Reconstruction, 1850–1874," in *Mobile: The New History of Alabama's First City*, ed. Michael Thompson (Tuscaloosa: University of Alabama Press, 2001), 90, 95–100. In June 1861, the *Mobile Advertiser* merged with the *Mobile Register* to become the *Mobile Advertiser and Register*, which for the duration of the war was a pro-Confederate newspaper under the editorship of John Forsyth.

73. Martis, *Historical Atlas*, 135; *Clarke County Journal*, July 30 and August 6, 1863; *Mobile Daily Advertiser and Register*, July 12, 1863; Election Files, folders 12 and 13, SG002475, ADAH.

74. Martis, *Historical Atlas*, 135; Election Files, folders 12 and 13, SG002475, ADAH.

75. *Alabama Beacon*, July 24, 1863; Brewer, *Alabama*, 493; Dorman, *Party Politics in Alabama*, 151; Martis, *Historical Atlas*, 135; Election Files, folders 12 and 13, SG002475, ADAH.

76. Martin, *Rich Man's War*, 115, 118; *Montgomery Daily Advertiser*, June 17, 1863; *Selma Daily Reporter*, June 28, 1863; *South Western Baptist*, July 30, 1863; Rogers, *Confederate Home Front*, 119.

77. Michael Jackson Daniel, "Red Hills and Piney Woods: A Political History of Butler County, Alabama, in the Nineteenth Century" (PhD diss., University of Alabama, 1985), 155; Estill, "Franklin B. Sexton," 38:276–77; Rable, *Confederate Republic,* 186; Coulter, *Confederate States of America,* 139–40; "Proceedings of the Confederate Congress," 46 (1928): 255; Murray, "Gubernatorial Politics," 361; *Selma Daily Reporter,* July 16, July 17, and July 31, 1863.

78. Martis, *Historical Atlas,* 135; Election Files, folder 12, SG002475, ADAH; Reuben Mitchell to Lewis Parsons, August 5, 1863, Parsons Papers, folder 1, box 1, LPR248, ADAH; *Montgomery Daily Advertiser,* June 17; *Montgomery Weekly Advertiser,* August 5, and August 12, 1863.

79. Brewer, *Alabama,* 269, 701; McWhiney, "Were the Whigs a Class Party," 517; William L. Barney, *The Secessionist Impulse: Alabama and Mississippi in 1860* (1974; Tuscaloosa: University of Alabama Press, 2004), 250; Rhoda Coleman Ellison, *History and Bibliography of Alabama Newspapers in the Nineteenth Century* (Tuscaloosa: University of Alabama Press, 1954), 56, 183; Smith, *History and Debates of the Convention,* 128; Martis, *Historical Atlas,* 135; Election Files, folders 12 and 13, SG002475, ADAH; Alexander and Beringer, *Anatomy of the Confederate Congress,* 40. After the election, Captain Fowler returned to his battery, and he subsequently fought with valor at the Battle of Chickamauga. See *Official Records,* 1st ser., vol. 30, pt. 2 (1890): 286–87.

80. Alderman and Gordon, *J. L. M. Curry,* 173–74; *Official Records,* 4th ser., vol. 3 (1900): 126–37; Brewer, *Alabama,* 542, 683. Charles P. Roland describes this session of the Confederate Congress as "a body of desperate, confused, and bitter men [whose] mood was ripe for measures at once heroic and vindictive." Roland, *The Confederacy* (Chicago: University of Chicago Press, 1960), 127. A few days after his oration, Curry returned to Talladega, and he later accepted a commission in the Fifth Alabama Cavalry.

81. Martis, *Historical Atlas,* 75; Rable, *Confederate Republic,* 225; Andrew, "Essential Nationalism of the People," 142–43. It should be noted that in Georgia, most incumbents lost to military veterans who espoused a continuation of the war effort. Conversely, virtually the whole of North Carolina's incoming delegation was both antiwar and anti-Confederate.

82. Christopher Lyle McIlwain, *Civil War Alabama* (Tuscaloosa: University of Alabama Press, 2016), 167, 220–21; Brewer, *Alabama,* 286–87; Wilfred Buck Yearns, "The Peace Movement in the Confederate Congress," *Georgia Historical Quarterly* 41, no. 1 (1957): 14; Jackson, "Work of the Alabama Delegation," 179–84; "Proceedings of the Confederate Congress," 51 (1958): 52. Confederate newspapers (and early histories of the period) explain Cobb's death as an accident, the congressman apparently killing himself when he dropped a pistol and was struck in the torso by the ensuing discharge.

83. McIlwain, *1865 Alabama,* 18–21; Warner and Yearns, *Biographical Register,* 66; Thomas B. Alexander, "Persistent Whiggery in Alabama and the Lower South, 1860–1867," *Alabama Review* 12, no. 1 (1959): 41–42; Coulter, *Confederate States of America,* 143; Alexander and Beringer, *Anatomy of the Confederate Congress,* 27, 342; Beringer,

"Unconscious 'Spirit of Party,'" 322; *The Papers of Andrew Johnson*, ed. Paul H. Bergeron, vol. 8, *May–August 1865* (Knoxville: University of Tennessee Press, 1989), 143–44; *The Papers of Andrew Johnson*, ed. Paul H. Bergeron, vol. 9, *September 1865–January 1866* (Knoxville: University of Tennessee Press, 1989), 385.

84. E. W. Sikes, *The Confederate States Congress* (Raleigh, NC: Edwards and Broughton, 1903), 21; Jackson, "Work of the Alabama Delegation," 181, 184; Martis, *Historical Atlas*, 107; Warner and Yearns, *Biographical Register*, 78; *JCCSA* 7:350; "Proceedings of the Confederate Congress," 51 (1958): 113–14, 201–2, 218, 243; Robbins, "Confederate Nationalism," 145, 147; Fehrenbacher, *Sectional Crisis*, 144; Adam Ramey, "National Survival and the Confederate Congress," *Historical Methods* 46, no. 1 (2013): 36.

85. Rable, *Confederate Republic*, 280–81; "Proceedings of the Confederate Congress," 51 (1958): x, 6–8, 166, 310, 316–18; *JCCSA* 7:276–77, 659–60. Toward the end, William Smith also faced possible expulsion, but he resigned his seat "under the shadow of an impeachment." See McIlwain, *1865 Alabama*, 21. Vandiver's comment comes from the foreword to the "Proceedings."

86. Bensel, "Southern Leviathan," 121; Rable, *Confederate Republic*, 281; *JCCSA* 7:84–85, 451–52; Yearns, *Confederate Congress*, 181–83.

87. Bruce Levine, *Confederate Emancipation: Southern Plans to Free and Arm Slaves during the Civil War* (New York: Oxford University Press, 2006), 118; *JCCSA* 7:612–13; "Proceedings of the Confederate Congress," 50 (1953): 137; 52 (1959): 331, 337; Philip D. Dillard, *Jefferson Davis's Final Campaign: Confederate Nationalism and the Fight to Arm Slaves* (Macon, GA: Mercer University Press, 2017), 267.

Chapter 2

1. *Montgomery Weekly Advertiser*, October 21, 1863; Alabama Legislature, *House Journal* 1863, executive message, 90; Malcolm C. McMillan, "Alabama," in *The Confederate Governors*, ed. Wilfred Buck Yearns (Athens: University of Georgia Press, 1985), 30.

2. Malcolm C. McMillan, *The Alabama Confederate Reader* (Tuscaloosa: University of Alabama Press, 1963), 236; Yearns, *Confederate Governors*, 6–8; Michael Albert Powell, "Confederate Federalism: A View from the Governors (PhD diss., University of Maryland, 2004), 1, 7, 257–58. For further concurrence in the generally cooperative and nationalistic behavior of the South's war governors, see William C. Davis, *Look Away! A History of the Confederate States of America* (New York: Free Press, 2002), 323–40.

3. Benjamin F. Riley, *Makers and Romance of Alabama History* (n.p.: n.p., 1915), 185; William Garrett, *Reminiscences of Public Men in Alabama, for Thirty Years* (Atlanta: Plantation, 1872), 722; Willis Brewer, *Alabama: Her History, Resources, War Record, and Public Men; From 1540 to 1872* (Montgomery: Barrett and Brown, 1872), 127; Mike Bunn, *Civil War Eufaula* (Charleston, SC: History Press, 2013), 25.

4. J. Mills Thornton III, *Politics and Power in a Slave Society: Alabama, 1800–1860* (Baton Rouge: Louisiana State University Press, 1978), 207; James Benson Sellers,

Slavery in Alabama (Tuscaloosa: University of Alabama Press, 1950), 249; Bunn, *Civil War Eufaula*, 36; William Russell Smith, *The History and Debates of the Convention of the People of Alabama* (Montgomery, AL: White, Pfister, 1861), 395.

5. Kenneth Michael Murray, "Gubernatorial Politics and the Confederacy" (PhD diss., Columbia University, 1977), 12–13, 53–74; Malcolm C. McMillan, *The Disintegration of a Confederate State: Three Governors and Alabama's Wartime Home Front, 1861–1865* (Macon, GA: Mercer University Press, 1986), 30–33; Alabama Legislature, *House Journal*, 1862, election returns, 117–18.

6. *The War of the Rebellion: A Compilation of the Official Records of the Union and Confederate Armies* (*Official Records*), 4th ser., vol. 1 (Washington, DC: Government Printing Office, 1900), 771–74; McMillan, *Disintegration of a Confederate State*, 33–34.

7. Emory M. Thomas, *The Confederacy as a Revolutionary Experience* (Englewood Cliffs, NJ: Prentice-Hall, 1971), 134; *Supplement to the Official Records of the Union and Confederate Armies* (*Supplement*), ed. Janet B. Hewett (Wilmington, NC: Broadfoot, 1999), 94:155; Powell, "Confederate Federalism," 262; see also Murray, "Gubernatorial Politics," 39.

8. *Supplement* 94:157; McMillan, *Disintegration of a Confederate State*, 124; Powell, "Confederate Federalism," 125.

9. *Population of the United States in 1860: The Eighth Census* (Washington, DC: Government Printing Office, 1864), 2–3; McMillan, *Disintegration of a Confederate State*, 23; Alabama Legislature, *House Journal*, 1862, executive message, 95. For Alabama troop strength, see also Thomas Alton Smith, "Mobilization of the Army in Alabama, 1859–1865" (master's thesis, Alabama Polytechnic Institute, 1953).

10. Anne Kendrick Walker, ed., "Governor John Gill Shorter: Miscellaneous Papers, 1861–1863," *Alabama Review* 11 (1958): 231, 267–78; Ralph N. Brannen, "John Gill Shorter: War Governor of Alabama" (master's thesis, Alabama Polytechnic Institute, 1956), 37, 41.

11. Powell, "Confederate Federalism," 125, 138; McMillan, *Disintegration of a Confederate State*, 40; Janet E. Kaufman, "Sentinels on the Watchtower: The Confederate Governors and the Davis Administration" (PhD diss., American University, 1977), 259.

12. Murray, "Gubernatorial Politics," 349; McMillan, *Disintegration of a Confederate State*, 41; Kaufman, "Sentinels on the Watchtower," 258; Walter L. Fleming, "Conscription and Exemption in Alabama during the Civil War," *Gulf States Historical Magazine* 2 (1904): 317; Douglas Clare Purcell, "Military Conscription in Alabama during the Civil War" *Alabama Review* 34, no. 2 (1981): 102–4; *The Papers of Jefferson Davis*, vol. 8, *1862* (Baton Rouge: Louisiana State University Press, 1995), 497, 542; *Official Records*, 4th ser., vol. 2 (1900): 255.

13. Murray, "Gubernatorial Politics," 364–65; Albert B. Moore, *Conscription and Conflict in the Confederacy* (New York: Hillary House, 1963), 107, 160; Alabama Legislature, *House Journal*, 1862, executive message, 6–7; Purcell, "Military Conscription in Alabama," 101; *Official Records*, 4th ser., vol. 2 (1900): 754.

14. Alabama Legislature, *House Journal*, 1862, executive message, 18; Governor

Shorter to Joel D. Murphree, July 18, 1863, Governors' Papers: Shorter, reel 14, SG024882, Alabama Department of Archives and History (ADAH).

15. Joseph W. Danielson, *War's Desolating Scourge: The Union's Occupation of North Alabama* (Lawrence: University of Kansas Press, 2012), 117–27; McMillan, *Disintegration of a Confederate State*, 34–35; *Supplement* 94:254; *Papers of Jefferson Davis*, 8:490; Christopher Lyle McIlwain, *Civil War Alabama* (Tuscaloosa: University of Alabama Press, 2016), 99–105.

16. McMillan, *Disintegration of a Confederate State*, 35–36, McIlwain, *Civil War Alabama*, 115–18; *Official Records*, 2nd ser., vol. 5 (1899): 946–47, 969; *Clarke County Journal*, May 28, 1863; *Montgomery Daily Advertiser*, May 8, 1863; Governor Shorter to Thomas J. Foster, June 11, 1863, Governors' Papers: Shorter, reel 14, SG024882, ADAH.

17. Arthur W. Bergeron Jr., *Confederate Mobile* (Baton Rouge: Louisiana State University Press, 1991), 30, 58–61; *Papers of Jefferson Davis*, 8:459, 468; McMillan, *Disintegration of a Confederate State*, 36–37; Brannen, "John Gill Shorter," 26–27.

18. McMillan, *Disintegration of a Confederate State*, 52–54; Bergeron, *Confederate Mobile*, 109–10; *Supplement* 94:650; Jeffrey N. Lash, "A Yankee in Gray: Danville Leadbetter and the Defense of Mobile Bay, 1861–1863" *Civil War History* 37, no. 3 (1991): 208–14.

19. Governor Shorter to William F. Samford, March 2 and May 12, 1863, Governors' Papers: Shorter, reel 6, folder 30, SG006472, ADAH; *Supplement* 94:649; 95:191.

20. *Montgomery Weekly Advertiser*, May 29, 1863; *Sumter Independent*, July 11, 1863; Brannen, "John Gill Shorter," 46–48; Alabama Legislature, *House Journal*, 1863, executive message, 75–77; Stephanie McCurry, *Confederate Reckoning: Power and Politics in the Civil War South* (Cambridge, MA: Harvard University Press, 2010), 278; Jaime Amanda Martinez, *Confederate Slave Impressment in the Upper South* (Chapel Hill: University of North Carolina Press, 2013), 2–4, 32.

21. *Montgomery Weekly Advertiser*, May 22 and June 3, 1863; *Alabama Beacon*, June 5, 1863; T. J. Seals to Governor Shorter, May 15, 1863, and R. T. Scott to Governor Shorter, June 21, 1863, Governors' Papers: Shorter, reel 15, SG024882, ADAH.

22. "Delegates to the Alabama Secession Convention," *Alabama Historical Quarterly* 3, no. 3/4 (1941): 420; Brewer, *Alabama*, 460; McMillan, *Disintegration of a Confederate State*, 73–74.

23. Riley, *Makers and Romance*, 214, 217; McMillan, *Disintegration of a Confederate State*, 75; Brewer, *Alabama*, 461; William Warren Rogers Jr., *Confederate Home Front: Montgomery during the Civil War* (Tuscaloosa: University of Alabama Press, 1999), 33; "Delegates to the Alabama Secession Convention," 420.

24. Garrett, *Reminiscences of Public Men*, 723; McMillan, *Disintegration of a Confederate State*, 74–75; Emma Beall Culver, "Thomas Hill Watts, a Statesman of the Old Regime," *Transactions of the Alabama Historical Society* 4 (1904): 431–33; McMillan, *Alabama Confederate Reader*, 29.

25. Joseph Wheeler, *Confederate Military History*, vol. 8, *Alabama* (Wilmington, NC:

Broadfoot, 1987), 111; *Papers of Jefferson Davis*, 8:314; McMillan, *Alabama Confederate Reader*, 132.

26. Rembert W. Patrick, *Jefferson Davis and His Cabinet* (Baton Rouge: Louisiana State University Press, 1944), 305–9; Wilfred Buck Yearns, *The Confederate Congress* (Athens: University of Georgia Press, 1960), 75–76; Richard Bensel, "Southern Leviathan: The Development of Central State Authority in the Confederate States of America," *Studies in American Political Development* 2, no. 1 (1987): 101–2; John Brawner Robbins, "The Confederacy and the Writ of Habeas Corpus," *Georgia Historical Quarterly* 55, no. 1 (1971): 85–86; Edward Younger, ed., *Inside the Confederate Government: The Diary of Robert Garlick Hill Kean* (Cambridge: Oxford University Press, 1957), 93; *Papers of Jefferson Davis*, 9:395.

27. *Montgomery Daily Advertiser*, May 10, 1863; *Clarke County Journal*, May 21 and June 25, 1863; *Jacksonville Republican*, May 16, 1863; *Montgomery Weekly Advertiser*, May 23, 1863.

28. Wheeler, *Confederate Military History*, 8:411; Younger, *Inside the Confederate Government*, 67; *Alabama Beacon*, April 17, 1863; Garrett, *Reminiscences of Public Men*, 586–87; Riley, *Makers and Romance*, 279–80; "Delegates to the Alabama Secession Convention," 390–91; *Southern Advertiser*, June 16, 1863; Murray, "Gubernatorial Politics," 399; Mary Ann Neely, ed., *The Works of Matthew Blue: Montgomery's First Historian* (Montgomery, AL: New South Books, 2010), 11–16; *Clarke County Journal*, March 19, 1863.

29. Culver, "Thomas Hill Watts," 434; *Southern Advertiser*, July 29, 1863; McIlwain, *Civil War Alabama*, xii; *Autauga Citizen*, June 25, 1863; *Alabama Beacon*, July 10, 1863; *Clarke County Journal*, July 9, 1863.

30. Campaign circulars, Watts Family Papers, folder 5, box 3, LPR 237, ADAH; *Montgomery Weekly Advertiser*, July 29, 1863; McIlwain, *Civil War Alabama*, 126; *Sumter Independent*, August 15, 1863; *Selma Daily Reporter*, July 18, 1863. The *Montgomery Daily Mail* also endorsed Watts for governor, through its masthead.

31. *Mobile Daily Advertiser and Register*, July 8, 1863; *Selma Daily Reporter*, July 11, 1863; *Montgomery Weekly Advertiser*, July 15, 1863; McMillan, *Disintegration of a Confederate State*, 43–48, 68; Bessie Martin, *A Rich Man's War, A Poor Man's Fight: Desertion of Alabama Troops from the Confederate Army* (1932; Tuscaloosa: University of Alabama Press, 2003), 174–81; McCurry, *Confederate Reckoning*, 162, 195, 210; Phyllis LaRue Legrand, Destitution and Relief of the Indigent Soldiers' Families of Alabama during the Civil War" (master's thesis, Auburn University, 1964), 2–3, 49–55.

32. Michael Brem Bonner, *Confederate Political Economy: Creating and Managing a Southern Corporatist Nation* (Baton Rouge: Louisiana State University Press, 2016), 13, 120–48, 168–77; Powell, "Confederate Federalism," 164; McIlwain, *Civil War Alabama*, 139; Donald Louis Stelluto Jr., "A Light Which Reveals Its True Meaning: State Supreme Courts and the Confederate Constitution" (PhD diss., University of Maryland, 2004), 122–24; William H. Brantley, *Chief Justice Stone of Alabama* (Birmingham, AL: Birmingham, 1943), 156–59; Robbins, "Confederacy and the Writ of Habeas Corpus," 89–90.

33. Ira Berlin et al., eds., *Free at Last: A Documentary History of Slavery, Freedom,*

and the Civil War (New York: New Press, 1992), 134–35; McCurry, *Confederate Reckoning*, 321; *Montgomery Weekly Advertiser*, July 15, 1863. William C. Bibb is not to be confused with his nephew William J. Bibb, who was also from Montgomery but was an outspoken unionist.

34. *Official Records*, 4th ser., vol. 2 (1900): 582, 593, 632; *Alabama Beacon*, June 26, 1863; Huntsville petition, May 13, 1863, Governors' Papers: Shorter, folder 36, reel 6, SG006472, ADAH; Walker, "Governor John Gill Shorter," 281; James P. Tarry to Governor Shorter, July 13, 1863, Governors' Papers: Shorter, reel 8, SG024882, ADAH.

35. Governor Shorter to James P. Tarry, July 15, 1863, Governors' Papers: Shorter, reel 4, SG024884, ADAH; *Clarke County Journal*, July 23, 1863; *Montgomery Weekly Advertiser*, July 22, 1863; *Mobile Weekly Advertiser and Register*, July 25, 1863; Governor Shorter to M. J. Saunders, July 27, 1863, Governors' Papers: Shorter, reel 4, SG024884, ADAH.

36. McMillan, *Disintegration of a Confederate State*, 65; *Mobile Weekly Advertiser and Register*, August 1, 1863; J. J. Carter to Governor Shorter, July 20, 1863, Governors' Papers: Shorter, reel 15, SG024882, ADAH; J. D. Williams to Governor Shorter, July 28, 1863, Governors' Papers: Shorter, folder 26, reel 6, SG006472, ADAH; John Clisby to Governor Shorter, July 22, 1863, Governors' Papers: Shorter, reel 8, SG024882, ADAH; Walker, "Governor John Gill Shorter," 281–83.

37. Alabama Legislature, *House Journal*, 1863, 110–11; Election Files of the Alabama Secretary of State, folder 9, SG002475, ADAH; *Selma Daily Reporter*, August 13, 1863; *Southern Advertiser*, September 2, 1863; *Montgomery Weekly Mail*, August 19, 1863.

38. McMillan, *Disintegration of a Confederate State*, 55; J. R. Siler of Pike County complained several weeks after the election that he had yet to be compensated for damages to his impressed slaves. Siler to Governor Shorter, September 15, 1863, Governors' Papers: Shorter, folder 9, SG006472, ADAH.

39. *Mobile Daily Advertiser and Register*, August 16, 1863; Henry M. McKiven, "John Gill Shorter, 1861–1863," in *Alabama Governors*, ed. Samuel L. Webb and Margaret E. Armbrester (Tuscaloosa: University of Alabama Press, 2001), 73; John Brawner Robbins, "Confederate Nationalism: Politics and Government in the Confederate South, 1861–1865" (PhD diss., Rice University, 1964), 96; *Papers of Jefferson Davis*, 9:416; Yearns, *Confederate Governors*, 30.

40. Thomas Watts to Jefferson Davis, September 8, 1863, Watts Family Papers, folder 5, box 3, LPR237, ADAH; *Autauga Citizen*, August 13, 1863; *Clarke County Journal*, August 13, 1863; *Montgomery Weekly Advertiser*, August 5 and August 26, 1863; *Mobile Daily Advertiser and Register*, August 7, 1863; *Selma Daily Reporter*, August 5, 1863.

41. McMillan, *Alabama Confederate Reader*, 239–40; McIlwain, *Civil War Alabama*, 144; *Sumter Independent*, October 31, 1863; *Talladega Reporter*, excerpt in Watts Family Papers, folder 5, box 3, LPR237, ADAH; *Selma Daily Reporter*, October 24, 1863; *Montgomery Weekly Advertiser*, November 18, 1863; Culver, "Thomas Hill Watts," 434.

42. Alabama Legislature, *House Journal*, 1863, 16; McIlwain, *Civil War Alabama*, 133; McMillan, *Disintegration of a Confederate State*, 65–67.

43. McIlwain, *Civil War Alabama*, 139–42; *Mobile Daily Advertiser and Register*, November 29, 1863; *Mobile Telegraph*, October 27, 1863; *Selma Morning Dispatch*, November 6, 1863; *Mobile Tribune*, November 1, 1863.

44. *Clarke County Journal*, December 10, 1863; Culver, "Thomas Hill Watts," 434–35; Thomas Hill Watts, *Inaugural Address* (Montgomery, AL: Montgomery Advertiser Book and Job Office, 1863), 16; Edward Moren to Mary Frances, December 2, 1863, Moren Papers, LPR55, ADAH.

45. R. Douglas Hurt, *Agriculture and the Confederacy: Policy, Productivity, and Power in the Civil War South* (Chapel Hill: University of North Carolina Press, 2015), 201–2; Powell, "Confederate Federalism," 210; *Official Records*, 4th ser., vol. 3 (1900): 37; McMillan, *Disintegration of a Confederate State*, 84–91.

46. Walter L. Fleming, *Civil War and Reconstruction in Alabama* (New York: Columbia University Press, 1905), 94; *Supplement* 95:421, 603, 725; McMillan, *Disintegration of a Confederate State*, 97, 115; Moore, *Conscription and Conflict*, 242–43, 251; *Official Records*, 4th ser., vol. 3 (1900): 463–64; McMillan, *Alabama Confederate Reader*, 248–50; Kaufman, "Sentinels on the Watchtower," 269, 272–74, 279.

47. McMillan, *Disintegration of a Confederate State*, 99, 101–5, 109; Culver, "Thomas Hill Watts," 437; McIlwain, *Civil War Alabama*, 199–200, 212. For a lively and informative account of Rousseau's Raid, see John S. Sledge, *These Rugged Days: Alabama in the Civil War* (Tuscaloosa: University of Alabama Press, 2017), 100–18.

48. McMillan, *Alabama Confederate Reader*, 308; *Montgomery Daily Advertiser*, March 3, 1865; McIlwain, *Civil War Alabama*, 252–53; McMillan, *Disintegration of a Confederate State*, 118–20.

49. McMillan, *Disintegration of a Confederate State*, 124–25.

50. Frank E. Vandiver, *Rebel Brass: The Confederate Command System* (Baton Rouge: Louisiana State University Press, 1956), 39; Powell, "Confederate Federalism," 264; E. Merton Coulter, *The Confederate States of America, 1861–1865* (Baton Rouge: Louisiana State University Press, 1950), 399; *Official Records*, 4th ser., vol. 2 (1900): 235.

Chapter 3

1. Kenneth C. Martis, *The Historical Atlas of the Congresses of the Confederate States of America, 1861–1865* (New York: Simon and Schuster, 1994), 67.

2. May Spencer Ringold, *The Role of the State Legislatures in the Confederacy* (Athens: University of Georgia Press, 1966), 37; *Public Acts of the Alabama General Assembly*, 1862, 37–42, 201; Grady McWhiney, Warner O. Moore, and Robert F. Pace, eds., "*Fear God and Walk Humbly": The Agricultural Journal of James Mallory, 1843–1877* (Tuscaloosa: University of Alabama Press, 1997), 325. At least ten incumbents accepted commissions in the Confederate army and so did not stand for reelection.

3. *Selma Morning Dispatch*, November 18, 1863; Ringold, *Role of the State Legislatures*, 7.

4. Beverly Wilson Palmer, ed., *The Selected Papers of Thaddeus Stevens* (Pittsburgh: University of Pittsburgh Press, 1997), 2:89–90; *The War of the Rebellion: A Compilation of the Official Records of the Union and Confederate Armies* (*Official Records*), 4th ser.,

vol. 3 (Washington, DC: Government Printing Office, 1900), 397–98; Christopher Lyle McIlwain, *Civil War Alabama* (Tuscaloosa: University of Alabama Press, 2016), 121–22; J. Morgan to L. E. Parsons, August 28, 1863, Parsons Papers, box 1, folder 1, LPR248, Alabama Department of Archives and History (ADAH); Allen W. Jones, "Unionism and Disaffection in South Alabama: The Case of Alfred Holley," *Alabama Review* 24, no. 2 (1971): 124.

5. Michael Jackson Daniel, "Red Hills and Piney Woods: A Political History of Butler County, Alabama, in the Nineteenth Century" (PhD diss., University of Alabama, 1985), 140, 155; Jon L. Wakelyn, *Confederates against the Confederacy: Essays on Leadership and Loyalty* (Westport, CT: Praeger, 2002), 39, 42, 45–49; Glenn and Virginia Linden, eds., *Disunion, War, Defeat, and Recovery in Alabama: The Journal of Augustus Benners, 1850–1885* (Macon, GA: Mercer University Press, 2007), 8–9, 104–5; Alabama Legislature, *House Journal*, 1862, 20–22; Wiley Sword, *Southern Invincibility: A History of the Confederate Heart* (New York: St. Martin's Press, 1999), 52–59, 107.

6. Mike Bunn, *Civil War Eufaula* (Charleston, SC: History Press, 2013), 25; John H. Clisby to Governor Shorter, July 22, 1863, Governors' Papers: Shorter, reel 8, SG024882, ADAH; Joseph Wheeler, *Confederate Military History*, vol. 8, *Alabama* (Wilmington, NC: Broadfoot, 1987), 675–76; Donald Bradford Dodd, "Unionism in Confederate Alabama," (PhD diss., University of Georgia, 1969), 67.

7. George C. Bradley and Richard L. Dahlen, *From Conciliation to Conquest: The Sack of Athens and the Court-Martial of Colonel John B. Turchin* (Tuscaloosa: University of Alabama Press, 2006), 109, 118–19, 168–69.

8. "Alabama Civil War Service Database," ADAH, updated May 23, 2017, http://www.archives.alabama.gov/civilwar/search.cfm; *Memorial Record of Alabama* (Madison, WI: Brant and Fuller, 1893), 2:1047. Kilpatrick was the longtime law partner of Congressman James S. Dickinson. Timothy H. Ball, *A Glance into the Great South-East, or Clarke County, Alabama, and Its Surroundings, from 1540 to 1877* (Tuscaloosa, AL: Willco, 1962), 552.

9. "Alabama Civil War Service Database"; *Autauga Citizen*, May 7 and July 16, 1863; Leonidas Howard to Bolling Hall, June 15, 1863, Bolling Hall Family Papers, folder 5, box 52, LPR39, ADAH.

10. This study generally categorizes Alabama's wartime politicians as either former Democrats or former Whigs, but the short-lived American party (better known as the Know-Nothings) played an important role in the sectional crisis of the 1850s. As the data shows, some of the legislators discussed herein were affiliated with this third party at one time or another. For a fuller discussion, see Robert Farrell, "No Foreign Despots on Southern Soil: The Know-Nothing Party in Alabama, 1850–1857," *Alabama Review* 72, no. 2 (2019): 99–122.

11. Edward Moren to Mary Frances Moren, August 18 and August 20, 1863, Edward Moren Papers, LPR55, ADAH; Alabama Legislature, *Senate Journal*, 1863, 6–7.

12. Alabama Legislature, *House Journal*, 1863, 17–18; Alabama Legislature, *Senate Journal*, 1863, 20; Alexander White to L. E. Parsons, August 20, 1863, Parsons Papers, box 1, folder 1, LPR248, ADAH.

13. Alabama Legislature, *Senate Journal*, 1863, 66–67; *Public Acts of the Alabama General Assembly*, 1863, 52–53.

14. Edward Moren to Mary Frances Moren, August 24, 1863, Edward Moren Papers, LPR55, ADAH.

15. Eric H. Walther, *William Lowndes Yancey and the Coming of the Civil War* (Chapel Hill: University of North Carolina Press, 2006), 368–70; William L. Barney, *The Secessionist Impulse: Alabama and Mississippi in 1860* (1974; Tuscaloosa: University of Alabama Press, 2004), 295; *Chattanooga Daily Rebel*, August 25, 1863; Alabama Legislature, *Senate Journal*, 1863, 29–30.

16. *The Papers of Andrew Johnson*, ed. Paul H. Bergeron, vol. 9, *September 1865–January 1866* (Knoxville: University of Tennessee Press, 1989), 142; Ezra J. Warner and Wilfred Buck Yearns, *Biographical Register of the Confederate Congress* (Baton Rouge: Louisiana State University Press, 1975), 129; Willis Brewer, *Alabama: Her History, Resources, War Record, and Public Men; From 1540 to 1872* (Montgomery, AL: Barret and Brown, 1872), 563; Malcolm C. McMillan, *The Alabama Confederate Reader* (Tuscaloosa: University of Alabama Press, 1963), 29–30; Paul Avery Meigs, *The Life of Senator Robert Jemison, Junior* (Tuscaloosa: University of Alabama Press, 1928), 50–51; Alabama Legislature, *Senate Journal*, 1862, 25, 168, 177; McIlwain, *Civil War Alabama*, 58.

17. Alabama Legislature, *Senate Journal*, 1863, 41–42; *Montgomery Weekly Advertiser*, August 26, 1863.

18. Helen Jeanette Jackson, "The Work of the Alabama Delegation in the Confederate Congress" (master's thesis, Emory University, 1953), 104, 130, 177, 184; Warner and Yearns, *Biographical Register*, 130; *Journal of the Congress of the Confederate States of America, 1861–1865* (*JCCSA*), 7 vols. (Washington, DC: Government Printing Office, 1904–5), 3:712; Hermione Dannelly, "The Life and Times of Robert Jemison, Jr., during the Civil War and Reconstruction" (master's thesis, University of Alabama, 1942), 59, 70; Wilfred Buck Yearns, *The Confederate Congress* (Athens: University of Georgia Press, 1960), 12, 56; Christopher Lyle McIlwain, *1865 Alabama: From Civil War to Uncivil Peace* (Tuscaloosa: University of Alabama Press, 2017), 12, 64, 234.

19. *Montgomery Weekly Advertiser*, September 2, 1863.

20. Brewer, *Alabama*, 358–59; Ruth Ketring Nuermberger, *The Clays of Alabama: A Planter-Lawyer-Politician Family* (Tuscaloosa: University of Alabama Press, 1958), 81–82, 111, 178; H. E. Sterkx, *Partners in Rebellion: Alabama Women in the Civil War* (Cranbury, NJ: Associated University Press, 1970), 76–77; C. Vann Woodward, ed., *Mary Chestnut's Civil War* (New Haven, CT: Yale University Press, 1981), 570.

21. J. Mills Thornton III, *Politics and Power in a Slave Society: Alabama, 1800–1860* (Baton Rouge: Louisiana State University Press, 1978), 334–39; Nuermberger, *Clays of Alabama*, 122, 126, 136–38, 158, 163.

22. Nuermberger, *Clays of Alabama*, 168–70; McMillan, *Alabama Confederate Reader*, 43–44.

23. Nuermberger, *Clays of Alabama*, 190; Brewer, *Alabama*, 77.

24. *JCCSA*, 2:154, 261; 3:148, 253, 311; "Proceedings of the Confederate Congress," *Southern Historical Society Papers*, 47 (1930): 10, 49, 149; 49 (1943): 85, 132–33; Jackson, "Work of the Alabama Delegation," 85, 92–93, 104, 118, 161, 167; Nuermberger, *Clays*

of Alabama, 198, 201–4, 213; Ada Sterling, ed., *A Belle of the Fifties: Memoirs of Mrs. Clay of Alabama* (New York: Doubleday, Page, 1905), 202; Wilfred Buck Yearns, *The Confederate Congress* (Athens: University of Georgia Press, 1960), 76, 117.

25. Warner and Yearns, *Biographical Register*, 52; "Proceedings of the Confederate Congress," 45 (1925): 220; 47 (1930): 40–42; Nuermberger, *Clays of Alabama*, 194, 196, 205–6; Ian Binnington, "They Have Made a Nation: Confederates and Confederate Nationalism" (PhD diss., University of Illinois Urbana-Champaign, 2004), 136, 250–51; William M. Robinson, *Justice in Grey: A History of the Judicial System in the Confederate States of America* (Cambridge, MA: Harvard University Press, 1941), 427–28, 435.

26. Woodward, *Mary Chestnut's Civil War*, 138–39; William C. Davis, *Jefferson Davis: The Man and His Hour* (New York: Harper Collins, 1991), 393, 442–43; *The Papers of Jefferson Davis*, ed. Lynda Lasswell Crist, vol. 8, *1862* (Baton Rouge: Louisiana State University Press, 1995), 99, 128; *The Papers of Jefferson Davis*, ed. Lynda Lasswell Crist, vol. 9, *January–September 1863* (Baton Rouge: Louisiana State University Press, 1997), 122; Sterling, *Belle of the Fifties*, 194; Felicity Allen, *Jefferson Davis: Unconquerable Heart* (Columbia: University of Missouri Press, 1999), 352.

27. Sterling, *Belle of the Fifties*, 194, 196; McIlwain, *Civil War Alabama*, 84, 96–98; McMillan, *Alabama Confederate Reader*, 176–77; Albert D. Kirwan, ed., *The Confederacy* (Cleveland, OH: World, 1958), 266; Nuermberger, *Clays of Alabama*, 213; Yearns, *Confederate Congress*, 19; Joe A. Mobley, *Weary of War: Life on the Confederate Home Front* (Westport, CT: Praeger, 2008), 129.

28. *Mobile Weekly Advertiser and Register*, November 21, 1863; *Selma Morning Dispatch*, November 18, 1863; *Mobile Tribune*, November 15, 1863; *Montgomery Weekly Advertiser*, September 2 and November 18, 1863. The other names bandied about for senator included William Brooks, John Cochran, John Forsyth, George Goldthwaite, Thomas Judge, James Pugh, Samuel Rice, John Shorter, Richard Walker, and William Wood.

29. Edwin Anderson Alderman and Armistead Churchill Gordon, *J. L. M. Curry: A Biography* (New York: MacMillan, 1911), 172; *Huntsville Confederate*, September 7, 1863; Thornton, *Politics and Power*, 335; "Proceedings of the Confederate Congress," 49 (1943): 248; Nuermberger, *Clays of Alabama*, 197–98, 226–27; George C. Rable, *The Confederate Republic: A Revolution against Politics* (Chapel Hill: University of North Carolina Press, 1994), 228–29.

30. William Warren Rogers Jr., *Confederate Home Front: Montgomery during the Civil War* (Tuscaloosa: University of Alabama Press, 1999), 71–72, 91; *Papers of Andrew Johnson*, ed. Paul H. Bergeron, vol. 8, *May–August 1865* (Knoxville: University of Tennessee Press, 1989), 216; *Official Records*, 4th ser., vol. 3 (1900): 394; Walther, *William Lowndes Yancey*, 235–36, 247–48, 314; Walter L. Fleming, "The Peace Movement in Alabama: The Peace Society, 1863–1865," *South Atlantic Quarterly* 2 (1903): 252.

31. Alabama Legislature, *Senate Journal*, 1863, 138–53.

32. *Mobile Tribune*, November 21, 1863.

33. Nuermberger, *Clays of Alabama*, 225; Alabama Legislature, *Senate Journal*, 1863, 153–55.

34. Alabama Legislature, *Senate Journal*, 1863, 155–56.

35. Alabama Legislature, 160–65; Linden and Linden, *Disunion, War, Defeat, and Recovery in Alabama*, 111. The voting patterns of Ezekiel A. Powell in the Senate and Thomas P. Lewis in the House are too inconsistent to place them in either the war Confederate or peace Confederate camp.

36. Yearns, *Confederate Congress*, 56; Brewer, *Alabama*, 354–56; Donald Louis Stelluto Jr., "A Light Which Reveals Its True Meaning: State Supreme Courts and the Confederate Constitution" (PhD diss., University of Maryland, 2004), 95, 122–23; William H. Brantley, *Chief Justice Stone of Alabama* (Birmingham, AL: Birmingham, 1943), 159. Walker owned forty-two slaves.

37. *Huntsville Confederate*, December 7 and December 22, 1862; *Clarke County Journal*, November 26 and December 3, 1863; *Montgomery Weekly Advertiser*, December 2, 1863; Woodward, *Mary Chestnut's Civil War*, 500. The *Huntsville Confederate* was hardly impartial in its support for Clay; the managing editor was J. Withers Clay, the senator's brother.

38. Jackson, "Work of the Alabama Delegation," 130, 181, 184; Martis, *Historical Atlas*, 97–98; McIlwain, *Civil War Alabama*, 380; "Proceedings of the Confederate Congress," 52 (1959): 297; *JCCSA*, 4:387, 670–71.

39. Alabama Legislature, *House Journal*, 1862, 246; 1863, executive message, 14; Alabama Legislature, *Senate Journal*, 1863, 216–17. Alabama was not alone in pursuing militia legislation. Several other southern states were simultaneously wrestling with their own ideas on how best to use their respective militias. Ringold, *Role of the State Legislatures*, 13–23.

40. McMillan, *Disintegration of a Confederate State*, 65–67; McIlwain, *Civil War Alabama*, 133.

41. Alabama Legislature, *Senate Journal*, 1863, 18, 20; Alabama Legislature, *House Journal*, 1863, 19; *Montgomery Weekly Mail*, August 19 and August 26, 1863.

42. "An Act to Reorganize the Militia of the State of Alabama," *Public Acts of the Alabama General Assembly*, 1863, 3; Abstract of the State Adjutant General's Report on the Militia (1863), Parsons Papers, folder 4, box 1, LPR248, ADAH; Alabama Legislature, *House Journal*, 1863, 38; *Senate Journal*, 1863, 44.

43. "An Act to Reorganize the Militia of the State of Alabama," *Public Acts of the Alabama General Assembly*, 1863, 4–5, 8; "An Act Declaring Who Shall Be Exempt from Militia Duty," *Public Acts of the Alabama General Assembly*, 1863, 12–13; Alabama Legislature, *Senate Journal*, 1863, 45–51; Alabama Legislature, *House Journal*, 1863, 43, 47–48, 55–60. The county reserves operated very much like the home guard, though the latter was apparently a volunteer organization that was presumably absorbed into the former in accordance with the Class 1 provisions of the Militia Act.

44. Alabama Legislature, *Senate Journal*, 1863, 44, 46, 50–51, 59; Alabama Legislature, *House Journal*, 1863, 38, 60–61; *Jacksonville Republican*, August 29, 1863; Linden and Linden, *Disunion, War, Defeat, and Recovery in Alabama*, 109.

45. *Clarke County Journal*, August 27, 1863; McMillan, *Disintegration of a Confederate State*, 67, 99; Fleming, *Civil War and Reconstruction in Alabama*, 92; Marion Bailey Brunson, *Pea River Reflections: Intimate Glimpses of Area Life during Two Centuries*

(Tuscaloosa, AL: Portals Press, 1975), 55–62; Stephen V. Ash, "A Wall around Slavery: Safeguarding the Peculiar Institution on the Confederate Periphery, 1861–1865," in *Nineteenth-Century America: Essays in Honor of Paul H. Bergeron*, ed. W. Todd Groce and Stephen V. Ash (Knoxville: University of Tennessee Press, 2005), 55–73.

46. G. Ward Hubbs, *Guarding Greensboro: A Confederate Company in the Making of a Southern Community* (Athens: University of Georgia Press, 2003), 163–64; Bruce Levine, *Confederate Emancipation: Southern Plans to Free and Arm Slaves during the Civil War* (New York: Oxford University Press, 2006), 24–25.

47. Alabama Legislature, *House Journal*, 1863, 39–42.

48. Robert F. Durden, *The Gray and the Black: The Confederate Debate on Emancipation* (Baton Rouge: Louisiana State University Press, 1972), 32; Alabama Legislature, *House Journal*, 1863, 61; *Official Records*, 4th ser., vol. 2 (1900): 767; Linden and Linden, *Disunion, War, Defeat, and Recovery in Alabama*, 135; The Alabama Senate also approved the resolution, though there is no record of a vote or any debate. Alabama Legislature, *Senate Journal*, 1863, 60. See also Philip D. Dillard, *Jefferson Davis's Final Campaign: Confederate Nationalism and the Fight to Arm Slaves* (Macon, GA: Mercer University Press, 2017), 8–9.

49. *Clarke County Journal*, August 20, 1863; *Southern Advertiser*, September 2, 1863; Durden, *Gray and the Black*, 33; McIlwain, *Civil War Alabama*, 134.

50. Jabez L. M. Curry to Robert Jemison Jr., October 23, 1863, Robert Jemison Jr. Papers, folder 8, box 753.007, W. S. Hoole Special Collections Library, University of Alabama.

51. Alabama Legislature, *House Journal*, 1863, 258.

Chapter 4

1. Wartime Recollections of Robert M. Sands, Regimental Files (Third Alabama Infantry), folder 8, SG024887, Alabama Department of Archives and History (ADAH).

2. Joseph Allan Frank, *With Ballot and Bayonet: The Political Socialization of American Civil War Soldiers* (Athens: University of Georgia Press, 1998), 91, 172.

3. Gary W. Gallagher, *The Confederate War: How Popular Will, Nationalism, and Military Strategy Could Not Stave Off Defeat* (Cambridge, MA: Harvard University Press, 1997), 53, 73; Jason Phillips, *Diehard Rebels: The Confederate Culture of Invincibility* (Athens: University of Georgia Press, 2007), 2, 54, 76; Charles Royster, *The Destructive War: William Tecumseh Sherman, Stonewall Jackson, and the Americans* (New York: Alfred A. Knopf, 1991), 187.

4. James M. McPherson, *For Cause and Comrades: Why Men Fought in the Civil War* (New York: Oxford University Press, 1997), 100; Reid Mitchell, *Civil War Soldiers* (New York: Viking Press, 1988), 10, 161, 172; Frank, *With Ballot and Bayonet*, 154–55. See also Ian Binnington, "They Have Made a Nation: Confederates and Confederate Nationalism" (PhD diss., University of Illinois Urbana-Champaign, 2004), 183–224.

5. Randall C. Jimerson, *The Private Civil War: Popular Thought during the Sectional Conflict* (Baton Rouge: Louisiana State University Press, 1988), 230; Kenneth W. Noe, *Reluctant Rebels: The Confederates Who Joined the Army after 1861* (Chapel Hill:

University of North Carolina Press, 2010), 209; Kenneth W. Noe, "Alabama, We Will Fight for Thee: The Initial Motivations of Later-Enlisting Confederates," *Alabama Review* 62, no. 3 (2009): 184; Kristopher A. Teters, "Fighting for the Cause? An Examination of the Motivations of Alabama's Confederate Soldiers from a Class Perspective," in *The Yellowhammer War: The Civil War and Reconstruction in Alabama*, ed. Kenneth W. Noe (Tuscaloosa: University of Alabama Press, 2013), 90, 103; Bell I. Wiley, *The Life of Johnny Reb: The Common Soldier of the Confederacy* (Indianapolis, IN: Bobbs-Merrill, 1943), 104, 127.

6. *Mobile Daily Register*, October 4, 1863; Thomas Warrick to Martha Warrick, August 9, 1863, Thomas Warrick Papers, folder 2, SPR 420, ADAH. For general attitudes among soldiers, see Wiley, *Life of Johnny Reb*; and James I. Robertson Jr., *Soldiers Blue and Gray* (Columbia: University of South Carolina Press, 1988).

7. *The War of the Rebellion: A Compilation of the Official Records of the Union and Confederate Armies* (*Official Records*), 1st ser., vol. 26, pt. 2 (Washington: Government Printing Office, 1889), 548–57; *Huntsville Confederate*, October 7, 1863; Mauriel Phillips Joslyn, "Comrades of the Southern Cross," *North and South* 4, no. 1 (2000): 27–29; Bessie Martin, *A Rich Man's War, A Poor Man's Fight: Desertion of Alabama Troops from the Confederate Army* (1932; Tuscaloosa: University of Alabama Press, 2003), 116–17.

8. Walter L. Fleming, *Civil War and Reconstruction in Alabama* (New York: Columbia University Press, 1905), 86; James M. McPherson, *Ordeal by Fire: The Civil War and Reconstruction* (New York: McGraw-Hill, 1982), 172; Louis Roycraft Smith, "A History of Sumter County, Alabama, through 1886" (master's thesis, University of Alabama, 1988), 141. For details on every Confederate unit from Alabama, see Willis Brewer, *Alabama: Her History, Resources, War Record, and Public Men; From 1540 to 1872* (Montgomery, AL: Barrett and Brown, 1872); and Stewart Sifakis, *Compendium of the Confederate Armies: Alabama* (New York: Facts on File, 1991).

9. Henry B. Wood to Allen Wood, May 22, [1862], Regimental Files (Twelfth Alabama Infantry), folder 9, SG024894, ADAH. See also Wayne Wood, *The Marble Valley Boys: Marble Valley, Coosa County, Alabama* (Birmingham, AL: Banner Press, 1986), 36–37.

10. Resolution, February 1, 1863, Regimental Files (Twenty-Ninth Alabama Infantry), folder 11, SG024900, ADAH; Henry W. Pond to Ebenezer Pond, February 19, 1863, Regimental Files (Thirteenth Alabama Infantry), folder 6, SG024895, ADAH.

11. Elias Davis to Georgiana A. Davis, April 10 and May 25, 1863, Regimental Files (Tenth Alabama Infantry), folder 6, SG024893, ADAH; Judith Lee Hallock, ed., *The Civil War Letters of Joshua K. Callaway* (Athens: University of Georgia Press, 1997), 79; Address by John P. Hubbard, April 30, 1863, Regimental Files (Fifty-Seventh Alabama Infantry), folder 13, SG024908, ADAH.

12. Chandra Manning, *What This Cruel War Was Over: Soldiers, Slavery, and the Civil War* (New York: Alfred A. Knopf, 2007), 132; Phillips, *Diehard Rebels*, 119–20; *Mobile Weekly Advertiser and Register*, August 22, 1863.

13. Phillips, *Diehard Rebels*, 118; Joseph T. Glatthaar, *General Lee's Army: From Victory to Collapse* (New York: Free Press, 2008), 283–85; Lisa Laskin, "'The Army Is Not

Near So Much Demoralized as the Country Is': Soldiers in the Army of Northern Virginia and the Confederate Home Front," in *The View from the Ground: Experiences of Civil War Soldiers*, ed. Aaron Sheehan-Dean (Lexington: University Press of Kentucky, 2007), 91; Frank Anderson Chappell, ed., *Dear Sister: Civil War Letters to a Sister in Alabama* (Huntsville, AL: Branch Springs, 2002), 161; Elias Davis to Georgiana Davis, July 26, 1863, Regimental Files (Tenth Alabama Infantry), folder 6, SG024893, ADAH; Ebenezer B. Coggin to Anne E. Coggin, July 19 and August 25, 1863, Ebenezer B. Coggin Papers, folder 3, SPR419, ADAH.

14. John G. Barrett, ed., *Yankee Rebel: The Civil War Journal of Edmund DeWitt Patterson* (Chapel Hill: University of North Carolina Press, 1966), 119; John C. Carter, ed., *Welcome the Hour of our Conflict: William Cowan McClellan and the 9th Alabama* (Tuscaloosa: University of Alabama Press, 2007), 250; Thomas S. Taylor to Matilda Taylor, August 26, 1863, Regimental Files (Sixth Alabama Infantry), folder 6, SG0024891, ADAH.

15. Michael B. Ballard, *Vicksburg: The Campaign That Opened the Mississippi* (Chapel Hill: University of North Carolina Press, 2004), 418, 430; Richard M. McMurry, ed., *An Uncompromising Secessionist: The Civil War of George Knox Miller, Eighth (Wade's) Confederate Cavalry* (Tuscaloosa: University of Alabama Press, 2007), 136, 142; Ann K. Blomquist and Robert A. Taylor, eds., *This Cruel War: The Civil War Letters of Grant and Malina Taylor, 1862–1865* (Macon, GA: Mercer University Press, 2000), 150–51, 204–5; Samuel H. Sprott, *Cush: A Civil War Memoir*, ed. Louis R. Smith and Andrew Quist (Livingston, AL: Livingston Press, 1999), 65.

16. Mark A. Weitz, *More Damning Than Slaughter: Desertion in the Confederate Army* (Lincoln: University of Nebraska Press, 2005), 150, 156; Martin, *Rich Man's War*, 38–43; Lucille Griffith, ed., *Yours till Death: Civil War Letters of John W. Cotton* (Tuscaloosa: University of Alabama Press, 1951), 65; Robert Partin, "An Alabama Confederate Soldier's Report to His Wife," *Alabama Review* 3, no. 1 (1950): 34.

17. Stephens Croom to William W. Croom, July 19, 1863, Croom Collection, folder 12, box 3A, Doy Leale McCall Rare Book and Manuscript Library, University of South Alabama; Statement by James D. Harwell, Regimental Files (Twentieth Alabama Infantry), folder 16, SG024897, ADAH; George E. Brewer, "History of the Twenty-Third Alabama Regiment," Regimental Files (Twenty-Third Alabama Infantry), folder 9, SG024898, ADAH; Larry D. Stephens, *Bound for Glory: A History of the 30th Alabama Infantry Regiment, C.S.A.* (Ann Arbor, MI: Sheridan Books, 2005), 148–49; Terry Whittington, "In the Shadow of Defeat: Tracking the Vicksburg Parolees," *Journal of Mississippi History* 64, no. 4 (2002), 327; *Eutaw Whig and Observer*, September 17, 1863. The commentary here pertains also to the smaller rebel garrison that surrendered at Port Hudson, Louisiana, on July 9, 1863. Among the paroled regiments was the First Alabama Infantry, which had fully reconstituted by October.

18. Larry J. Daniel, *Soldiering in the Army of Tennessee: A Portrait of Life in the Confederate Army* (Chapel Hill: University of North Carolina Press, 1991), 147; H. E. Sterkx, *Partners in Rebellion: Alabama Women in the Civil War* (Cranbury, NJ: Associated University Press, 1970), 196; Edward N. Brown to Fannie Brown, July 24, 1863, Edward

Norphlet Brown Papers, SPR337, ADAH; Ray Mathis, ed., *In the Land of the Living: Wartime Letters by Confederates from the Chattahoochee Valley of Alabama and Georgia* (Troy, AL: Troy State University Press, 1981), 72–73. For further insight into the patriotic character of the Army of Tennessee, see Wiley Sword, *Southern Invincibility: A History of the Confederate Heart* (New York: St. Martin's Press, 1999), 184–95.

19. Hallock, *Civil War Letters of Joshua K. Callaway*, 110–11, 113–16, 166. For a fuller biographical sketch of Callaway, see Peter S. Carmichael, *The War for the Common Soldier: How Men Thought, Fought, and Survived in Civil War Armies* (Chapel Hill: University of North Carolina Press, 2018), 36–47.

20. Phillips, *Diehard Rebels*, 95; Anne Sarah Rubin, *A Shattered Nation: The Rise and Fall of the Confederacy, 1861–1868* (Chapel Hill: University of North Carolina Press, 2005), 83; Edmund Waller Henderson, "History of the Thirty-Sixth Alabama Infantry," Regimental Files (Thirty-Sixth Alabama Infantry), folder 11, SG024903, ADAH.

21. Carter, *Welcome the Hour of Conflict*, 234; Alabama Legislature, *House Journal*, 1862, 26, 65, 97, 148; Josiah Henry Benton, *Voting in the Field: A Forgotten Chapter of the Civil War* (Boston: privately printed, 1915), 34–35; *Montgomery Weekly Advertiser*, June 17, 1863; *Southern Advertiser*, August 5, 1863. In discussing the Confederate elections more broadly, William L. Barney incorrectly assumes that Alabama soldiers did cast ballots in 1863. Barney, *Flawed Victory: A New Perspective on the Civil War* (New York: Praeger, 1975), 113.

22. Wiley, *Life of Johnny Reb*, 330–31; McPherson, *Ordeal by Fire*, 355; Malcolm C. McMillan, *The Disintegration of a Confederate State: Three Governors and Alabama's Wartime Home Front, 1861–1865* (Macon, GA: Mercer University Press, 1986), 68; Kenneth C. Martis, *The Historical Atlas of the Congresses of the Confederate States of America, 1861–1865* (New York: Simon and Schuster, 1994), 57, 135; Oscar Osburn Winther, "The Soldier Vote in the Election of 1864," *New York History* 25, no. 4 (1944): 457–58; Benjamin P. Thomas and Harold M. Hyman, *Stanton: The Life and Times of Lincoln's Secretary of War* (New York: Alfred A. Knopf, 1962), 334; Henry C. Semple to Emily Semple, April 7, 1863, Henry C. Semple Papers, LPR5, ADAH; David Herbert Donald, "Died of Democracy," in *Why the North Won the Civil War*, ed. David Herbert Donald (Baton Rouge: Louisiana State University Press, 1960), 90. Thomas and Hyman contend that many furloughed Union soldiers, whose ballots are not included in the absentee tally, probably voted for Lincoln in large numbers. Wiley and McPherson posit, respectively, that between one-third and two-fifths of rebel soldiers were younger than twenty-one. McMillan records 39,356 votes in the gubernatorial contest, while Martis records 35,251 votes in the congressional races.

23. Hubert Jennings Thompson, "The Civil War Correspondence of James B. Daniel" (master's thesis, Samford University, 1980), 125; James B. Mitchell to his father, May 24, 1863, Regimental Files (Thirty-Fourth Alabama Infantry), folder 4, SG024903, ADAH; *Montgomery Weekly Advertiser*, June 2, 1863; M. T. Sanders to Governor Shorter, July 17, 1863, Governors' Papers: Shorter, reel 8, SG024882, ADAH; Allen W. Jones, ed., "A Georgia Confederate Soldier Visits Montgomery, Alabama, 1862–1863," *Alabama Historical Quarterly* 25, no. 2 (1963): 109.

24. "The Soldiers for Judge Watts" circular, July 18, 1863, Watts Family Papers, folder 5, box 3, LPR237, ADAH.

25. *Montgomery Weekly Advertiser*, April 12 and April 24, 1863; *Southern Advertiser*, June 16 and July 29, 1863.

26. *Southern Advertiser*, June 17, 1863.

27. Calvin J. C. Munroe to Terry Munroe, July 16, 1863, Regimental Files (Twenty-Fifth Alabama Infantry), folder 11, SG024899, ADAH; *Clarke County Journal*, September 3, 1863.

28. Jackson County Returns, Election Files of the Alabama Secretary of State, folder 12, SG002475, ADAH. The same folder also includes a list of 103 soldiers from the Twenty-First Alabama Infantry Regiment, stationed around Mobile Bay, who ostensibly participated in the congressional election in the state's Ninth District, but for whom these men voted is not recorded; nor is it clear whether these ballots were validated by the registrar.

29. Tommy Brown, "Of All the Hardy Sons of Toil: Class and Race in Antebellum Southcentral and Southeastern Alabama," *Alabama Review* 68, no. 3 (2015): 249–50; *Spirit of the South*, June 23 and June 28, 1863; Colonel J. P. Amerine to Governor Shorter, July 29, 1863, Governors' Papers: Shorter, folder 36, reel 8, SG006472, ADAH; *Southern Advertiser*, June 24, 1863.

30. W. Stanley Hoole, ed., "The Letters of Captain Joab Goodson, 1862–1864," *Alabama Review* 10 (1957): 146–47; Bolling Hall Jr. to Bolling Hall Sr., August 17, 1863, Bolling Hall Family Papers, folder 6, LPR39, ADAH; Carter, *Welcome the Hour of Conflict*, 233, 245. The McClellan brothers' father, Thomas McClellan, represented Limestone County at the Secession Convention as a cooperationist who voted against the ordinance.

31. *Eutaw Whig and Observer*, April 30, 1863; *Alabama Beacon*, July 17, 1863; *Southern Advertiser*, June 10, 1863; George E. Brewer, *History of Coosa County, Alabama* (Wetumpka, AL: Wetumpk, 1955), 208, 212.

32. Colonel Jeptha Edwards of the Forty-Ninth Alabama Infantry won his race for representative of DeKalb County, but he was captured at Port Hudson, Louisiana, a month before the election, and he remained in prison for the duration of the war. His political proclivity was probably war Confederate, but this is sheer conjecture. See Brewer, *Alabama*, 662.

33. Frank, *With Ballot and Bayonet*, 169; *Montgomery Weekly Advertiser*, September 16, 1863; *Southern Advertiser*, August 26, 1863.

34. McMurry, *An Uncompromising Secessionist*, 148; Thomas S. Taylor to Matilda Taylor, November 16, 1863, Regimental Files (Sixth Alabama Infantry), folder 6, SG024891, ADAH; Edward N. Brown to Fannie Brown, December 11, 1863, Edward Norphlet Brown Papers, SPR337, ADAH; A. Reed Taylor, "The War History of Two Soldiers: A Two-Sided View of the Civil War," *Alabama Review* 23, no. 2 (1970): 97; Manning, *What This Cruel War Was Over*, 135. See also Jimerson, *Private Civil War*, 216–18.

35. G. Ward Hubbs, ed., *Voices from Company D: Diaries by the Greensboro Guards,*

Fifth Alabama Infantry Regiment, Army of Northern Virginia (Athens: University of Georgia Press, 2003), 196; *Democratic Watchtower*, August 26 and October 28, 1863; *Mobile Daily Register*, October 4, 1863.

36. *Montgomery Weekly Advertiser*, September 23, 1863.

37. Marc W. Kruman, "Dissent in the Confederacy: The North Carolina Experience," *Civil War History* 27, no. 4 (1981): 310; *Official Records*, 4th ser., vol. 2 (1900): 726–27. Likewise, George C. Rable finds that a majority of soldiers in Georgia, Mississippi, and Virginia voted for prowar candidates in those states' midwar elections. *The Confederate Republic: A Revolution against Politics* (Chapel Hill: University of North Carolina Press, 1994), 163, 218, 220, 224.

38. "Letters from the Front," *Confederate Veteran* 26 (1918): 198; Norman M. Shapiro, "Daniel Coleman Diary," *Huntsville Historical Review* 26, no. 2 (1999): 30; McMurry, *Uncompromising Secessionist*, 149; Griffith, *Yours till Death*, 84. Regarding the battle's outcome, Wiley Sword notes that citizens and soldiers alike "expressed a renewal of the Southern hope that the war would end soon . . . and even greater success was anticipated." Sword, *Southern Invincibility*, 215.

39. *Mobile Weekly Advertiser and Register*, June 27, 1863; Benjamin Buford Williams, "Alexander B. Meek," Encyclopedia of Alabama, updated October 3, 2011, http://www.encyclopediaofalabama.org/article/h-1127; Williams, "Two Uncollected Civil War Poems of Alexander Beaufort Meek," *Alabama Historical Quarterly* 25, no. 2 (1963): 116–18.

40. Newton N. Davis to Bettie Davis, December 2, December 11, and December 20, 1863, Davis Papers, folder 3, SPR342, ADAH; Mattie Lou Teague Crow, ed., *The Diary of a Confederate Soldier: John Washington Inzer, 1834–1928* (Huntsville, AL: Strode, 1977), 12–14, 65–66, 68; Grady McWhiney and Perry D. Jamieson, *Attack and Die: Civil War Military Tactics and the Southern Heritage* (Tuscaloosa: University of Alabama Press, 1982), 170–91; Elias Davis to Mrs. R. T. Lathem, December 13, 1863, Regimental Files (Tenth Alabama Infantry), folder 6, SG024893, ADAH.

41. J. J. D. Renfroe, *"The Battle Is God's": A Sermon Preached before Wilcox's Brigade on Fast Day* (Richmond: MacFarlane and Fergusson, 1863), 6, 15; Carmichael, *War for the Common Soldier*, 232–34.

42. Walter L. Fleming, "The Peace Movement in Alabama: The Peace Society, 1863–1865," *South Atlantic Quarterly* 2 (1903): 246; Frank, *With Ballot and Bayonet*, 84, 124–25; *Montgomery Weekly Mail*, September 23, 1863; Paul D. Escott, *Military Necessity: Civil-Military Relations in the Confederacy* (Westport, CT: Praeger, 2006), 178. In 1864, Alabama troops stationed in North Carolina openly threatened to lynch William Holden, an antiwar candidate for governor, if he won that state's election. Rable, *Confederate Republic*, 203.

Conclusion

1. *Montgomery Daily Mail*, September 28 and October 1, 1864; Alabama Legislature, *House Journal*, 1864, 161–65; Christopher Lyle McIlwain, *Civil War Alabama* (Tuscaloosa: University of Alabama Press, 2016), 213–15; Parsons's Peace Resolution,

Parsons Papers, folder 6, box 2, LPR 248, Alabama Department of Archives and History (ADAH).

2. Alabama Legislature, *House Journal*, 1864, 183, 202; *Montgomery Daily Mail*, September 27, 1864; *Southern Advertiser*, September 30, 1864.

3. *Montgomery Daily Mail*, December 10, 1864; *Southern Advertiser*, December 9, 1864; Alabama Legislature, *House Journal*, 1864, 418–22, 429.

4. Alabama Legislature, *House Journal*, 1864, 255–57, 427; *Jacksonville Republican*, December 8, 1864; McIlwain, *Civil War Alabama*, 224; "Against Reconstruction with the Federal Government of the United States," *Public Acts of Alabama*, 1864, 24. Among the yea votes was Thomas P. Cottle, who had replaced Alfred Holley and was likely a war Confederate.

5. For a succinct and trenchant distillation of the internal-versus-external debate, see James M. McPherson, "American Victory, American Defeat," in *Why the Confederacy Lost*, ed. Gabor S. Boritt (New York: Oxford University Press, 1992): 17–42.

6. Carl von Clausewitz, *On War*, trans. and ed. Peter Paret and Michael Howard (Princeton, NJ: Princeton University Press, 1976), 483. "Help from abroad" might have come from Great Britain or France, but after 1862 neither of those countries expressed any serious desire to intervene in the American conflict.

7. *Supplement to the Official Records of the Union and Confederate Armies*, ed. Janet B. Hewett (Wilmington, NC: Broadfoot, 1999), 95:805.

8. Ezekiel A. Powell, "Fifty-Five Years in West Alabama," *Alabama Historical Quarterly* 4, no. 4 (1942): 610; Alabama Legislature, *House Journal*, 1864, 442. Powell's and Crenshaw's sentiments comport with Robert E. Bonner's observation that the longer the war lasted, the more southern politicians strove to model their duties after the "Revolutionary heroism" of the Confederate army. Bonner, *Mastering America: Southern Slaveholders and the Crisis of American Nationhood* (New York: Cambridge University Press, 2009), 253, 257.

9. *Mobile Daily Advertiser and Register*, November 13, 1863; Henry St. Paul, *Our Home and Foreign Policy* (Mobile, AL: Daily Register and Advertiser, 1863), 11, 13; Frank E. Vandiver, "The Confederacy and the American Tradition," in *The Civil War: A Second American Revolution?*, ed. William E. Parrish (New York: Holt, Rinehart and Winston, 1970), 134; Wiley Sword, *Southern Invincibility: A History of the Confederate Heart* (New York: St. Martin's Press, 1999), 359; Don E. Fehrenbacher, *Sectional Crisis and Southern Constitutionalism* (Baton Rouge: Louisiana State University, 1995), 142.

10. James Horace Bass, "The Georgia Gubernatorial Elections of 1861 and 1863," *Georgia Historical Quarterly* 17, no. 3 (1933): 179–88; Rod Andrew, "The Essential Nationalism of the People: Georgia's Confederate Congressional Election of 1863," in *Inside the Confederate Nation: Essays in Honor of Emory M. Thomas*, ed. Lesley J. Gordon and John C. Inscoe (Baton Rouge: Louisiana State University Press, 2005), 128–43; George C. Rable, *Damn Yankees: Demonization and Defiance in the Confederate South* (Baton Rouge: Louisiana State University Press, 2015), 126–27.

11. Michael I. Handel, *Masters of War: Classical Strategic Thought*, 3rd ed. (London: Frank Cass, 2001), 207. Related to the "rational calculus of war" is a concept that Carl

von Clausewitz called the "culminating point." This point is the difficult-to-discern moment when continued military action, in the absence of an immediate decision, is less and less likely to achieve success. In hindsight, at the strategic level, the Confederacy reached its culminating point at Chickamauga in September 1863. Any chance for reconstruction on southern terms needed to occur right after that battle and before the subsequent disaster at Chattanooga in November. Thereafter, even though Confederate forces remained potent, the Union army held the initiative and dominated the battlefield for the duration of the war. See Clausewitz, *On War*, 566–73.

12. Glenn Linden and Virginia Linden, eds., *Disunion, War, Defeat, and Recovery in Alabama: The Journal of Augustus Benners, 1850–1885* (Macon, GA: Mercer University Press, 2007), 104; *Southern Advertiser*, August 26, 1863; Wilfred Buck Yearns, *The Confederate Congress* (Athens: University of Georgia Press, 1960), 183.

Bibliography

GOVERNMENT DOCUMENTS

Alabama Legislature. *House Journals*. 1862–64.

Alabama Legislature. *Senate Journals*. 1862–63.

Journal of the Congress of the Confederate States of America, 1861–1865 (*JCCSA*). 7 vols. Washington, DC: Government Printing Office, 1904–5.

Population of the United States in 1860: The Eighth Census. Washington DC: Government Printing Office, 1864.

"Proceedings of the Confederate Congress." *Southern Historical Society Papers* (*SHSP*) 44–52 (1923–59).

Public Acts of the Alabama General Assembly. 1862–64.

Supplement to the Official Records of the Union and Confederate Armies. 100 vols. Edited by Janet B. Hewett. Wilmington, NC: Broadfoot, 1994–99.

The War of the Rebellion: A Compilation of the Official Records of the Union and Confederate Armies (*Official Records*). 70 vols. across 4 series. Washington, DC: Government Printing Office, 1880–1901.

MANUSCRIPT COLLECTIONS

Alabama Department of Archives and History (ADAH)

"Alabama Civil War Service Database." Updated May 23, 2017. http://www.archives.alabama.gov/civilwar/search.cfm.

Brown, Edward Norphlet. Papers. SPR337.

Coggin, Ebenezer B. Papers. SPR419.

Davis, Newton N. Papers. SPR342.

Election Files of the Alabama Secretary of State for 1863. SG002475.

Espy, Sarah Rousseau. Diary (1859–68). SPR2.

Governors' Papers: Shorter. SG024882, SG024884, SG006472.

Governors' Papers: Watts. SG024872, SG024884.

Hall, Bolling. Family Papers. LPR39.

Moren, Edward. Papers. LPR55.

Parsons, Lewis E. Papers. LPR248.

Regimental History Files for Confederate Military Units from Alabama. SG024887–908.

Semple, Henry C. Papers. LPR5.

Warrick, Thomas. Papers. SPR420.

Watts Family Papers. LPR237.

UNIVERSITY OF ALABAMA, W. S. HOOLE SPECIAL COLLECTIONS LIBRARY

Clayton, Henry D. Papers.

Jemison, Robert, Jr. Papers.

UNIVERSITY OF SOUTH ALABAMA, SPECIAL COLLECTIONS

Croom, Cicero Stephens. Papers.

NEWSPAPERS

Alabama Beacon (Greene County).

Alabama Reporter (Talladega County).

Autauga Citizen.

Chattanooga Daily Rebel.

Clarke County Journal.

Confederate Veteran.

Democratic Watchtower (Talladega County).

Eutaw Whig and Observer (Greene County).

Huntsville Confederate (Madison County).

Jacksonville Republican (Calhoun County).

Mobile Advertiser and Register.

Mobile Daily Advertiser and Register.

Mobile Telegraph.

Mobile Tribune.

Mobile Weekly Advertiser and Register.

Montgomery Daily Advertiser.

Montgomery Daily Mail.

Montgomery Weekly Advertiser.

Montgomery Weekly Mail.

Selma Morning Dispatch (Dallas County).

Selma Daily Reporter (Dallas County).

Southern Advertiser (Pike County).

South Western Baptist (Macon County).

Spirit of the South (Barbour County).

Sumter Independent.

BOOKS

Alderman, Edwin Anderson, and Armistead Churchill Gordon. *J. L. M. Curry: A Biography.* New York: Macmillan, 1911.

Alexander, Thomas B., and Richard E. Beringer. *The Anatomy of the Confederate Congress: A Study of the Influences of Member Characteristics on Legislative Voting Behavior, 1861–1865.* Nashville: Vanderbilt University Press, 1972.

Allen, Felicity. *Jefferson Davis: Unconquerable Heart.* Columbia: University of Missouri Press, 1999.

Amlund, Curtis Arthur. *Federalism in the Southern Confederacy*. Washington, DC: Public Affairs Press, 1966.

Ball, Douglas B. *Financial Failure and Confederate Defeat*. Chicago: University of Illinois Press, 1991.

Ball, Timothy H. *A Glance into the Great South-East, or Clarke County, Alabama, and Its Surroundings, from 1540 to 1877*. Tuscaloosa, AL: Willco, 1962.

Ballard, Michael B. *Vicksburg: The Campaign That Opened the Mississippi*. Chapel Hill: University of North Carolina Press, 2004.

Barney, William L. *Flawed Victory: A New Perspective on the Civil War*. New York: Praeger, 1975.

———. *The Secessionist Impulse: Alabama and Mississippi in 1860*. 1974. Tuscaloosa: University of Alabama Press, 2004.

Barrett, John G. *Yankee Rebel: The Civil War Journal of Edmund DeWitt Patterson*. Chapel Hill: University of North Carolina Press, 1966.

Benton, Josiah Henry. *Voting in the Field: A Forgotten Chapter of the Civil War*. Boston: Privately printed, 1915.

Bergeron, Arthur W, Jr. *Confederate Mobile*. Baton Rouge: Louisiana State University Press, 1991.

Beringer, Richard E., Herman Hattaway, Archer Jones, and William N. Still Jr. *Why the South Lost the Civil War*. Athens: University of Georgia Press, 1986.

Berlin, Ira, Barbara Fields, Steven F. Miller, Joseph P. Reidy, and Leslie S. Rowland. *Free at Last: A Documentary History of Slavery, Freedom, and the Civil War*. New York: New Press, 1992.

Blomquist, Ann K., and Robert A. Taylor, eds. *This Cruel War: The Civil War Letters of Grant and Malinda Taylor, 1862–1865*. Macon, GA: Mercer University Press, 2000.

Bogue, Alan G. *The Congressman's Civil War*. New York: Cambridge University Press, 1989.

Bonner, Michael Brem. *Confederate Political Economy: Creating and Managing a Southern Corporatist Nation*. Baton Rouge: Louisiana State University Press, 2016.

Bonner, Robert E. *Mastering America: Southern Slaveholders and the Crisis of American Nationhood*. New York: Cambridge University Press, 2009.

George C. Bradley, George C., and Richard L. Dahlen. *From Conciliation to Conquest: The Sack of Athens and the Court-Martial of Colonel John B. Turchin*. Tuscaloosa: University of Alabama Press, 2006.

Brantley, William H. *Chief Justice Stone of Alabama*. Birmingham, AL: Birmingham, 1943.

Brewer, George E. *History of Coosa County, Alabama*. Wetumpka, AL: Wetumpka, 1955.

Brewer, Willis. *Alabama: Her History, Resources, War Record, and Public Men; From 1540 to 1872*. Montgomery, AL: Barrett and Brown, 1872.

Brunson, Marion Bailey. *Pea River Reflections: Intimate Glimpses of Area Life during Two Centuries*. Tuscaloosa, AL: Portals Press, 1975.

Bunch, Jack A. *Roster of the Courts-Martial in the Confederate States of America*. Shippensburg, PA: White Mane, 2001.

Bunn, Mike. *Civil War Eufaula*. Charleston, SC: History Press, 2013.

Carmichael, Peter S. *The War for the Common Soldier: How Men Thought, Fought, and Survived in Civil War Armies*. Chapel Hill: University of North Carolina Press, 2018.

Carter, John C., ed. *Welcome the Hour of Conflict: William Cowan McClellan and the 9th Alabama*. Tuscaloosa: University of Alabama Press, 2007.

Chappell, Frank Anderson, ed. *Dear Sister: Civil War Letters to a Sister in Alabama*. Huntsville, AL: Branch Springs, 2002.

Clausewitz, Carl von. *On War*. Translated and edited by Peter Paret and Michael Howard. Princeton, NJ: Princeton University Press, 1976.

Cooper, Edward S. *Traitors: The Secession Period, November 1860–July 1861*. Madison, NJ: Fairleigh Dickinson University Press, 2008.

Cooper, William J. *Jefferson Davis and the Civil War Era*. Baton Rouge: Louisiana State University Press, 2008.

Coulter, E. Merton. *The Confederate States of America, 1861–1865*. Baton Rouge: Louisiana State University Press, 1950.

Crow, Mattie Lou Teague, ed. *The Diary of a Confederate Soldier: John Washington Inzer, 1834–1928*. Huntsville, AL: Strode, 1977.

Curry, Jabez L. M. *Civil History of the Government of the Confederate States*. Richmond, VA: B. F. Johnson, 1901.

———. *Progress of Anti-Slaveryism*. Washington, DC: Lemuel Towers, 1859.

Daniel, Larry J. *Soldiering in the Army of Tennessee: A Portrait of Life in a Confederate Army*. Chapel Hill: University of North Carolina Press, 1991.

Danielson, Joseph W. *War's Desolating Scourge: The Union's Occupation of North Alabama*. Lawrence: University Press of Kansas, 2012.

Davis, Jefferson. *The Papers of Jefferson Davis*. 14 vols. Edited by Haskell Monroe, James McIntosh, Lynda Lasswell Crist, and Mary Seaton Dix. Baton Rouge: Louisiana State University Press, 1971–2015.

Davis, William C. *Jefferson Davis: The Man and His Hour*. New York: Harper Collins, 1991.

———. *Look Away! A History of the Confederate States of America*. New York: Free Press, 2002.

Dedmondt, Glen. *The Flags of Civil War Alabama*. Gretna, LA: Pelican, 2001.

Denman, Clarence Phillips. *The Secession Movement in Alabama*. Freeport, NY: Books for Libraries Press, 1971.

Dew, Charles B. *Apostles of Disunion: Southern Secession Commissioners and the Causes of the Civil War*. Charlottesville: University Press of Virginia, 2001.

Dickinson, Jack L., ed. *If I Should Fall in Battle: The Civil War Diary of James P. Stephens*. Huntington, WV: John Deaver Drinko Academy, 2003.

Dillard, Philip D. *Jefferson Davis's Final Campaign: Confederate Nationalism and the Fight to Arm Slaves*. Macon, GA: Mercer University Press, 2017.

Dorman, Lewy. *Party Politics in Alabama from 1850 through 1860*. Montgomery: Alabama State Department of Archives and History, 1935.

Duncan, Katherine McKinstry, and Larry Joe Smith. *The History of Marshall County, Alabama*. Vol. 1, *Pre-History to 1939*. Albertville, AL: Thompson Press, 1969.

Durden, Robert F. *The Gray and the Black: The Confederate Debate on Emancipation*. Baton Rouge: Louisiana State University Press, 1972.

Easby-Smith, Anne. *William Russell Smith of Alabama: His Life and Works*. Philadelphia: Dolphin Press, 1931.

Edwards, Laura F. *Scarlett Doesn't Live Here Anymore: Southern Women in the Civil War Era*. Chicago: University of Illinois Press, 2000.

Ellison, Rhoda Coleman. *Early Alabama Publications: A Study in Literary Interests*. Tuscaloosa: University of Alabama Press, 1947.

———. *History and Bibliography of Alabama Newspapers in the Nineteenth Century*. Tuscaloosa: University of Alabama Press, 1954.

Escott, Paul D. *The Confederacy: The Slaveholders' Failed Venture*. Santa Barbara, CA: Praeger, 2010.

———. *Military Necessity: Civil-Military Relations in the Confederacy*. Westport, CT: Praeger, 2006.

Farmer, Margaret Pace. *One Hundred Fifty Years in Pike County, Alabama, 1821–1971*. Anniston, AL: Higginbotham, 1973.

Fehrenbacher, Don E. *Sectional Crisis and Southern Constitutionalism*. Baton Rouge: Louisiana State University Press, 1995.

Fleming, Walter L. *Civil War and Reconstruction in Alabama*. New York: Columbia University Press, 1905.

Frank, Joseph Allen. *With Ballot and Bayonet: The Political Socialization of American Civil War Soldiers*. Athens: University of Georgia Press, 1998.

Ferguson, Yale H., and Richard W. Mansbach. *Polities: Authority, Identities, and Change*. Columbia: University of South Carolina Press, 1996.

Gallagher, Gary W. *The Confederate War: How Popular Will, Nationalism, and Military Strategy Could Not Stave Off Defeat*. Cambridge, MA: Harvard University Press, 1997.

Garrett, William. *Reminiscences of Public Men in Alabama, for Thirty Years*. Atlanta: Plantation, 1872.

Glatthaar, Joseph T. *General Lee's Army: From Victory to Collapse*. New York: Free Press, 2008.

Griffith, Lucille, ed. *Yours till Death: Civil War Letters of John W. Cotton*. Tuscaloosa: University of Alabama Press, 1951.

Hahn, Steven. *A Nation under Our Feet: Black Political Struggles in the Rural South from Slavery to the Great Migration*. Cambridge, MA: Belknap Press, 2003.

Hallock, Judith Lee, ed. *The Civil War Letters of Joshua K. Callaway*. Athens: University of Georgia Press, 1997.

Handel, Michael I. *Masters of War: Classical Strategic Thought*. 3rd ed. London: Frank Cass, 2001.

The Heritage of Clarke County, Alabama. Heritage of Alabama 13. Clanton, AL: Heritage, 2001.

The Heritage of Pike County, Alabama. Heritage of Alabama 55. Clanton, AL: Heritage, 2001.

The Heritage of Tuscaloosa County, Alabama. Heritage of Alabama 63. Clanton, AL: Heritage, 1999.

Hubbs, G. Ward. *Guarding Greensboro: A Confederate Company in the Making of a Southern Community*. Athens: University of Georgia Press, 2003.

———, ed. *Voices from Company D: Diaries by the Greensboro Guards, Fifth Alabama Infantry Regiment, Army of Northern Virginia*. Athens: University of Georgia Press, 2003.

Hurt, R. Douglas. *Agriculture and the Confederacy: Policy, Productivity, and Power in the Civil War South*. Chapel Hill: University of North Carolina Press, 2015.

Hutchison, Coleman. *Apples and Ashes: Literature, Nationalism, and the Confederate States of America*. Athens: University of Georgia Press, 2012.

Jemison, E. Grace. *Historic Tales of Talladega*. Montgomery, AL: Paragon Press, 1959.

Jewett, Clayton E., ed. *Rise and Fall of the Confederacy: The Memoir of Senator Williamson S. Oldham, CSA*. Columbia: University of Missouri Press, 2006.

Jimerson, Randall C. *The Private Civil War: Popular Thought during the Sectional Conflict*. Baton Rouge: Louisiana State University Press, 1988.

Johnson, Andrew. *The Papers of Andrew Johnson*. 16 vols. Edited by LeRoy P. Graf, Ralph W. Haskins, and Paul H. Bergeron. Knoxville: University of Tennessee Press, 1967–2000.

Jones, John B. *A Rebel War Clerk's Diary at the Confederate States Capital*. 2 vols. Philadelphia: Lippincott, 1866.

Kirwan, Albert D., ed. *The Confederacy*. Cleveland, OH: World, 1958.

Laine, J. Gary, and Morris M. Penny. *Law's Alabama Brigade in the War between the Union and the Confederacy*. Shippensburg, PA: White Mane, 1996.

Levine, Bruce. *Confederate Emancipation: Southern Plans to Free and Arm Slaves during the Civil War*. New York: Oxford University Press, 2006.

———. *The Fall of the House of Dixie: The Civil War and the Social Revolution That Transformed the South*. New York: Random House, 2013.

Linden, Glenn, and Virginia Linden, eds. *Disunion, War, Defeat, and Recovery in Alabama: The Journal of Augustus Benners, 1850–1885*. Macon, GA: Mercer University Press, 2007.

Manning, Chandra. *What This Cruel War Was Over: Soldiers, Slavery, and the Civil War*. New York: Alfred A. Knopf, 2007.

Martin, Bessie. *A Rich Man's War, A Poor Man's Fight: Desertion of Alabama Troops from the Confederate Army*. 1932. Tuscaloosa: University of Alabama Press, 2003.

Martinez, Jaime Amanda. *Confederate Slave Impressment in the Upper South*. Chapel Hill: University of North Carolina Press, 2013.

Martis, Kenneth C. *The Historical Atlas of the Congresses of the Confederate States of America, 1861–1865*. New York: Simon and Schuster, 1994.

Mathis, Ray, ed. *In the Land of the Living: Wartime Letters by Confederates from the Chattahoochee Valley of Alabama and Georgia*. Troy, AL: Troy State University Press, 1981.

McCardell, John. *The Idea of a Southern Nation: Southern Nationalists and Southern Nationalism, 1830–1860*. New York: W. W. Norton, 1979.

McCurry, Stephanie. *Confederate Reckoning: Power and Politics in the Civil War South*. Cambridge, MA: Harvard University Press, 2010.

McIlwain, Christopher Lyle. *Civil War Alabama*. Tuscaloosa: University of Alabama Press, 2016.

———. *1865 Alabama: From Civil War to Uncivil Peace*. Tuscaloosa: University of Alabama Press, 2017.

McMillan, Malcolm C. *The Alabama Confederate Reader*. Tuscaloosa: University of Alabama Press, 1963.

———. *The Disintegration of a Confederate State: Three Governors and Alabama's Wartime Home Front, 1861–1865*. Macon, GA: Mercer University Press, 1986.

McMurray, Richard M., ed. *An Uncompromising Secessionist: The Civil War of George Knox Miller, Eighth (Wade's) Confederate Cavalry*. Tuscaloosa: University of Alabama Press, 2007.

McPherson, James M. *For Cause and Comrades: Why Men Fought in the Civil War*. New York: Oxford University Press, 1997.

———. *Ordeal by Fire: The Civil War and Reconstruction*. New York: McGraw-Hill, 1982.

McWhiney, Grady, and Perry D. Jamieson. *Attack and Die: Civil War Military Tactics and the Southern Heritage*. Tuscaloosa: University of Alabama Press, 1982.

McWhiney, Grady, Warner O. Moore, and Robert F. Pace, eds. *"Fear God and Walk Humbly": The Agricultural Journal of James Mallory, 1843–1877*. Tuscaloosa: University of Alabama Press, 1997.

Meigs, Paul Avery. *The Life of Senator Robert Jemison, Junior*. Tuscaloosa: University of Alabama, 1928.

Memorial Record of Alabama. 2 vols. Madison, WI: Brant and Fuller, 1893.

Mitchell, Reid. *The American Civil War, 1861–1865*. New York: Routledge, 2013.

———. *Civil War Soldiers*. New York: Viking Press, 1988.

Mobley, Joe A. *Weary of War: Life on the Confederate Home Front*. Westport, CT: Praeger, 2008.

Moore, Albert B. *Conscription and Conflict in the Confederacy*. New York: Hillary House, 1963.

Neeley, Mary Ann, ed. *The Works of Matthew Blue, Montgomery's First Historian*. Montgomery, AL: New South Books, 2010.

Nelson, Scott, and Carol Sheriff. *A People at War: Civilians and Soldiers in America's Civil War, 1854–1877*. New York: Oxford University Press, 2008.

Nevins, Allan. *The War for the Union*. 4 vols. New York: Konecky and Konecky, 1959–71.

Noe, Kenneth W. *Reluctant Rebels: The Confederates Who Joined the Army after 1861*. Chapel Hill: University of North Carolina Press, 2010.

Nuermberger, Ruth Ketring. *The Clays of Alabama: A Planter-Lawyer-Politician Family*. Tuscaloosa: University of Alabama Press, 1958.

Ott, Victoria E. *Confederate Daughters: Coming of Age during the Civil War*. Carbondale: Southern Illinois University Press, 2008.

Palmer, Beverly Wilson, ed. *The Selected Papers of Thaddeus Stevens*. 2 vols. Pittsburgh, PA: University of Pittsburgh Press, 1997.

Patrick, Rembert W. *Jefferson Davis and His Cabinet*. Baton Rouge: Louisiana State University Press, 1944.

Phillips, Jason. *Diehard Rebels: The Confederate Culture of Invincibility*. Athens: University of Georgia Press, 2007.

Quigley, Paul. *Shifting Grounds: Nationalism and the American South, 1848–1865*. New York: Oxford University Press, 2012.

Rable, George C. *Civil Wars: Women and the Crisis of Southern Nationalism*. Chicago: University of Illinois Press, 1989.

———. *The Confederate Republic: A Revolution against Politics*. Chapel Hill: University of North Carolina Press, 1994.

———. *Damn Yankees! Demonization and Defiance in the Confederate South*. Baton Rouge: Louisiana State University Press, 2015.

Renfroe, J. J. D. *"The Battle Is God's": A Sermon Preached before Wilcox's Brigade on Fast Day*. Richmond, VA: MacFarlane and Fergusson, 1863.

Representative Men of the South. Philadelphia: Charles Robson, 1880.

Rice, Jessie Pearl. *J. L. M. Curry: Southerner, Statesman and Educator*. New York: Kings Crown Press, 1949.

Riley, Benjamin F. *Makers and Romance of Alabama History*. N.p.: N.p., 1915.

Ringold, May Spencer. *The Role of the State Legislatures in the Confederacy*. Athens: University of Georgia Press, 1966.

Robertson, James I., Jr. *Soldiers Blue and Gray*. Columbia: University of South Carolina Press, 1988.

Robinson, Armstead L. *Bitter Fruits of Bondage: The Demise of Slavery and the Collapse of the Confederacy, 1861–1865*. Charlottesville: University of Virginia Press, 2005.

Robinson, William M. *Justice in Grey: A History of the Judicial System in the Confederate States of America*. Cambridge, MA: Harvard University Press, 1941.

Rogers, William Warren, Jr. *Confederate Home Front: Montgomery during the Civil War*. Tuscaloosa: University of Alabama Press, 1999.

Rogers, William Warren, Sr., Robert David Ward, Leah Rawls Atkins, and Wayne Flynt. *Alabama: The History of a Deep South State*. Tuscaloosa: University of Alabama Press, 1994.

Roland, Charles P. *The Confederacy*. Chicago: University of Chicago Press, 1960.

Royster, Charles. *The Destructive War: William Tecumseh Sherman, Stonewall Jackson, and the Americans.* New York: Alfred A. Knopf, 1991.

Rubin, Anne Sarah. *A Shattered Nation: The Rise and Fall of the Confederacy, 1861–1868.* Chapel Hill: University of North Carolina Press, 2005.

Schwab, John Christopher. *The Confederate States of America, 1861–1865: A Financial and Industrial History of the South during the Civil War.* New York: Charles Scribner's Sons, 1904.

Sellers, James Benson. *Slavery in Alabama.* Tuscaloosa: University of Alabama Press, 1950.

Severance, Ben H. *Portraits of Conflict: A Photographic History of Alabama in the Civil War.* Fayetteville: University of Arkansas Press, 2012.

Sexton, Rebecca Grant, ed. *A Southern Woman of Letters: The Correspondence of August Jane Evans Wilson.* Columbia: University of South Carolina Press, 2002.

Sifakis, Stewart. *Compendium of the Confederate Armies: Alabama.* New York: Facts on File, 1991.

Sikes, E. W. *The Confederate States Congress.* Raleigh, NC: Edwards and Broughton, 1903.

Sledge, John S. *These Rugged Days: Alabama in the Civil War.* Tuscaloosa: University of Alabama Press, 2017.

Smith, William Russell. *The History and Debates of the Convention of the People of Alabama.* Montgomery, AL: White, Pfister, 1861.

———. *The Royal Ape: A Dramatic Poem.* Richmond, VA: West and Johnson, 1863.

Smith, Winston. *The People's City: The Glory and Grief of an Alabama Town, 1850–1874.* Demopolis, AL: Marengo County Historical Society, 2003.

Sprott, Samuel H. *Cush: A Civil War Memoir.* Edited by Louis R. Smith and Andrew Quist. Livingston, AL: Livingston Press, 1999.

Stephens, Larry D. *Bound for Glory: A History of the 30th Alabama Infantry Regiment, C.S.A.* Ann Arbor, MI: Sheridan Books, 2005.

Sterkx, H. E. *Partners in Rebellion: Alabama Women in the Civil War.* Cranbury, NJ: Associated University Press, 1970.

Sterling, Ada, ed. *A Belle of the Fifties: Memoirs of Mrs. Clay of Alabama.* New York: Doubleday, Page, 1905.

Storey, Margaret M. *Loyalty and Loss: Alabama's Unionists in the Civil War and Reconstruction.* Baton Rouge: Louisiana State University Press, 2004.

St. Paul, Henry. *Our Home and Foreign Policy.* Mobile, AL: Daily Register and Advertiser, 1863.

Sword, Wiley. *Southern Invincibility: A History of the Confederate Heart.* New York: St. Martin's Press, 1999.

Tatum, Georgia Lee. *Disloyalty in the Confederacy.* New York: AMS Press, 1934.

Tharin, Robert S. *Arbitrary Arrests in the South, or Scenes from the Experience of an Alabama Unionist.* New York: John Bradburn, 1863.

Thomas, Benjamin P., and Harold M. Hyman. *Stanton: The Life and Times of Lincoln's Secretary of War.* New York: Alfred A. Knopf, 1962.

Thomas, Emory M. *The Confederacy as a Revolutionary Experience.* Englewood Cliffs, NJ: Prentice-Hall, 1971.

Thornton, J. Mills, III. *Politics and Power in a Slave Society: Alabama, 1800–1860.* Baton Rouge: Louisiana State University Press, 1978.

Todd, Richard C. *Confederate Finance.* Athens: University of Georgia Press, 1954.

Vandiver, Frank E. *Rebel Brass: The Confederate Command System.* Baton Rouge: Louisiana State University Press, 1956.

Wakelyn, Jon L. *Confederates against the Confederacy: Essays on Leadership and Loyalty.* Westport, CT: Praeger, 2002.

———, ed. *Southern Pamphlets on Secession, November 1860–April 1861.* Chapel Hill: University of North Carolina Press, 1996.

Walker, Anne Kendrick. *Backtracking in Barbour County: A Narrative of the Last Alabama Frontier.* Richmond, VA: Dietz Press, 1941.

Walther, Eric H. *William Lowndes Yancey and the Coming of the Civil War.* Chapel Hill: University of North Carolina Press, 2006.

Warner, Ezra J., and Wilfred Buck Yearns. *Biographical Register of the Confederate Congress.* Baton Rouge: Louisiana State University Press, 1975.

Waters, Spencer A., and Betty R. Waters. *Lawrence County.* Vol. 2, *Genealogical Records.* N.p.: B. R. Waters, 2009.

Watts, Thomas Hill *Inaugural Address.* Montgomery, AL: Montgomery Advertiser Book and Job Office, 1863.

Weitz, Mark A. *More Damning Than Slaughter: Desertion in the Confederate Army.* Lincoln: University of Nebraska Press, 2005.

Wheeler, Joseph. *Confederate Military History.* Vol. 8, *Alabama.* Wilmington, NC: Broadfoot, 1987.

Wiley, Bell I., ed. *Letters of Warren Akin, Confederate Congressman.* Athens: University of Georgia Press, 1959.

———. *The Life of Johnny Reb: The Common Soldier of the Confederacy.* Indianapolis, IN: Bobbs-Merrill, 1943.

Williams, Benjamin Buford. *A Literary History of Alabama: The Nineteenth Century.* Rutherford, NJ: Fairleigh Dickinson University Press, 1979.

Williams, David. *A People's History of the Civil War: Struggles for the Meaning of Freedom.* New York: New Press, 2005.

Wood, Wayne. *The Marble Valley Boys: Marble Valley, Coosa County, Alabama.* Birmingham, AL: Banner Press, 1986.

Woodward, C. Vann, ed. *Mary Chestnut's Civil War.* New Haven, CT: Yale University Press, 1981.

Yearns, Wilfred Buck. *The Confederate Congress.* Athens: University of Georgia Press, 1960.

———, ed. *The Confederate Governors.* Athens: University of Georgia Press, 1985.

Younger, Edward, ed. *Inside the Confederate Government: The Diary of Robert Garlick Hill Kean.* New York: Oxford University Press, 1957.

ARTICLES AND CHAPTERS

Adams, E. Bryding. "William Frye, Artist." *Alabama Heritage* 32 (1994): 30–38.

Alexander, Thomas B. "Persistent Whiggery in Alabama and the Lower South, 1860–1867." *Alabama Review* 12, no. 1 (1959): 35–52.

———. "Persistent Whiggery in the Confederate South, 1860–1877." *Journal of Southern History* 27, no. 3 (1961): 305–29.

Andrew, Rod. "The Essential Nationalism of the People: Georgia's Confederate Congressional Election of 1863." In *Inside the Confederate Nation: Essays in Honor of Emory M. Thomas,* edited by Lesley J. Gordon and John C. Inscoe, 128–46. Baton Rouge: Louisiana State University Press, 2005.

Ash, Stephen V. "A Wall around Slavery: Safeguarding the Peculiar Institution on the Confederate Periphery, 1861–1865." In *Nineteenth-Century America: Essays in Honor of Paul H. Bergeron,* edited by W. Todd Groce and Stephen V. Ash, 55–73. Knoxville: University of Tennessee Press, 2005.

Atkins, Leah. "Williamson R. W. Cobb and the Graduation Act of 1854." *Alabama Review* 28, no. 1 (1975): 16–31.

Bass, James Horace. "The Georgia Gubernatorial Elections of 1861 and 1863." *Georgia Historical Quarterly* 17, no. 3 (1933): 167–88.

Bensel, Richard. "Rejoinder to 'Why No Parties? Investigating the Disappearance of Democratic-Whig Divisions in the Confederacy.'" *Studies in American Political Development* 13, no. 2 (1999): 263–78.

———. "Southern Leviathan: The Development of Central State Authority in the Confederate States of America." *Studies in American Political Development* 2, no. 1 (1987): 68–136.

Beringer, Richard E. "A Profile of the Members of the Confederate Congress." *Journal of Southern History* 33, no. 4 (1967): 518–41.

———. "The Unconscious 'Spirit of Party' in the Confederate Congress." *Civil War History* 18, no. 4 (1972): 312–33.

Bradley, Robert. "Tattered Banners: Alabama's Civil War Flags." *Alabama Heritage* 96 (2010): 10–21.

Brown, Tommy. "Of All the Hardy Sons of Toil: Class and Race in Antebellum Southcentral and Southeastern Alabama." *Alabama Review* 68, no. 3 (2015): 213–50.

Burnett, Lonnie. "Precipitating a Revolution: Alabama's Democracy in the Election of 1860." In *The Yellowhammer War: The Civil War and Reconstruction in Alabama,* edited by Kenneth W. Noe, 15–33. Tuscaloosa: University of Alabama Press, 2013.

Culver, Emma Beall. "Thomas Hill Watts, a Statesman of the Old Regime." *Transactions of the Alabama Historical Society* 4 (1904): 415–39.

Cunningham, H. H. "Confederate General Hospitals: Establishment and Organization." *Journal of Southern History* 20, no. 3 (1954): 376–94.

"Delegates to the Alabama Secession Convention." *Alabama Historical Quarterly* 3, no. 3/4 (1941): 368–426.

Donald, David Herbert. "Died of Democracy." In *Why the North Won the Civil War*, edited by David Herbert Donald, 79–90. Baton Rouge: Louisiana State University Press, 1960.

Estill, Mary S., ed. "Franklin B. Sexton: Diary of a Confederate Congressman, 1862–1863." *Southwestern Historical Quarterly* 38, no. 4 (1935): 270–301; 39, no. 1 (1935): 33–65.

Farrell, Robert. "No Foreign Despots on Southern Soil: The Know-Nothing Party in Alabama, 1850–1857." *Alabama Review* 72, no. 2 (2019): 99–122.

Fleming, Walter L. "Conscription and Exemption in Alabama during the Civil War." *Gulf States Historical Magazine* 2 (1904): 310–325.

——. "The Peace Movement in Alabama: The Peace Society, 1863–1865." *South Atlantic Quarterly* 2 (1903): 114–24, 246–60.

Flynn, Stuart, and T. J. Beitelman. "Demopolis: City of the People." *Alabama Heritage* 59 (2001): 18–27.

Franklin, John Hope. "The Southern Expansionists of 1846." *Journal of Southern History* 25, no. 3 (1959): 323–38.

Hill, Louise B. "State Socialism in the Confederate States of America." *Southern Sketches* 1st ser., no. 9 (1936): 3–31.

Hoole, W. Stanley, ed. "The Letters of Captain Joab Goodson, 1862–1864." *Alabama Review* 10 (1957): 126–53, 215–31.

Horton, Paul. "Submitting to the Shadow of Slavery: The Secession Crisis and Civil War in Alabama's Lawrence County." *Civil War History* 44, no. 2 (1998): 111–36.

Jones, Allen W., ed. "A Georgia Confederate Soldier Visits Montgomery, Alabama, 1862–1863." *Alabama Historical Quarterly* 25, no. 2 (1963): 99–113.

———. "Unionism and Disaffection in South Alabama: The Case of Alfred Holley." *Alabama Review* 24, no. 2 (1971): 114–32.

Joslyn, Mauriel Phillips. "Comrades of the Southern Cross." *North and South* 4, no. 1 (2000): 27–33.

Kruman, Marc W. "Dissent in the Confederacy: The North Carolina Experience." *Civil War History* 27, no. 4 (1981): 293–313.

Lash, Jeffrey N. "A Yankee in Gray: Danville Leadbetter and the Defense of Mobile Bay, 1861–1863." *Civil War History* 37, no. 3 (1991): 197–218.

Laskin, Lisa. "'The Army Is Not Near So Much Demoralized as the Country Is': Soldiers in the Army of Northern Virginia and the Confederate Home Front." In *The View from the Ground: Experiences of Civil War Soldiers*, edited by Aaron Sheehan-Dean, 91–120. Lexington: University of Kentucky Press, 2007.

McKiven, Henry M. "John Gill Shorter, 1861–1863." In *Alabama Governors*, edited by Samuel L. Webb and Margaret E. Armbrester, 70–73. Tuscaloosa: University of Alabama Press, 2001.

———. "Secession, War, and Reconstruction, 1850–1874." In *Mobile: The New History of Alabama's First City*, edited by Michael Thompson, 95–125. Tuscaloosa: University of Alabama Press, 2001.

McMillan, Malcolm C. "Alabama." In *The Confederate Governors*, edited by Wilfred Buck Yearns, 15–40. Athens: University of Georgia Press, 1985.

McPherson, James M. "American Victory, American Defeat." In *Why the Confederacy Lost*, edited by Gabor S. Boritt, 15–42. New York: Oxford University Press, 1992.

McWhiney, Grady. "Were the Whigs a Class Party in Alabama?" *Journal of Southern History* 23, no. 4 (1957): 510–22.

Mering, John Vollmer. "Persistent Whiggery in the Confederate South: A Reconsideration." *South Atlantic Quarterly* 69, no. 1 (1970): 124–43.

Noe, Kenneth W. "Alabama, We Will Fight for Thee: The Initial Motivations of Later-Enlisting Confederates." *Alabama Review* 62, no. 3 (2009): 163–89.

"Our Harman Heritage Research Center." J & W Enterprises. Accessed August 25, 2019. http://www.harmanheritage.net/genealogy/.

Owsley, Frank L. "Defeatism in the Confederacy." *North Carolina Historical Review* 3 (1926): 446–56.

Partin, Robert. "An Alabama Confederate Soldier's Report to His Wife." *Alabama Review* 3, no. 1 (1950): 22–35.

Potter, David M. "Jefferson Davis and the Political Factors in Confederate Defeat." In *Why the North Won the Civil War*, edited by David Herbert Donald, 91–112. Baton Rouge: Louisiana State University Press, 1960.

Powell, Ezekiel A. "Fifty-Five Years in West Alabama." *Alabama Historical Quarterly* 4, no. 4 (1942): 459–663.

Purcell, Douglas Clare. "Military Conscription in Alabama during the Civil War." *Alabama Review* 34, no. 2 (1981): 94–106.

Ramey, Adam. "National Survival and the Confederate Congress." *Historical Methods* 46, no. 1 (2013): 31–41.

Robbins, John Brawner. "The Confederacy and the Writ of Habeas Corpus." *Georgia Historical Quarterly* 55, no. 1 (1971): 83–101.

Shapiro, Norman M. "Daniel Coleman Diary." *Huntsville Historical Review* 26, no. 2 (1999): 1–46.

Shields, Johanna Nicol. "A Social History of Antebellum Alabama Writers." *Alabama Review* 42, no. 3 (1989): 163–91.

Taylor, A. Reed. "The War History of Two Soldiers: A Two-Sided View of the Civil War." *Alabama Review* 23, no. 2 (1970): 83–109.

Teters, Kristopher A. "Fighting for the Cause? An Examination of the Motivations of Alabama's Confederate Soldiers from a Class Perspective." In *The Yellowhammer War: The Civil War and Reconstruction in Alabama*, edited by Kenneth W. Noe, 90–106. Tuscaloosa: University of Alabama Press, 2013.

Vandiver, Frank E. "The Civil War as an Institutionalizing Force." In *Essays on the American Civil War*, edited by Frank E. Vandiver, Martin Hardwick Hall, and Homer L. Kerr, 73–87. Austin: University of Texas Press, 1968.

———. "The Confederacy and the American Tradition." In *The Civil War: A Second American Revolution?*, edited by William E. Parrish, 129–36. New York: Holt, Rinehart and Winston, 1970.

Walker, Anne Kendrick, ed. "Governor John Gill Shorter: Miscellaneous Papers, 1861–1863." *Alabama Review* 11 (1958): 208–32, 267–85.

Whittington, Terry. "In the Shadow of Defeat: Tracking the Vicksburg Parolees." *Journal of Mississippi History* 64, no. 4 (2002): 307–30.

Williams, Benjamin Buford. "Alexander B. Meek." Encyclopedia of Alabama. Updated October 3, 2011. http://www.encyclopediaofalabama.org/article/h-1127.

———. "Two Uncollected Civil War Poems of Alexander Beaufort Meek." *Alabama Historical Quarterly* 25, no. 2 (1963): 114–19.

Winther, Oscar Osburn. "The Soldier Vote in the Election of 1864." *New York History* 25, no. 4 (1944): 440–58.

Yearns, Wilfred Buck. "The Peace Movement in the Confederate Congress." *Georgia Historical Quarterly* 41, no. 1 (1957): 1–18.

THESES AND DISSERTATIONS

Binnington, Ian. "They Have Made a Nation: Confederates and Confederate Nationalism." PhD diss., University of Illinois Urbana-Champaign, 2004.

Brannen, Ralph N. "John Gill Shorter: War Governor of Alabama." Master's thesis, Alabama Polytechnic Institute, 1956.

Daniel, Michael Jackson. "Red Hills and Piney Woods: A Political History of Butler County, Alabama, in the Nineteenth Century." PhD diss., University of Alabama, 1985.

Dannelly, Hermione. "The Life and Times of Robert Jemison, Jr., during the Civil War and Reconstruction." Master's thesis, University of Alabama, 1942.

Davidson, Mary Jane. "James Lawrence Pugh: A Half Century in Politics." Master's thesis, Auburn University, 1971.

Dodd, Donald Bradford. "Unionism in Confederate Alabama." PhD diss., University of Georgia, 1969.

Jackson, Helen Jeanette. "The Work of the Alabama Delegation in the Confederate Congress." Master's thesis, Emory University, 1953.

Jenkins, Jeffery A. "Examining Contemporary Congressional Theories Historically: Essays on the Congress of the Confederate States of America." PhD diss., University of Illinois Urbana-Champaign, 1999.

Kaufman, Janet E. "Sentinels on the Watchtower: The Confederate Governors and the Davis Administration." PhD diss., American University, 1977.

Legrand, Phyllis LaRue. "Destitution and Relief of the Indigent Soldiers' Families of Alabama during the Civil War." Master's thesis, Auburn University, 1964.

Murray, Kenneth Michael. "Gubernatorial Politics and the Confederacy." PhD diss., Columbia University, 1977.

Powell, Michael Albert. "Confederate Federalism: A View from the Governors." PhD diss., University of Maryland, 2004.

Robbins, John Brawner. "Confederate Nationalism: Politics and Government in the Confederate South, 1861–1865." PhD diss., Rice University, 1964.

Smith, Louis Roycraft. "A History of Sumter County, Alabama, through 1886." PhD diss., University of Alabama, 1988.

Smith, Thomas Alton. "Mobilization of the Army of Alabama, 1859–1865." Master's thesis, Alabama Polytechnic Institute, 1953.

Stelluto, Donald Louis, Jr. "A Light Which Reveals Its True Meaning: State Supreme Courts and the Confederate Constitution." PhD diss., University of Maryland, 2004.

Thompson, Hubert Jennings. "The Civil War Correspondence of James B. Daniel." Master's thesis, Samford University, 1980.

Yamaguchi, Elizabeth H. "Macon County, Alabama: Its Land and Its People from Prehistory to 1870." Master's thesis, Auburn University, 1981.

Index

Page numbers in italics indicate figures or tables.